HAND STITCHED Crazy Patchwork

HAND STITCHED Crazy
Patchwork

HAZEL Blomkamp

SEARCH PRESS

ACKNOWLEDGEMENTS

Darren Willson for his help with
the illustrations and guidance with
the software;

Pat van Wyk and Margie Breetzke for
making the appliqued examples of two
of the designs;

John Blomkamp for always urgently
sorting out any computer problems;

My husband Peter for the continuing
support that he gives me.

First published in 2016
Reprinted June 2016
Search Press Limited
Wellwood, North Farm Road,
Tunbridge Wells, Kent TN2 3DR

Originally published in 2016 by Metz Press
1 Cameronians Avenue, Welgemoed 7530
South Africa

ISBN 978-1-78221-348-2

Publisher	Wilsia Metz
Project manager	Nikki Metz
Photographer	Ivan Naudé
Illustrator	Darren Willson
Designer	Liezl Maree
Proofreader	Pat Barton
Reproduction	Robert Wong, Color Fuzion

Printed and bound in China by 1010 Printing
International Ltd

Contents

Introduction

Crazy patchwork has its roots in an environment far removed from the way we live our lives today. It arose out of necessity and thrift in a harsh world devoid of abundance and Internet shopping, when every scrap of fabric was so precious that it was used and re-used, until it was too threadbare to use again.

From these rudimentary beginnings, a practical task performed by hard-working, ingenious colonial women developed, with increased wealth, into an art form. It acquired additional decoration. Working from a sentimental starting point, much of the embellishment was symbolic of the artist's life, or that of the person for whom the finished work was intended. Personal objects were attached and interests depicted. Along with that, scraps of lace, buttons or braid were collected and to this day, crazy patch artists are likely to have cupboards and boxes filled with findings that they have collected, because they might be useful.

But, there is another way.

For some years, I have been harbouring a desire to embellish crazy patch from scratch. In other words, make everything that goes onto it myself with a needle, threads and beads. Anyone who is passionate about one form of needle art will probably have learnt other forms too, and I am no different. So, I reasoned, why not combine all the needle art skills acquired in my life so far – and the logical medium for that is crazy patchwork.

In the first half, you will find the techniques gallery. Whilst the techniques are provided specifically for the projects in the second half of the book, they can be adapted for use in your own quilting, embroidery and crazy patch projects.

These include:
- Embellishment techniques: bead embroidery stitches, embroidery stitches, silk ribbon embroidery stitches, combination embroidery and silk ribbon embroidery edgings, beading, needle lace, needle weaving and tatting techniques;
- Patchwork and quilting techniques: how to make crazy patch using both free hand techniques and working from paper templates, simple quilting techniques and tips for finishing off.

The second half of the book features five projects.

- The first three are completely from scratch. Even the patches are created with a needle and thread.
- The fourth project combines a panel of traditional crazy patch and a Jacobean embroidery panel.
- The fifth project is traditional crazy patch, each embellishment having been made with a needle or a shuttle.

Other than the raw materials, nothing has been specifically bought, or pulled from my stash. I don't have a stash.

For the courageous among you, some elements of the projects can be done with appliqué techniques, as shown in the work of Margie Breetzke and Pat van Wyk. They have taken two of the projects and recreated them using these techniques, adding additional embroidery and beadwork, in line with a developing trend among quilters to further embellish their work.

This book is intended for both embroidery and quilt artists. I hope you'll be inspired and that your fingers will itch to stitch.

Hazel

General tips

YOU MUST BE ABLE TO SEE PROPERLY

There is a lot of fine work in this book. Make sure your spectacles have sufficient magnification to cope with that. I wear two pairs: multifocals with a pair of plus 1.5 readers in front of them. This creates a telescope and is more comfortable than grappling with one of those magnifying glasses that hang around your neck.

GOOD LIGHT

You don't want to have to restrict yourself to only being able to work during daylight hours, so you will need a good light or lights. At the moment, I am using two angle-poise lamps fitted with 15-watt cool-white energy saver bulbs. They are set up on either side of me as I stitch. Because they are angle-poise, I pull them closer or push them away, depending on what I am stitching. They are proving to be the best lighting system I've had so far.

HOOPS AND FRAMES

They improve the tension of your work and stop the fabric from puckering. You cannot produce good work without them. The projects in this book use:
- The Morgan no-slip hoop 12 and 14" lap stand;
- A 24" light duty scroll frame;
- A 30" heavy duty scroll frame.

FABRIC GUARDS

No matter how often you wash your hands, or how clean you keep your working environment, a grubby ring is likely to form at the place where the fabric meets the outer ring of the hoop. To avoid this problem, make a fabric guard.

Measure the circumference of your hoop. Add 2" (50 mm) for a small hoop and 4" (100 mm) for a large hoop. Using that measurement, cut a strip of fabric that is 10" (250 mm) wide.

Fold the strip in half, with right sides together, and sew a seam to join the ends of the strip, making it into a tube.

Stitch a 1½" (15 mm) casing by turning in a hem at top and bottom.

Calculate how much narrow elastic you will need by tightly stretching a piece around the circumference of the hoop and adding 1" (25 mm). Cut two pieces and thread them into the top and bottom casings, stitch them together and close the gaps of the casings.

Once you have stretched the working fabric into the hoop, stretch the fabric guard around the perimeter of the hoop, protecting the edge of the embroidery, and tucking the excess working fabric on the outside of the hoop into the part of the fabric guard that lies below the hoop.

USE A THREAD CONDITIONER

It strengthens your thread, makes silk and rayon threads less lively and delays the stripping of metallic thread. Beeswax is good, but the best is a silicone thread conditioner. This leaves no residue.

USE SUPERGLUE

I don't like using a thimble but find that a hole develops in the tip of the finger that I use to push the needle through the fabric. I place a blob of superglue on that spot, hold my finger in the air for a few minutes and let it dry. Once that blob is dry it will be rock hard and a needle will not penetrate it. It peels off after a few hours. I promise. Ignore the neurotics who predict dire health problems. They're wrong. I've used it for years and I'm fine.

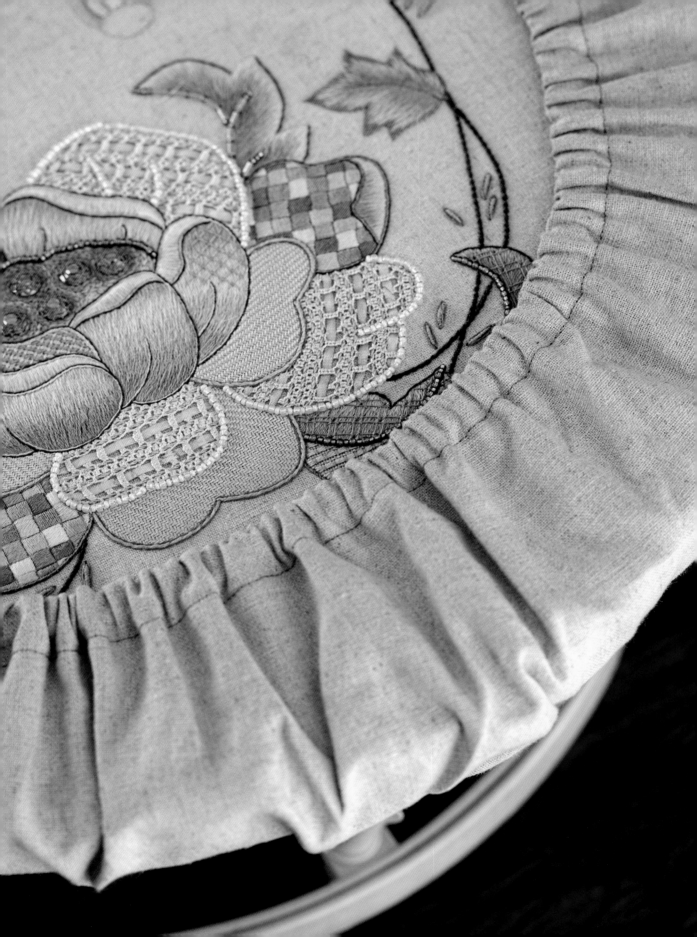

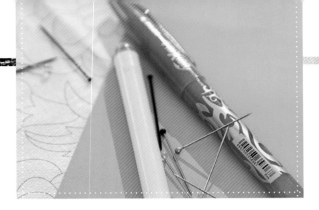

START YOUR STITCHES WITH A KNOT

Yes, a knot. This is the 21st Century. We do needlework for our pleasure, not to be judged. While the back of your work should not look like a bird's nest, it does not have to look the same as the front. We're humans, not machines.

TRANSFERRING YOUR DESIGN

The line drawings for all of the designs in this book are at the back. The easiest way to transfer them onto your fabric is with dressmaker's carbon. Like most things in life, I do what works best for me. And dressmaker's carbon, or chalk paper, is my choice.

- Make a photocopy of the drawing, adjusting the size where recommended.
- Pin the photocopy to the fabric, taking care to place it in the centre. Don't get too fussy about the grain, just get it as straight as you can.
- Place a sheet of dressmaker's carbon, ink side down, between the photocopy and the fabric.

Using the hard tip of a ballpoint pen – preferably one that has no ink in it (I have a dry pen in my toolbox for this task) – go over each and every line pressing hard. And I do mean pressing hard. You should end up with a sore finger. If you don't press hard enough the lines won't transfer.

Another alternative is to pin the photocopy to the underside of the fabric. Place it on a light box and trace the lines with a pencil, a blue washout pen, or a Pilot Frixion pen.

And if the above is all too much for you, order a print pack from our website!

PENS

The blue washout pen is controversial because it has been known to cause brown lines that won't wash out. Brown lines and stains will be avoided if you follow two simple guidelines:

- Always rinse your embroidery in cold water before putting it into any detergent;
- Do not allow the lines to fade. If you draw something onto fabric with a washout pen, grow bored with it and put it away in a cupboard for a while, when you come back to it those lines will have faded to brown and you won't get rid of them.

Provided you avoid these pitfalls, you can use a washout pen with impunity. It is still the easiest way to draw something onto fabric.

The Pilot Frixion pen is my second choice. The lines don't wash out but if you want to get rid of them, just press them with a warm iron. The ink is formulated to disappear if heat is applied to it.

WASHING YOUR EMBROIDERY

We are living in the 21st century with good dyes and non-shrinking fabrics. You can wash your needlework. Provided you have checked that all the dyes are colour-fast – which they should be if you have used good quality thread – you MUST wash it. It brings the colours to life and the sheen of the thread reappears.

- Rinse it well in cold water to get rid of any lines that you may have drawn with a washout pen.
- Soak it for a few hours in tepid water mixed with a tablespoon or two of good detergent.
- Swish it around a bit before rinsing it in cold water.
- If you find there are marks – perhaps chalk paper lines – that haven't washed out, scrub them gently with pure soap on a toothbrush.
- Rinse again to make sure that no soap or detergent remains.
- Squeeze out the excess water, place it flat on a towel and roll up the towel.
- Squeeze the towel with the embroidery inside it to get rid of any remaining excess water.
- Stretch the damp embroidery in a hoop or frame that is larger than the embroidered area and place it in front of an open window, out of direct sunlight, to dry in the breeze.

If you have stretched it well you will probably not need to iron it when it is dry. If you do need to iron it, turn it wrong side up on a folded towel and press the back with an iron set on medium heat.

Tools and materials

All the tools and materials used in this book are listed and described below.

TOOLS

CUTTING
- Large **dressmaking** scissors for cutting fabric
- A rotary cutter (optional)
- Small, sharp scissors for cutting threads

NEEDLES
- Embroidery/crewel needles: Sizes 7 and 10
- Tapestry needles: Sizes 26 and 28
- Chenille needles: Size 18, 20 or 22
- Quilting needles: Size 10, 11 or 12
- Bead embroidery needles: Size 10 or 12

TRACING
Dressmaker's carbon OR a light box for transferring designs onto fabric used in conjunction with either a blue tailor's pen, a Pilot Frixion pen or a soft pencil.

GENERAL TOOLS
- A sewing machine and good quality thread
- Embroidery hoops – 14"
- Scroll frames – 24" and 30"
- Thread conditioner
- A beading mat or beading tray
- A seam ripper or stitch cutter for unpicking
- A pair of tweezers to get rid of fluff when you are unpicking
- A spinster twisting-tool for cord making

FABRIC

Linen cotton blend: I've used a quality linen/cotton blend 200gsm fabric for the embroidery in this book. It washes well, does not lose its shape and has a weave that is close enough for fine stitching.

Quilting fabric: It is best to use pure cotton quilting fabrics. Pay a bit more and go for good quality. It's a false economy to use anything less as it will show in the finished product.

Dupion silk: Although it is the most luxurious of all fabrics, it does come with some drawbacks. It is coloured with vegetable dyes, which are not colourfast and may fade or even change colour when washed. Silk also tears easily, so you should be gentle with it when stitching.

Cotton voile: Lightweight and smooth, cotton voile in either white or Ecru is the perfect fabric to use as backing. Because of its weight it is also useful when sandwiching before quilting.

THREADS AND THEIR NEEDLES

When embroidering, you should endeavour to use quality threads. Their dyes should be colourfast; they should not break easily and should not develop fluff balls while you are working with them. The threads used in this book are available worldwide and fulfil the criteria mentioned here.

Stranded cotton: Usually six-stranded, this thread comes in skeins of 8 m. It has a lustrous sheen and you can embroider with as many strands as you wish.

This book uses stranded cotton from the DMC range. Use a size 7 or 10 embroidery needle when stitching with stranded cotton.

Satin thread: This six-stranded thread is ideal for adding texture and dimension to your work. It is inclined to be lively, but can be tamed by running it through a thread conditioner. This book uses threads from the DMC satin range. Use a size 6 or 7 embroidery needle when stitching with rayon thread.

Perlé thread: This twisted thread is available in a variety of sizes and colours, with a sheen that is remarkably effective. It is easy to work with and is ideal for many needle lace, tatting and weaving techniques. This book uses thread from the DMC and Chameleon ranges of perlé threads. Use a size 26 chenille or a size 26 tapestry needle when stitching with perlé thread.

Tatting cotton: This book uses DMC Special Dentelles #80 and Lizbeth #40 and #80 for needle lace, tatting and weaving techniques. The thread tangles easily. To guard against this, run it through a thread conditioner. Use a size 7 embroidery needle or a size 26 tapestry needle when stitching with these threads.

Metallic thread: Although manufactured from 100% polyester yarn, metallic threads have the appearance of metal. These threads shred easily so you should work with short pieces and re-thread often. Thread conditioner provides lubrication and protection, so should be used. You should use a size 6 or 7 embroidery needle when stitching with metallic threads.

BEADS AND CRYSTALS

Beads: Cheap beads are badly shaped, of uneven sizing and have holes that are off-centre. The best beads come from Japan and this book mostly uses beads from the Miyuki range of Japanese seed beads. The glass pearls, fire polished beads and long bugles come from Czechoslovakia. If you think that it's not worth paying extra for better beads, then don't bother with the beading techniques in this book. The result of your efforts will be iffy.

All of the items that have their instructions in the beading techniques gallery should be worked with fine beading thread. The dyes used in Superlon thread are least likely to run, but it is nevertheless worth checking. Wind a little onto a plastic floss card and dip it into water that has just boiled. Thereafter, press the card onto a white paper towel. If the colour runs, plunge it into hot water a few more times until the paper towel stays white. Then it's good to use, with a size 10 or 12 beading or bead embroidery needle.

As a general rule, bead embroidery using stranded cotton, the colour of which should be similar to the shade of the bead. It is sometimes better, though, when attaching single beads, to use a thread colour that is identical to the background fabric.

Because the holes in the beads are small and you will need to pass the needle through, sometimes more than once, you have the choice of using a bead embroidery needle, a size 12 quilting needle or a size 11 sharps needle. My preference is for the quilting needles. They are short and bend less. All of these needles have an extremely small eye so you should use only one strand of thread, which you then double over for extra strength.

Crystals: To be called crystal, glass must use a minimum of 24% lead or metal oxide in its manufacture. The sizing of crystal rhinestones and beads is metric and indicates either the diameter or the length of the glass object. This book uses Swarovski flat back crystals.

Techniques gallery

CREATING A PANEL OF CRAZY PATCH

Machine pieced crazy patchwork (free-hand)

Apart from a variety of fabrics for the patches, you will need a base fabric on which to work. This can be a piece of seed-cloth, linen or cotton fabric. Work out approximately how large you would like the crazy patch panel to be and cut the base fabric larger, so that you will have a border of at least 6" (150 mm) all the way around to accommodate an embroidery hoop.

Stop the edges fraying by stitching along each side with an overlocker or conventional sewing machine set on the zigzag stitch.

IT IS IMPORTANT TO PRESS THE FABRIC WITH AN IRON AFTER EACH STEP DESCRIBED BELOW.

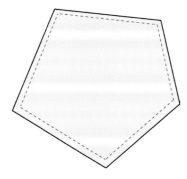

Start by cutting a five-sided shape from fabric no. 1. This will give you a variety of angles to work with. Pin it flat in the centre of the base fabric and stitch each side down, ¼" (5 mm) from the edge, with your sewing machine set on straight stitch.

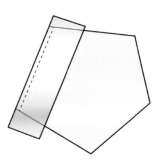

Cut a strip of fabric no. 2. This strip should be long enough to over-run the edges of one side of the centre block. Pin it flat along this side and stitch down leaving a seam allowance of ¼" (5 mm).

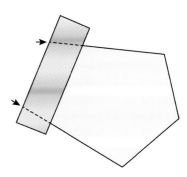

Flip the strip back and press it with a warm iron. Using a ruler to help you, trim the extra length away so that it follows the line of the original patch, as indicated in the diagram above.

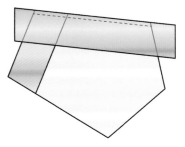

Cut a strip of fabric no. 3. This strip should be long enough to over-run the edges of one side of the centre block plus the strip that you have just added. Pin it flat along this side and stitch down leaving a seam allowance of ¼" (5 mm).

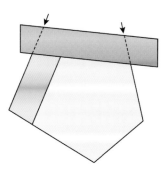

Flip the strip back and press it with a warm iron. Using a ruler to help you, trim the extra length away so that it follows the line of the original patch, as indicated in the diagram above.

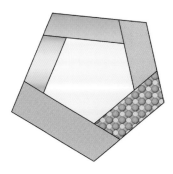

TOP TIP

The best tools for trimming strips and patches are a rotary cutter, a quilters' ruler and a self-healing cutting mat.

Keep adding strips, or rectangles, of different fabrics in this way until you get back to where you started. This completes one round.

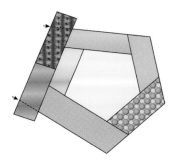

Start the second row by adding a strip adjacent to the first strip of fabric no. 2 that you added.

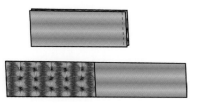

To add variety and extra detail, it is often useful to join two fabrics into one strip as indicated in the two diagrams above. You can also vary the width of the strips of fabric.

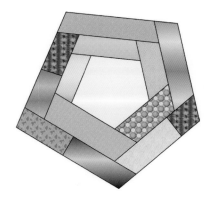

Two rounds have been completed in the diagram above. You can continue making the entire panel in this way. This can, though, make the finished product somewhat circular and even a bit boring.

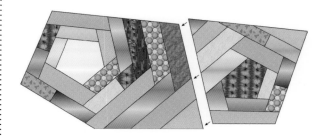

To make the panel more interesting cut a five-sided panel and begin to make a separate piece of crazy patchwork. Assemble this one by joining the patches before you stitch them onto the base fabric. Referring to the diagram above, work both of the pieces of crazy patch until you have the same angle on each one.

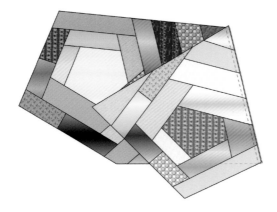

With right sides together, place the new piece over the existing panel. Stitch them together with a straight stitch, as indicated on the right of the above diagram.

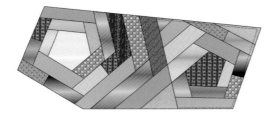

After it has been pressed with an iron, pin and stitch the three remaining sides to the base fabric with straight stitch.

Continue adding strips and rectangles of fabric by stitching them to the base fabric, or making separate pieced sections, which are then stitched to the existing crazy patchwork.

Template-pieced crazy patchwork

The template-pieced method of crazy patchwork allows you to follow a particular pattern, as you would need to do if you want to work the projects in this book. It also allows you to do repeats of a free-hand pieced panel.

Start by taking a photocopy plus an additional copy for each section of the crazy patch pattern. For example, Savannah winter will require three additional copies.

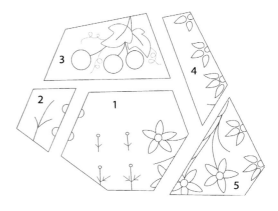

Working with one of the photocopies and keeping to the solid lines that are the outlines of each patch, cut out each numbered block with a pair of scissors.

Referring to the list of fabrics that you should use for each block, pin each block to the relevant fabric and cut out, leaving a seam allowance of at least ¼" (6 mm). It is easy to forget this seam allowance. Don't. You need it for the pattern to work.

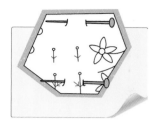

Making sure that the paper pattern stays in the same place, move the top pin to the upper edge. Remove the bottom pin, slip a piece of chalk paper (dressmaker's carbon) between the pattern and the fabric patch, with the ink side facing down onto the fabric and put the pin back where it was to limit movement of the pattern and the patch.

Working on a semi-hard surface (a magazine or soft cover book works well) and using a ballpoint pen (if you have one without any ink in it, that would be first prize), trace over every line. This will include the embroidery lines and the outline of the patch. You need to press very hard when you are tracing. Very hard. It's a job for an arm wrestler.

It is worth checking, before moving anything, that the lines have transferred. Remove the bottom pin and, keeping everything stable, lift the pattern and carbon slightly to expose the fabric patch. Go over the lines again if you haven't pressed hard enough. This time pressing even harder.

Carefully remove the chalk paper, replace the pin, slip the chalk paper under the top half of the pattern and repeat, going over the lines on the top half that you will have missed.

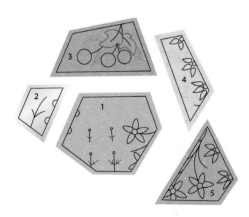

Make sure that, somewhere along the way, you have numbered each patch – on the back is usually a good idea – so that you know what each one is.

Now working with the second photocopy that you made, using a light box, or holding it up to the light – a light box really will make your life much simpler – pin block 1 in place making sure that what you have transferred to the fabric lines up with what is on the paper.

IT IS IMPORTANT TO PRESS THE FABRIC WITH AN IRON AFTER EACH STEP DESCRIBED BELOW.

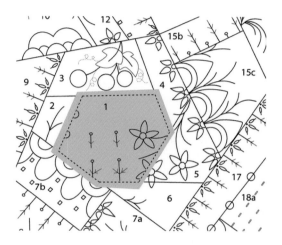

With your sewing machine set on straight stitch of average length, stitch patch 1 to the paper on all five sides. Stitch on the drawn outline of the fabric patch.

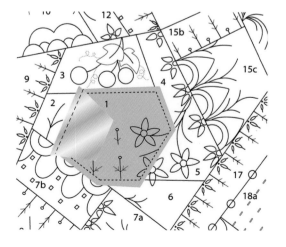

With right sides together, lining it up correctly, pin and stitch patch 2 to the edge of block 1 on the drawn line of that edge. Flip it back and press with an iron.

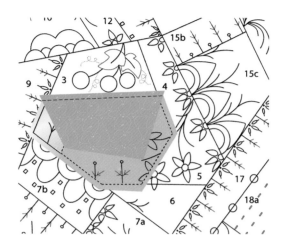

Continue adding patches in this way, following their numerical sequence, until you get to the point where you need to start a separate piece which will be added to the existing work.

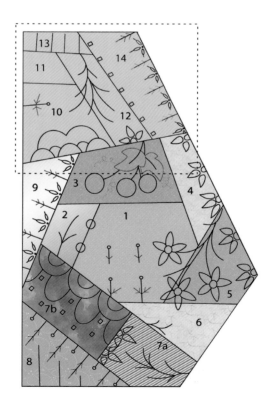

Working with the third photocopy and leaving a border as depicted by the dotted lines in the diagram above, cut out the next section that you need to work with.

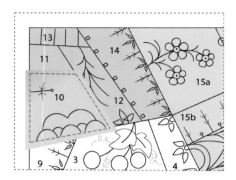

Add the block that follows on numerically from the last block you added to the previous section of the work, pinning and stitching it to the new piece of paper.

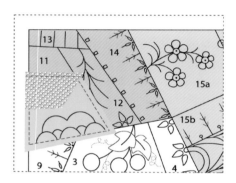

With right sides together, lining it up correctly, pin and stitch the next sequential patch to the edge of the first block on the drawn line of that edge. Flip it back and press with an iron.

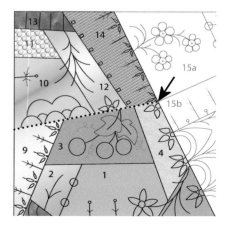

When you have completed the separate section, with right sides together, pin and stitch it to the, first, completed section.

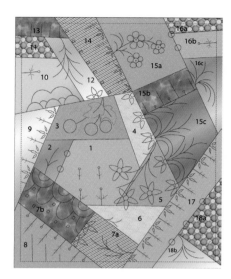

- Complete the crazy patchwork panel, adding each section according to the pattern.
- Remove the paper from the back of the panel.
- Cut a piece of foundation fabric that will accommodate a border of approximately 6″ (150 mm) all the way around the panel. Overlock or hem the edges of this fabric.
- Pin the crazy patch panel to the foundation and tack it down, all the way around, about ¼″ (6 mm) in from the raw edge, as indicated by the dotted line in the diagram above. It is better to tack (rather than machine stitch) the line as you will want to unpick it when you have finished the project.
- This will be the finished edge of the panel and the point to which you will embellish.
- It is worth pointing out at this stage that during embroidered, tatted, needle lace and silk ribbon embroidery embellishment, it is not necessary to stop mid-stitch when you reach this line. Continue over the line in order to complete a stitch in such a way that it will not be distorted. Anything that involves beads, however, should be spaced to end before the tacking line, as it will not be possible to stitch through the beads.
- Neaten off the raw edges on the outside edge of the panel so that they will not fray during the embellishment of the panel.

And now you are good to go. Have fun adding your embellishments!

EMBROIDERY STITCHES

Backstitch

Working from right to left, bring the needle up a stitch length before the end of the line you wish to stitch. Go in at the end of the line, coming up again a stitch length away from the beginning of the stitch you are working. Go into the hole that you came out of for the first stitch, coming up again a stitch length away from the beginning of the stitch you are working. Repeat as necessary, keeping the stitch length as even as possible.

Battlement couching

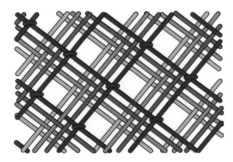

Work a layer of long straight stitches across the area. These can be vertical or diagonal. Work another layer of straight stitches that are placed at right angles to the first layer (lightest layer). Work three more layers in the three shades moving steadily darker (or lighter, depending on what you are creating). Work small, straight couching stitches over the intersection of the last layer of trellis stitches.

Bullion knot

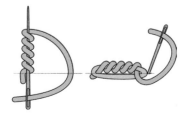

Come out of the fabric at the start of the space you wish to fill and go in again at the end of that space. Come out again at the start of the space but don't pull the needle all the way through the fabric. Twist the thread around the needle as many times as you require. Holding the twists with the thumb and forefinger of your other hand, pull the needle through. Pull the working thread until the knot lies flat and take the needle back into the fabric at the start of the space.

Buttonhole and blanket stitch

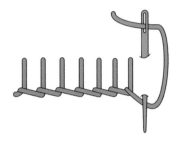

These stitches are formed in the same way. The difference between the two is that buttonhole stitches are placed close together, while blanket stitches have gaps between them. Working from left to right, bring the needle up on the bottom edge where you require the ridge. Take the needle in at the top edge, and out again at the bottom edge, with the thread looped under the needle. Pull through and repeat as required. Secure at the end with a small couching stitch over the last one at the ridge edge.

Chain stitch

Bring the needle up on the line and pull through. Take the needle back into the same hole, loop the thread under the needle and pull through, creating a rounded stitch that is held by the working thread. Staying inside the loop, go back into the same hole, loop the thread under the needle and pull through. Repeat as required and catch the last loop with a small couching stitch.

Chevron stitch

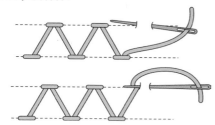

Working along two parallel lines, bring the needle up on the line at the starting point on the bottom line. Moving from left to right work a small backstitch, coming up half way back on the line of the backstitch and pulling through to tighten. Go into the fabric on the top line and pull through. Work a small backstitch, coming up halfway back on the line of the backstitch and pulling through to tighten. Go into the fabric on the bottom line and pull through. Repeat as required, finishing off with a complete backstitch.

Coral stitch

Working from left to right, bring your needle up at the beginning of the line. Make a small stitch under the line, taking the working thread over and then under the needle. Pull through, first backwards and then forwards to tighten the small knot.

Couching stitch

Use two threaded needles. Bring the first one up at the beginning of the line and lay it down. Using the second needle, catch that thread with small stitches placed at intervals along the line. These stitches should not have a tight tension.

Cretan stitch (straight)

Straight Cretan stitch is worked along two parallel lines. Starting at bottom left and working to the right, begin with a small straight stitch. Come up halfway along the stitch on the left and go in at the top coming out immediately below and tightening to catch the long stitch. Go in at the bottom, coming out immediately above, tighten to catch the long stitch. Finish with a short, straight stitch that catches the stitch before it.

Detached buttonhole stitch

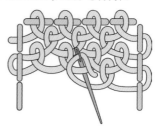

Surround the area that you intend to fill with small back-stitches which will be what you use to anchor the detached buttonhole stitch. Bring your needle up on the side, at the starting point indicated in the diagram, go over and under the first horizontal backstitch, making sure that the working thread is under the needle. Pull through to form a buttonhole stitch. Continue to the end of the row and snake through the vertical backstitches at the end. The second and subsequent rows are anchored in the loops between the stitches.

Detached chain (lazy daisy stitch)

Bring the needle up at the starting point and pull through. Take the needle back into the same hole, loop the thread under the needle and pull through. Catch the loop with a small couching stitch.

Double detached chain

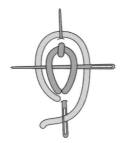

Work the smaller detached chain using the darker thread. Place a tapestry needle under the two sides of the main part of the stitch as indicated in the diagram. Using the lighter thread, came up below the first detached chain. Take the needle back into the same hole and manipulate it so that it comes out where you will want to catch the loop with a small couching stitch. Make the threads of the loop lie under both sides of the horizontal needle and, also, the needle that will catch it. Tighten the stitch, work the small couching stitch to catch the loop and remove the horizontal needle, making sure that the inner detached chain remains slightly raised in the middle.

Drizzle stitch

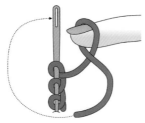

Bring the threaded needle up through the fabric, remove the thread from the eye of the needle. Put the needle back into the fabric just next to where you came up. Place the thread over your left index finger and rotate your finger to form a loop. Transfer that loop onto the needle, pull the work-ing thread so that it goes down to the base. This is a cast on stitch. Cast on as many stitches as you need. Without removing it from the fabric, rethread the needle and pull the thread down through the cast on stitches to the back of the fabric.

Extended French knot (pistil stitch)

Bring the needle up through the fabric, twist the thread over the needle once or twice and tighten. Go back into the fabric away from where you came out. Pull the twists that are around the needle down to the bottom. Hold the thread and pull the needle through to form the knot.

Feather stitch (basic)

Come up on the left of the lines and go in on the line, coming up below that slightly to the left of the line, catching the loop of the working thread before you tighten. Go in on the right of the line, coming up below that slightly to the right of the line, catching the loop of working thread before you tighten. Keep working on each side of the line in this way until you have covered its length. End off with a small couching stitch that catches the last stitch.

Feather stitch (variation)

Come up on the left and go in on the right of the line. Come up below that in the centre, picking up the loop of working thread as you tighten the stitch. Working down and diagonally to the right, do two more stitches in the same way. Change direction, working down and diagonally to the left. Keep working in this way until you have covered the length you wish to cover. Finish off with a small couching stitch that catches the last loop.

Fly stitch

Start at the tip of the shape with a straight stitch. Come up on the left of that stitch, go in at the same level on the right, leaving a loop. Come up in the bottom hole of the straight stitch. Catch the loop and pull through. Make a straight stitch.

French knot

Bring the needle up through the fabric, twist the thread over the needle once or twice and tighten. Go back into the fabric just next to where you came out. Pull the twists that are around the needle down to the bottom. Hold the thread and pull the needle through to form the knot.

Herringbone stitch

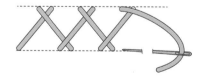

Going from left to right, come up on the bottom line. Working diagonally, go in on the top line and come up a little way back. Crossing over the first stitch, go back in on the bottom line, coming up a little way back. Keep going in this way until you have completed the row.

Knotted cable chain stitch

Bring the needle up at the beginning of the line. Make a small stitch under the line, take the working thread over and then under the needle. Pull through, first backwards and then forwards, to tighten the small knot. Pass the needle under the thread before the knot and pull the thread through. Go into the fabric on the other side of the knot and bring the needle up further down on the line, making sure that your thread is under the needle. Pull through to form a loop. Form the next knot by catching the fabric outside the loop and continuing as described above.

Layered buttonhole stitch

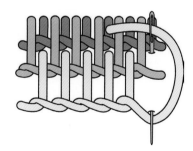

Referring to the diagram above, stitch the first line of buttonhole stitch as usual (dark). Start the next row (medium) above the ridge of the first row. Go into the fabric at the same level that you went into the fabric when stitching the first row, coming up at the bottom of the new row with the thread looped under the needle and pulling through. For the third and subsequent rows (light) start the row slightly above the ridge of the previous row. Go into the fabric immediately above the ridge of the first row with the thread looped under the needle and pulling through. Repeat as required. Fill in the vacant spaces between the buttonhole stitches with straight stitches, as depicted in the diagram for the woven variation, overleaf.

Layered buttonhole stitch (woven)

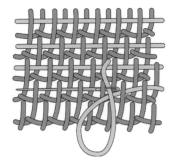

Following the instructions above, stitch layered buttonhole. Thereafter, usually with a different shade of thread, weave over and under the vertical legs of the buttonhole stitches, working over and under for the first row, then changing to under and over for the next, thereafter alternating for each woven row.

Long and short stitch

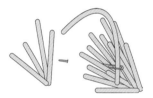

Work with 1 strand of thread. Starting in the middle of the shape working first to the right and then returning to the middle and working to the left, stitch the darkest colour at the base first. Work straight stitches of random lengths from top to bottom, fanning the stitches so that they favour the centre. Change to the medium colour thread for the next row, which is started slightly above the darkest colour. Work the stitches going into the fabric between the threads in the previous row. These stitches should also be of random lengths, making them alternately long and short on both ends. Change to the lightest colour for the top row. Following the top outline of the shape, work the final row going into the threads in the previous row. These stitches should also be of random lengths, with the ragged edge at the bottom of the row.

Outline stitch

It is usually best to do this stitch with one strand of thread. Working from left to right, come up at the beginning of the line. Go in on the line and before pulling the thread through, come up halfway back on the line. Pull through. Go into the fabric halfway further and come up just a little past halfway back, so that you are not coming up in the same hole as where the first stitch finished. Continue to the end of the outline.

Raised herringbone stitch

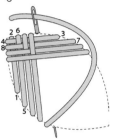

Bring your needle up at 1. Go in at 2, come up at 3 and go down at 4. Bring it up again at 5, go in at 6. Come up at 7 and go in at 8. Continue in this way until the shape has been filled. A subtle ridge will form in the centre of the leaf shape.

Running stitch

Stitch a continuous line by passing the needle over and under the fabric. Usually the gaps are half the length of the stitches.

Satin stitch

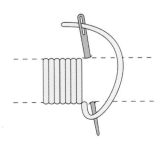

Working from left to right, bring your needle up at the bottom and in at the top, and coming out at the bottom again. Place your stitches close together so that no fabric is showing. It is usually best to work over the shortest side of a shape. Stitches can also be placed diagonally.

Sorbello stitch

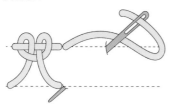

Working from left to right, bring your needle up on the top line. Make a straight stitch. Come up on the bottom line, work two detached buttonhole stitches over the straight stitch and go in on the bottom line. Come up on the top line again and repeat as necessary.

Split stitch

It is usually best to do this stitch with two strands of thread. Come up at the beginning of the line. Go in again a little way along and before pulling through, come up again in the middle of the stitch, taking the needle up between the two strands of thread. Pull through to tighten and finish the line with a straight stitch that is not split.

Stem stitch

Working from left to right, come up just above the line, go in just below the line, come up halfway back just above the line. Pull through.

Straight stitch

Bring your needle up at the beginning of the stitch and take it into the fabric at the end of the stitch. Stitches can be of equal or unequal length, or as directed in the instructions in your pattern.

Trellis couching

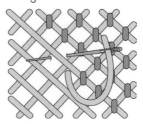

Work a layer of long straight stitches across the area. These can be vertical or diagonal. Work another layer of long straight stitches that are placed at right angles to the first layer. Work small, straight couching stitches over the intersection of the stitches.

Trellis couching with cross-stitch filling

Work a layer of pairs of long straight stitches across the area. These can be vertical or diagonal. Work another layer of pairs of long straight stitches that are placed at right angles to the first layer. Work four small, straight couching stitches over each thread of each intersection. Work from the outside into the middle of each intersection, each stitch going into the same hole.

Trellis couching with triangular filling

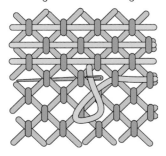

Using thread shade 1, work a layer of long diagonal straight stitches across the area. Work another layer of long straight stitches that are placed at right angles to the first layer. Work vertical small, straight couching stitches over the intersection of the stitches. These can be with the same thread, or another shade. Come through the fabric with a third shade on a tapestry needle. Weave under each couching stitch making a long horizontal line, which goes into the fabric when you reach the other side.

Twisted couching, twisted long and short stitch, twisted satin stitch

Refer to Working With Twisted Threads at the end of this section (p.28).

Up and down buttonhole stitch

Working from left to right, bring the needle up on the bottom edge where you require the ridge. Take the needle in at the top edge, and out again at the bottom edge, with the thread looped under the needle. Pull through. Go over the thread, insert the needle on the line, bringing it up again adjacent to the upper part of the stitch, as depicted. Making sure that the thread is looped under the needle, pull upwards and then downwards so that the small couching stitch holds the two stitches together.

Vermicelli couching

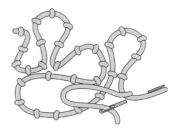

Thread a needle with two strands of thread and another with one strand of the same thread. Come through the fabric on the edge of the area you wish to cover with the two-strand needle and couch that thread with the one-strand needle into a series of rounded squiggles that go over all of the area, but never cross over each other. At the edges of the section go into the fabric and come up again further along, continuing the pattern.

Vermicelli couching 2-tone variation

To work 2-tone variation, follow the instructions for vermicelli couching above, working with two strands of cotton couched down with a single strand in the lighter of two shades. Make sure that the swirls are large enough to accommodate the second shade. The second shade requires a darker tone and is a single strand couched with a single strand, swirling in between the existing couching on both sides of each line.

Wheatear stitch

Working from top to bottom, work a detached chain stitch, starting just below and stretching to the beginning. Place a diagonal straight stitch on each side of this stitch. Come up slightly below, work a loop through all the threads of the straight and detached chain stitches. Place a diagonal straight stitch on each side of this loop. Repeat as required.

Whipped back stitch

To whip backstitch, bring your needle up adjacent to the beginning of the line of stitching. Take your needle and thread over, then under each stitch. It is advisable to use a tapestry needle when whipping. A contrasting colour thread is often effective.

Whipped chain stitch

To whip chain stitch, bring your needle up adjacent to the beginning of the line of stitching. Take your needle and thread over, then under each stitch. It is advisable to use a tapestry needle when whipping. A contrasting colour thread is often effective.

Whipped spider's web filling

Working from left to right, create a straight stitch ladder which forms the basis of this technique. Working from right to left, bring your needle up slightly past the last straight stitch in the ladder. Go under the first stitch. Go back over and under the same stitch and under the next straight stitch. Do continuous lines.

Whipped stem stitch

To whip stem stitch, bring your needle up adjacent to the beginning of the line of stem stitch. Take your needle and thread over, then under the section where that stitch and the next stitch lie adjacent to one another. It is advisable to use a tapestry needle when whipping. A contrasting colour thread is often effective.

Woven trellis

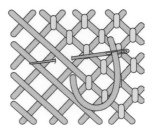

Using thread shade 1, work a layer of long straight stitches across the area. These can be horizontal or diagonal. Work another layer of long straight stitches that are placed at right angles to the first layer. Using thread shade 2, work small, straight couching stitches over the intersection of the long stitches.

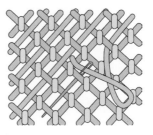

Using thread shade 3, weave over and under the shade 1 lines.

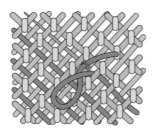

Using thread shade 4, and working at right angles, weave under the first of layer of trellis (shade 1 stitches) and over the weaving that you have just done (shade 3).

Twisted couching

When couching with twisted thread, use a size 22 or 24 che-nille needle for the twisted thread. Thread a separate needle with one strand of the same thread. Bring the twisted thread up at the beginning of the line, or outline, as you would with normal couching described previously in this gallery. Couch with the single thread. You should not, however, take your couching thread over the whole cord. Catch only the lowest twist with the single strand. Try to make this stitch invisible.

Twisted long and short stitch

Following the guidelines provided for long and short stitch described previously in this gallery, thread the twisted thread onto a size 20 or 22 chenille needle. Work with this thread in the normal manner to create the long and short stitch shading.

Twisted satin stitch

Following the guidelines provided for satin stitch described previously in this gallery, thread the twisted thread onto a size 20 or 22 chenille needle. Work with this thread in the normal manner to create the satin stitch.

WORKING WITH TWISTED THREAD

The easiest way to convert stranded cotton into cord with which to embroider is to acquire a Spinster tool. It is however possible to twist it by turning it between your index finger and thumb, or to place a pencil in the loop and turn that.

- Cut a two-strand length of thread that measures approximately 1 yd (1 m). Tie an overhand knot on each end of the thread. Loop one end over something that won't move, like a cup-hook or a door-knob. Loop the other end over the hook on the Spinster (or place a pencil in the loop), pull the yarn taut and wind the threads until they are firmly twisted together. Test from time to time by relaxing the tension and allowing the threads to twist around one another.

- When you are happy with the twist, double the twisted thread over by placing the two ends together. Hang the Spinster, or something heavy, at the fold so that it will twist together evenly and pull the threads off the hook. Holding the ends together, allow the thread to hang from your fingers and twist freely.
- Once they stop twisting, do an over-hand knot at the raw ends to keep them together. Snip off the raw end of the thread after the knot.
- Thread the folded end onto a size 20 or 22 chenille needle and embroider with it as if it were normal thread.

RIBBON EMBROIDERY STITCHES

Use a size 24 chenille needle for 2 mm ribbon, a size 22 chenille needle for 4 mm ribbon and a size 20 chenille needle for 7 mm ribbon.

It can be difficult to ease 7 mm ribbon through the fabric. If necessary, pierce the fabric in the correct spot using a tailor's awl.

How to thread the needle

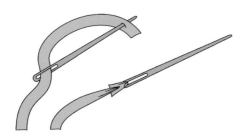

Take through the eye of the needle, pulling it through until you are able to pierce the ribbon at the raw end. Take the sharp end of the needle through the ribbon about ½" (10 mm) from the end and pull the ribbon down so that it sits securely in the eye of the needle.

Silk ribbon starting knot

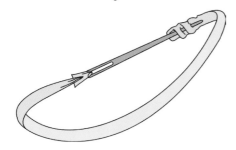

Run the sharp end of the needle through the ribbon a few times, starting at the raw end moving towards the needle. Pull the needle and the length of the ribbon through until the end and you will have a fine 'knot' at the end of the ribbon.

Silk ribbon stitch

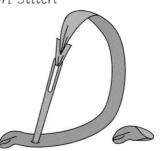

Bring the threaded needle up through the fabric. Lay the ribbon down. Allowing a slight loop to form, take the needle through the ribbon just before the end of the petal or leaf. Pull the ribbon through carefully, stopping just before you pull it all of the way through. You should end with a very slight point at the tip, the ribbon having folded in towards the point where it goes through the fabric.

French knot ribbon rose

Bring the threaded needle up through the fabric. Wind the ribbon once over the needle about 2¾" (70 mm) away from where it exits the fabric. Holding the ribbon taut, run the sharp end of the needle through the ribbon numerous times, starting immediately after where it folds over the needle and continuing down to the base. Go into the fabric at the base of the ribbon and gently pull through until the fold over the needle stops you from going any further. Using a single strand of cotton that is the same colour as the ribbon, strengthen the rose by coming up through all the folds of the ribbon and going back down again just next to where you come out, thereby creating an almost invisible stab stitch. Do a second stab stitch if necessary.

COMBINATION STITCHES

- All of these stitches are combinations of stitches found in the techniques galleries on the previous pages in this chapter.
- Assume that all of the stitches that are worked with stranded cotton use 2 strands, unless otherwise stated in brackets.
- Work the silk ribbon stitches and beads following the advice given in those techniques galleries.

Double chevron, lazy daisy, bead and straight stitch combination

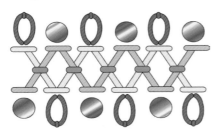

First line chevron stitch
Second line chevron stitch
Straight stitch
Lazy daisy or detached chain stitch
Bead

Double chevron, lazy daisy and bead combination

First line chevron stitch
Second line chevron stitch
Lazy daisy or detached chain trefoil
Lazy daisy or detached chain trefoil
Bead

Double chevron, lazy daisy, bead and straight stitch combination

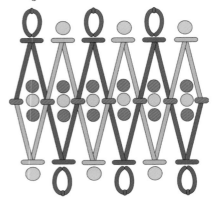

First line chevron stitch
Second line chevron stitch
Straight stitch
Lazy daisy or detached chain stitch

Bead couching

Bead

Double Cretan, straight stitch and bead combination I

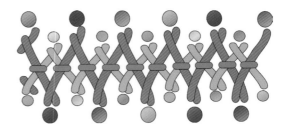

First line Cretan stitch
Second line Cretan stitch
Straight stitch
Larger bead
Smaller bead

Double Cretan, straight stitch and bead combination II

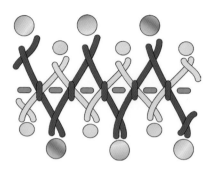

- ■ First line Cretan stitch, vertical straight stitch
- ■ Second line Cretan stitch
- ■ Horizontal straight stitch
- ■ Smaller bead
- ■ Larger bead

Double lazy daisy, fly stitch and bead combination

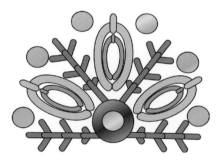

- ◉ Large bead held in place by small bead
- ■ Inner lazy daisy
- ■ Outer lazy daisy
- ■ Fly stitch
- ■ Small beads

Herringbone, double lazy daisy and beads combination

- ■ Herringbone stitch
- ■ Bead over intersections
- ■ Inner lazy daisy
- ■ Outer lazy daisy
- ■ Additional line of vertical beads

Knotted cable chain, lazy daisy and bead combination

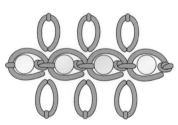

- ■ Knotted cable chain stitch
- ■ Bead
- ■ Lazy daisy stitch

Lazy daisy, straight stitch and bead combination I

- ■ Lazy daisy stitch
- ■ Straight stitch
- ■ Bead

Lazy daisy, straight stitch and bead combination II

- Horizontal lazy daisy stitch
- Vertical lazy daisy stitch
- Top diagonal straight stitches
- Top vertical and bottom diagonal straight stitches
- Bead

Lazy daisy, straight stitch and bead combination III

- Lazy daisy trefoil
- Lower lazy daisy leaf and diagonal straight stitches
- Bead

Lazy daisy and whipped backstitch combination

- Whipped back stitch and lazy daisy leaves
- Lazy daisy trefoils

Up and down buttonhole, extended French knot and lazy daisy combination

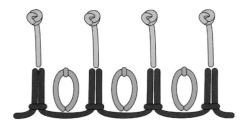

- Up and down buttonhole stitch
- Lazy daisy stitch
- Extended French knot

Simple bead-flower combination I

- Lower small bead
- Tila bead flowerpot
- Small bead flower stem
- Middle darker simple bead petal
- Outer two lighter simple bead petals

Simple bead-flower combination II

- Bead at bottom and top of bugle bead
- Bugle bead
- Middle darker simple bead petal
- Outer two lighter simple bead petals

Silk ribbon stitch, fly stitch and straight stitch combination I

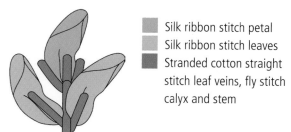

■ Silk ribbon stitch petal
■ Silk ribbon stitch leaves
■ Stranded cotton straight stitch leaf veins, fly stitch calyx and stem

Silk ribbon stitch, fly stitch and straight stitch combination II

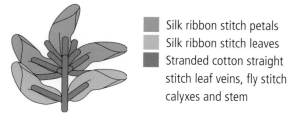

■ Silk ribbon stitch petals
■ Silk ribbon stitch leaves
■ Stranded cotton straight stitch leaf veins, fly stitch calyxes and stem

Silk ribbon stitch, French knot and straight stitch combination I

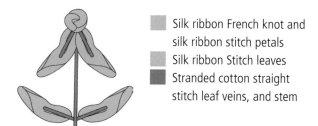

■ Silk ribbon French knot and silk ribbon stitch petals
■ Silk ribbon Stitch leaves
■ Stranded cotton straight stitch leaf veins, and stem

Silk ribbon stitch, French knot and straight stitch combination II

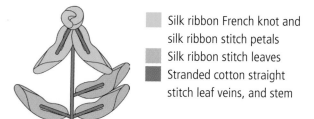

■ Silk ribbon French knot and silk ribbon stitch petals
■ Silk ribbon stitch leaves
■ Stranded cotton straight stitch leaf veins, and stem

Feather stitch, lazy daisy and bead combination

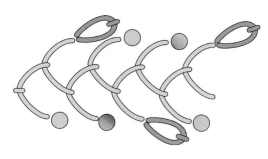

■ Feather stitch
■ Lazy daisy stitch
■ Bead colour 1
■ Bead colour 2

Feather stitch, silk ribbon stitch and French knot combination

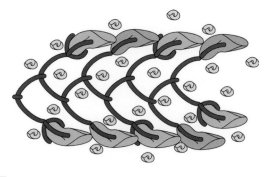

■ Silk ribbon stitch
■ Silk ribbon stitch
■ Feather stitch, fly stitch, straight stitch
■ French knot

NEEDLE LACE

General tips & basic knowledge

1. For ease of layout, the techniques are depicted on square blocks.

2. If you are new to needle lace techniques, try the techniques on a scrap of fabric.

3. Work in square blocks first, using a perlé no. 12, or even a no. 8. This gives you the opportunity to get to know the techniques and to get the feel of adjusting your stitching tension before you move onto filling shapes.

4. When you feel confident, draw some simple shapes onto the scrap of fabric and try those out, increasing and decreasing as necessary to fill shapes.

5. Once you move on to working on your embroidery pieces, Cordonette #80 or #40 tatting thread and perlé no. 12 are the best threads to use.

6. It is almost impossible to create a smooth edge to your needle lace. Try to be as even and smooth as you can but be aware that you will need to either outline the area or cover the edge in some way. Crewel stitches or beads are suitable for this task.

7. Always work with your fabric stretched taut in a hoop to prevent puckering.

8. Use a size 7 or 8 embroidery needle to work the back-stitches (BS) and a size 26 or 28 tapestry needle to work the detached buttonhole stitches (DBH).

9. Each shape that you wish to fill with needle lace should be surrounded with backstitch (BS). Use these stitches to anchor the lace.

10. Don't expect your backstitches (BS) to be perfect. It's not a perfect world. Use them as a guide and an anchor only. Adjust your tension and counting to suit the detached buttonhole stitches (DBH), not the backstitch (BS).

11. The majority of needle lace techniques use detached buttonhole stitches (DBH).

How to read the patterns in this gallery

1. Each instruction notes the length of the backstitches (BS) in the top row.

2. With the exception of those stitches in the section on Edges, it usually doesn't matter which direction you choose to stitch your needle lace. You make life easier for yourself if you choose to work the first row on the edge that will give you the longest and straightest row, decreasing or increasing from there.

3. To start the first row, come up at the side, approximately level with where the ridge of the detached buttonhole will lie. Alternatively, depending on where you have chosen to start, glide in as smoothly as you can from the backstitch (BS) curve.

4. A 'group' means two or more detached buttonhole stitches (DBH) that lie together, usually preceded and followed by a gap, or loop.

5. A 'loop' means a single strand, leading up to or away from a either a single detached buttonhole stitch or a group of buttonhole stitches, as described above.

6. LR means working from left to right; RL means working from right to left. Refer to Needle Lace Bottom Row for instructions to finish off a section of needle lace by attaching it to the backstitch (BS) at the bottom.

7. Always make sure that the beginning and end of each row are approximately level with one another.

8. When working further down, always make sure that you space your rows so that the sides of the needle lace are neither bunching up, nor stretching down too far. If you are unsure of where to come up at the beginning of a row, pull the last row down with the point of your needle, see how far it stretches, then come up for the start of your row approximately level with that point.

Needle Lace Bottom Row

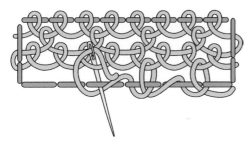

Continue working the detached buttonhole stitches until you reach the bottom of the section that you intend to fill. It does not matter whether you are working a right to left, or a left to right row. For the purposes of these instructions, assume you have worked a left to right row to correspond with the diagram on the left.

1. At the end of the row, instead of snaking through the backstitch take the needle through the fabric to the other side.

2. Bring the needle up directly below the backstitch at the bottom, just in from the corner on the right.

3. The last row continues the pattern of the technique and attaches the needle lace to the backstitch at the same time.

4. Depending on how far you need to travel to make the first buttonhole stitch in the pattern you may need to whip the first backstitch so that the loop which would otherwise form becomes lost. In the diagram above, this has not been necessary.

5. Working from right to left, form the detached buttonhole stitch which goes through the loop by taking the needle through the loop in the previous row and through the backstitch at the same time. Make sure that the working thread is below the tip of the needle.

6. Pull the needle through to form the detached buttonhole stitch, making sure that the lace pulls down and stretches over the shape that you have covered.

7. Whip the next backstitch to lose the loop and create the next detached buttonhole stitch.

8. Continue in this way until you reach the left corner. The needle lace should be attached and evenly stretched over the entire section.

9. Take your needle through the fabric to end off at the back.

Numbered stitches

NEEDLE LACE STITCH NO. 1

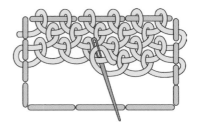

Preparation: BS outline
Top row stitch length: To accommodate 2 x DBH

1. Working LR, 2 x DBH into every BS along the top. Go through the nearest BS down the right hand side that is level with the ridge of the DBH in the row you have just done. Snake down through the next BS.

2. Working RL, do 1 x DBH into each gap between the DBH in the previous row, until you reach the end of the row. Snake down to start the next row.

Fill the space in this way and attach at the bottom.

NEEDLE LACE STITCH NO. 2

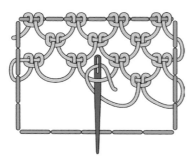

Preparation: BS outline
Top row stitch length: To accommodate 2 x DBH

1. Working LR, [2 x DBH into first BS, miss a BS]. Repeat [--] to end. Go through the nearest BS down the right hand side that is level with the ridge of the DBH in the row you have just done. Snake down through the next BS.
2. Working RL, 2 x DBH into each loop. Go through the nearest BS down the left hand side that is level with the ridge of the DBH in the row you have just done. Snake down to the next row.

Fill the space in this way and attach at the bottom.

NEEDLE LACE STITCH NO. 5

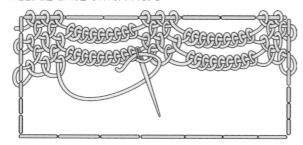

Preparation: BS outline
Top row stitch length: To accommodate 3 x DBH

1. Working LR, [3 x DBH into BS, miss 2 BS]. Repeat [--] to end. Go through the nearest BS down the right hand side that is level with the ridge of the DBH in the row you have just done. Snake down through the next BS.
2. # Working RL, [9 x DBH into large loop, 1 x DBH into small loop, 1 x DBH into small loop]. Repeat [--] to end. Snake down to the next row.
3. Working LR, [1 x DBH into each small loop, i.e. 1 at the end of the group of 9 DBH in the previous row, 1 between the 2 DBH in the middle, and 1 at the beginning of the next group of 9]. Repeat [--] to end. Snake down to the next row.#

Keep working the rows from # to # to fill the space and attach at the bottom.

NEEDLE LACE STITCH NO. 7

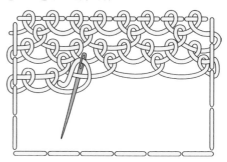

Preparation: BS outline
Top row stitch length: To accommodate 1 x DBH

1. Working LR, 1 x DBH into each BS. Go through the nearest BS down the right hand side that is level with the ridge of the DBH in the row you have just done. Snake down through the next BS.
2. # Working RL, [miss 1 small loop, 1 x DBH into next small loop]. Repeat [--] to end. Snake down to the next row.
3. Working LR, 2 x DBH into each large loop. Snake down through the next BS.
4. Working LR, 1 x DBH into the small loop between the groups of 2 DBH in the previous row. Miss 1 loop]. Snake down to the next row.#

Keep working the rows from # to # to fill the space and attach at the bottom.

NEEDLE LACE STITCH NO. 8

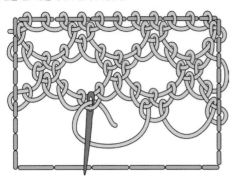

Preparation: BS outline
Top row stitch length: To accommodate 2 x DBH

1. Working LR, 2 x DBH into each BS. Go through the near-est BS down the right hand side that is level with the ridge of the DBH in the row you have just done. Snake down through the next BS.
2. Working RL, [miss 2 loops, 1 x DBH into next loop, 1 x DBH into next loop]. Repeat [--] to end. Snake down to the next row.
3. #Working LR, [3 x DBH into large loop, 1 x DBH into small loop]. Repeat [--] to end. Snake down to the next row.
4. Working RL, [miss 2 loops, 1 x DBH into next loop, 1 x DBH into next loop]. Make sure that you go into the two loops in the middle of the group of three in the previous row. Repeat [--] to end. Snake down to the next row. #

Keep working the rows from # to # to fill the space and attach at the bottom.

NEEDLE LACE STITCH NO. 15

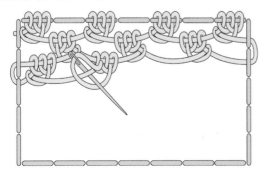

Preparation: BS outline
Top row stitch length: To accommodate 3 x DBH

1. Working LR, [3 x DBS into BS, needle over and then under the loop that led up to the group. Making sure that the working thread is lying under the needle; pull through to form a buttonhole stitch that lies horizontally below the group of two detached buttonhole stitches. This is called a Three Group Plus One (3G+1). Miss 1 x BS]. Repeat [--] to end. Go through the nearest BS down the right hand side that is level with the ridge of the DBH in the row you have just done. Snake down through the next BS.
2. #Working RL, work a 3G+1 into each large loop. Snake down to the next row.
3. Working LR, work a 3G+1 into each large loop. Snake down to the next row. #

Keep working the rows from # to # to fill the space and attach at the bottom leaving out the additional horizontal buttonhole.

NEEDLE LACE STITCH NO. 34

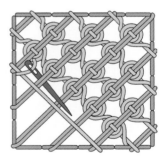

Preparation: BS outline
Top row stitch length: To accommodate 2 x DBH

1. Working diagonally over the space, stitch the first layer (darker lines). Come up outside and close to the backstitch line. Lay the thread at 45° across the whole area. Go over and under the nearest backstitch. Take the thread back to where you started, going under the backstitch line and into the fabric. Taking into account that the spacing of the stitches should allow space for the circles in the second layer, cover the entire shape with long diagonal double stitches.

2. The second layer (light lines) is worked at right angles to the first layer. Come up outside and close to the backstitch line and lay the thread at 45° across the whole area. Go over and under the nearest backstitch. This forms the middle line.

- Working in a circle, cross over the middle line, go under the side stitch (formed by the first layer of stitching), go over the middle line, go under the side stitch on the other side, go over the middle line at the top and go under the side stitch on the first side. This forms one circle.
- Do a second concentric circle. Go over the middle line, go under the side stitch on the other side, go over the middle line at the top and go under the side stitch on the first side. This forms the second circle. Go over the middle line and under the next side stitch formed by the first layer.
- Form the next two concentric circles by working in the opposite direction to the first two.

Keep working down the line in this way until you reach the bottom. Take your thread over the middle line, go under the backstitch line and into the fabric. Taking into account that the spacing of the stitches, complete the second layer of stitching.

Beaded needle lace stitches

BEADED NEEDLE LACE STITCH NO. 1
(based on Numbered Stitch 15)

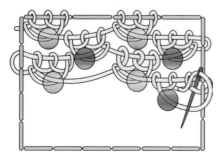

Preparation: BS outline
Top row stitch length: To accommodate 3 x DBH

1. Working LR, [3 x DBS into BS, pick up a bead and slide it to the bottom of the thread where it comes out of the DBH, needle over and then under the loop that led up to the group. Making sure that the working thread is lying under the needle; pull through to form a buttonhole stitch that lies horizontally below the group of two detached buttonhole stitches with the thread lying behind the bead. This is called a Three Group Plus One Beaded (3G+1B). Miss 1 x BS]. Repeat [--] to end. Go through the nearest BS down the right hand side that is level with the ridge of the DBH in the row you have just done. Snake down through the next BS.

2. #Working RL, work a 3G+1B into each large loop. Snake down to the next row.

3. Working LR, work a 3G+1B into each large loop. Snake down to the next row. #

Fill the space in this way and attach at the bottom.

BEADED NEEDLE LACE STITCH NO. 2
(based on Numbered Stitch 15)

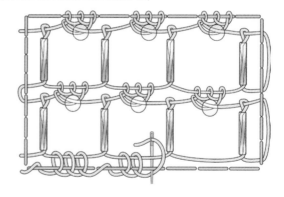

Preparation: BS outline
Top row stitch length: To accommodate 3 x DBH

1. Working LR, [3 x DBS into BS, pick up a bead and slide it to the bottom of the thread where it comes out of the DBH, needle over and then under the loop that led up to the group. Making sure that the working thread is lying under the needle; pull through to form a buttonhole stitch that lies horizontally below the group of two detached buttonhole stitches with the thread lying behind the bead. This is called a Three Group Plus One Beaded (3G+1B). Miss 1 x BS]. Repeat [--] to end. Go through the nearest BS down the right hand side that is level with the ridge of the DBH in the row you have just done. Snake down through the next

BS, taking note of the wider spacing that you will need to accommodate the bugle bead.

2. #Working RL. [Pick up a bugle bead. Work a DBH by going over and under the loop at the top, taking the thread back down the bead and going over the thread leading up to the bead to create the buttonhole formation]. Repeat [--] to end. Snake down to the next row.

3. Working LR, work a 3G+1B into each loop. Snake down to the next row, taking note of the wider spacing that you will need to accommodate the bugle bead.#

Keep working rows in this way until you have filled the required space. Try to end on a row that incorporates the bugle beads, so that you can finish off with groups of 3 at the bottom edge. Following the instructions for the bottom row in the General Tips, attach the detached buttonhole stitch to the backstitch at the bottom, leaving out the additional horizontal buttonhole and bead.

Needle lace edgings

NEEDLE LACE EDGING NO. 1 (INSERTION LACE)

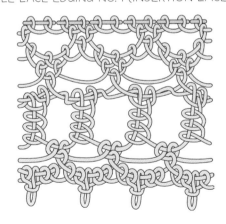

Preparation: BS line along top edge
Top row stitch length: To accommodate 2 x DBH

1. Working LR, 2 x DBH into each BS. Go into the fabric at the end of the row and come up again to start the next row where the ridge of DBH in that row will lie.

2. Working RL, [miss 2 loops, 1 x DBH into next loop, 1 x DBH into next loop]. Repeat [--] to end. Go into the fabric at the end of the row and come up again to start the next row where the ridge of DBH in that row will lie.

3. Working LR, [3 x DBH into large loop, 1 x DBH into small loop]. Repeat [--] to end. Go into the fabric at the end of the row and come up again to start the next row where the ridge of DBH in that row will lie.

4. Working RL, [miss 2 loops, 1 x DBH into next loop, 1 x DBH into next loop]. Make sure that you go into the two loops in the middle of the group of three in the previous row. Repeat [--] to end. Go into the fabric at the end of the row and come up again to start the next row where the ridge of DBH in that row will lie.

5. Working LR, [miss large loop, 1 DBH into small loop]. Repeat [--] to end. Go into the fabric, turn your work over and catch a bit of the fabric. Come up to the top in the same place. Working RL, whip once into each small loop and twice into each large loop. Go into the fabric at the end of the row and come up again to start the next row where the base of the gap formed in that row will lie.

6. Working LR, [2 x DBH into large loop, needle over and then under the loop that led up to the group. Making sure that the working thread is lying under the needle; pull through to form a buttonhole stitch that lies horizontally below the group of two detached buttonhole stitches. Work two more DBH in the same way. This is called a Two Group Plus Three (2G+3). Move to next large loop]. Repeat [--] to end. Go into the fabric at the end of the row and come up again to start the next row where the ridge of DBH in that row will lie.

7. Working RL, work 2 x DBH into each large loop. Go into the fabric at the end of the row and come up again to start the next row where the ridge of DBH in that row will lie.

8. Working LR, work 1 x DBH into each small loop. Go into the fabric at the end of the row and come up again to start the next row where the ridge of DBH in that row will lie.

9. Working RL, [2 x DBH, 1 x DBH with picot, 2 x DBH into large loop]. Repeat [--] to end and finish off the thread.

Thread 2 mm silk ribbon onto a size 22 (or larger) tapestry needle. Bring the needle up in the middle of the gap created by row 6. Weave the ribbon over and under the bars. Take the needle to the back of the fabric and end off the ribbon.

NEEDLE LACE EDGING NO. 2 (INSERTION LACE)

Preparation: BS line along top edge
Top row stitch length: To accommodate 2 x DBH

1. Working LR, 2 x DBH into each BS. Go into the fabric at the end of the row and come up again to start the next row where the ridge of DBH in that row will lie.

2. Working RL, [miss 2 loops, 1 x DBH into next loop, 1 x DBH into next loop]. Repeat [--] to end. Go into the fabric at the end of the row and come up again to start the next row where the ridge of DBH in that row will lie.

3. Working LR, [3 x DBH into large loop, 1 x DBH into small loop]. Repeat [--] to end. Go into the fabric at the end of the row and come up again to start the next row where the ridge of DBH in that row will lie.

4. Working RL, [miss 2 loops, 1 x DBH into next loop, 1 x DBH into next loop]. Make sure that you go into the two loops in the middle of the group of three in the previous row. Repeat [--] to end. Go into the fabric at the end of the row and come up again to start the next row where the ridge of DBH in that row will lie.

5. Working LR, [miss large loop, 1 DBH into small loop]. Repeat [--] to end. Go into the fabric, turn your work over and catch a bit of the fabric. Come up to the top in the same place. Working RL, whip once into each small loop

and twice into each large loop. Go into the fabric at the end of the row and come up again to start the next row where the base of the gap formed in that row will lie.

6. Working LR, [2 x DBH into large loop, needle over and then under the loop that led up to the group. Making sure that the working thread is lying under the needle; pull through to form a buttonhole stitch that lies horizontally below the group of two detached buttonhole stitches. Work two more DBH in the same way. This is called a Two Group Plus Three (2G+3). Move to next large loop]. Repeat [--] to end.

7. Go into the fabric, turn your work over and catch a bit of the fabric. Come up to the top in the same place. Working RL, whip once into each small loop and twice into each large loop. Go into the fabric at the end of the row and come up again to start the next row where the base of the gap formed in that row will lie.

8. Working LR, [2 x DBH into large loop, needle over and then under the loop that led up to the group. Making sure that the working thread is lying under the needle; pull through to form a buttonhole stitch that lies horizontally below the group of two detached buttonhole stitches. Work two more DBH in the same way. This is called a Two Group Plus Three (2G+3). Move to next large loop]. Repeat [--] to end. Go into the fabric at the end of the row and come up again to start the next row where the ridge of DBH in that row will lie.

9. Working RL, [2 x DBH, 1 x DBH with picot, 2 x DBH into large loop]. Repeat [--] to end and finish off the thread.

10. Thread 2 mm silk ribbon onto a size 22 (or larger) tapestry needle. Bring the needle up in the middle of the gap created by row 6. Weave the ribbon over and under the bars. Take the needle to the back of the fabric. Come up in the middle of the gap created by row 8. Weave the ribbon over and under the bars. Take the needle to the back of the fabric and end off the ribbon.

NEEDLE LACE EDGING NO. 3 (INSERTION LACE)

Preparation: BS line along top edge
Top row stitch length: To accommodate 2 x DBH

1. Working LR, 2 x DBH into each BS. Go into the fabric at the end of the row and come up again to start the next row where the ridge of DBH in that row will lie.
2. Working RL, [miss 2 loops, 1 x DBH into next loop, 1 x DBH into next loop]. Repeat [--] to end. Go into the fabric at the end of the row and come up again to start the next row where the ridge of DBH in that row will lie.
3. Working LR, [3 x DBH into large loop, 1 x DBH into small loop]. Repeat [--] to end. Go into the fabric at the end of the row and come up again to start the next row where the ridge of DBH in that row will lie.
4. Working RL, [miss 2 loops, 1 x DBH into next loop, 1 x DBH into next loop]. Make sure that you go into the two loops in the middle of the group of three in the previous row. Repeat [--] to end. Go into the fabric at the end of the row and come up again to start the next row where the ridge of DBH in that row will lie.
5. Working LR, [miss large loop, 1 DBH into small loop]. Repeat [--] to end. Go into the fabric, turn your work over and catch a bit of the fabric. Come up to the top in the

same place. Working RL, whip once into each small loop and twice into each large loop. Go into the fabric at the end of the row and come up again to start the next row where the base of the gap formed in that row will lie.
6. Working LR, [2 x DBH into large loop, needle over and then under the loop that led up to the group. Making sure that the working thread is lying under the needle; pull through to form a buttonhole stitch that lies horizontally below the group of two detached buttonhole stitches. Work two more DBH in the same way. This is called a Two Group Plus Three (2G+3). Move to next large loop]. Repeat [--] to end.
7. Go into the fabric, turn your work over and catch a bit of the fabric. Come up to the top in the same place. Working RL, whip once into each small loop and twice into each large loop. Go into the fabric at the end of the row and come up again to start the next row where the base of the gap formed in that row will lie.
8. Working LR, [2 x DBH into large loop, needle over and then under the loop that led up to the group. Making sure that the working thread is lying under the needle; pull through to form a buttonhole stitch that lies horizontally below the group of two detached buttonhole stitches. Work two more DBH in the same way. This is called a Two Group Plus Three (2G+3). Move to next large loop]. Repeat [--] to end. Go into the fabric at the end of the row and come up again to start the next row where the ridge of DBH in that row will lie.
9. Working RL, [2 x DBH into each available loop]. Repeat [--] to end.
10. Working RL, [1 x DBH, 1 x DBH with picot, 1 x DBH into large loop]. Repeat [--] to end and finish off the thread.
11. Thread 2 mm silk ribbon onto a size 22 (or larger) tapestry needle. Bring the needle up in the middle of the gap created by row 6. Weave the ribbon over and under the bars. Take the needle to the back of the fabric. Come up in the middle of the gap created by row 8. Weave the ribbon over and under the bars. Take the needle to the back of the fabric and end off the ribbon.

NEEDLE LACE EDGING NO. 4 (INSERTION LACE)

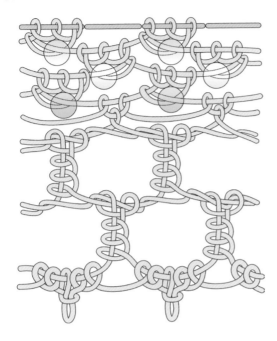

Preparation: BS line along top edge.
Top row stitch length: To accommodate 3 x DBH

1. Working LR, 3 x DBH into the first BS. Pick up a bead, pulling it down the thread to touch the third DBH. Take the needle over and then under the loop that led up to the group. Making sure that the working thread is lying under the needle; pull through to form a buttonhole stitch that lies horizontally below the group of three detached buttonhole stitches. Make sure that the working thread lies behind the bead. This is called a 3G+bead. Miss the next back stitch. Work a 3G+bead into the next back stitch and into every alternate backstitch until you reach the end. Go into the fabric at the end of the row and come up again to start the next row where the ridge of DBH in that row will lie.

2. Working RL, do a 3G+bead into each large loop in the previous row. Go into the fabric at the end of the row and come up again to start the next row where the ridge of DBH in that row will lie.

3. Working LR, do a 3G+bead into each large loop in the previous row. Go into the fabric at the end of the row and come up again to start the next row where the ridge of DBH in that row will lie.

4. Working RL, do 2 x DBH into each large loop. Go into the fabric at the end of the row and come up again to start the next row where the ridge of DBH in that row will lie.

5. Working LR, do 1 x DBH into the small loop between the 2 x DBH in the previous row. Go into the fabric, turn your work over and catch a bit of the fabric. Come up to the top in the same place. Working RL, whip once into each small loop and twice into each large loop. Go into the fabric at the end of the row and come up again to start the next row where the base of the gap formed in that row will lie.

6. Working LR, [2 x DBH into large loop, needle over and then under the loop that led up to the group. Making sure that the working thread is lying under the needle; pull through to form a buttonhole stitch that lies horizontally below the group of two detached buttonhole stitches. Work two more DBH in the same way. This is called a Two Group Plus Three (2G+3). Move to next large loop]. Repeat [--] to end.

7. Go into the fabric, turn your work over and catch a bit of the fabric. Come up to the top in the same place. Working RL, whip once into each small loop and twice into each large loop. Go into the fabric at the end of the row and come up again to start the next row where the base of the gap formed in that row will lie.

8. Working LR, [2 x DBH into large loop, needle over and then under the loop that led up to the group. Making sure that the working thread is lying under the needle; pull through to form a buttonhole stitch that lies horizontally below the group of two detached buttonhole stitches. Work two more DBH in the same way. This is called a Two Group Plus Three (2G+3). Move to next large loop]. Repeat [--] to end. Go into the fabric at the end of the row and come up again to start the next row where the ridge of DBH in that row will lie.

9. Working RL, [2 x DBH, 1 x DBH with picot, 2 x DBH into large loop]. Repeat [--] to end and finish off the thread.

10. Thread 2 mm silk ribbon onto a size 22 (or larger) tapestry needle. Bring the needle up in the middle of the gap created by row 6. Weave the ribbon over and under the bars. Take the needle to the back of the fabric. Come up in the middle of the gap created by row 8. Weave the ribbon over and under the bars. Take the needle to the back of the fabric and end off the ribbon.

NEEDLE LACE EDGING NO. 5 (INSERTION LACE)

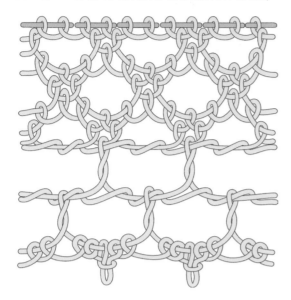

Preparation: BS line along top edge.
Top row stitch length: To accommodate 2 x DBH

1. Working LR, 2 x DBH into each BS. Go into the fabric at the end of the row and come up again to start the next row where the ridge of DBH in that row will lie.
2. Working RL, [miss 2 loops, 1 x DBH into next loop, 1 x DBH into next loop]. Repeat [--] to end. Go into the fabric at the end of the row and come up again to start the next row where the ridge of DBH in that row will lie.
3. Working LR, [3 x DBH into large loop, 1 x DBH into small loop]. Repeat [--] to end. Go into the fabric at the end of the row and come up again to start the next row where the ridge of DBH in that row will lie.
4. Working RL, [miss 2 loops, 1 x DBH into next loop, 1 x DBH into next loop]. Make sure that you go into the two loops in the middle of the group of three in the previous row.
5. Working LR, [3 x DBH into large loop, 1 x DBH into small loop]. Repeat [--] to end. Go into the fabric at the end of the row and come up again to start the next row where the ridge of DBH in that row will lie.
6. Working RL, [miss 2 loops, 1 x DBH into next loop, 1 x DBH into next loop]. Make sure that you go into the two loops in the middle of the group of three in the previous row. Repeat [--] to end. Go into the fabric, turn your work

over and catch a bit of the fabric. Come up to the top in the same place. Working LR, whip twice into each large loop. Go into the fabric at the end of the row and end off.
7. Bring your needle up on the left to start the next row where the base of the gap formed in that row will lie. Working LR, take your needle over and under the first loop in the row above, as you would for a DBH. Take the thread under and over the needle to create an additional twist, thereby creating what is referred to in these instructions as a tulle bar (TB). Do a TB into each loop in the row. When you reach the other side, go into the fabric, turn your work over and catch a bit of the fabric. Come up to the top in the same place. Working RL, whip twice into each large loop. Go into the fabric at the end of the row and come up again to start the next row where the base of the gap formed in that row will lie.
8. Working LR, do a TB into each loop in the row. Go into the fabric at the end of the row and come up again to start the next row where the ridge of DBH in that row will lie.
9. Working RL, [2 x DBH, 1 x DBH with picot, 2 x DBH into large loop]. Repeat [--] to end and finish off the thread.
10. Thread 2 mm silk ribbon onto a size 22 (or larger) tapestry needle. Bring the needle up in the middle of the gap created by row 6. Weave the ribbon over and under the bars. Take the needle to the back of the fabric. Come up in the middle of the gap created by row 7. Weave the ribbon over and under the bars. Take the needle to the back of the fabric and end off the ribbon.

NEEDLE LACE EDGING NO. 6 (INSERTION LACE)

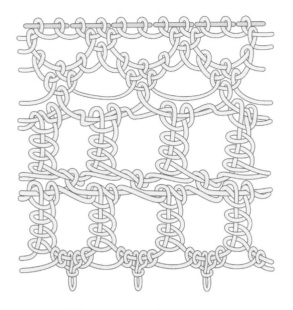

Preparation: BS line along top edge
Top row stitch length: To accommodate 2 x DBH

1. Working LR, 2 x DBH into each BS. Go into the fabric at the end of the row and come up again to start the next row where the ridge of DBH in that row will lie.
2. Working RL, [miss 2 loops, 1 x DBH into next loop, 1 x DBH into next loop]. Repeat [--] to end. Go into the fabric at the end of the row and come up again to start the next row where the ridge of DBH in that row will lie.
3. Working LR, [3 x DBH into large loop, 1 x DBH into small loop]. Repeat [--] to end. Go into the fabric at the end of the row and come up again to start the next row where the ridge of DBH in that row will lie.
4. Working RL, [miss 2 loops, 1 x DBH into next loop, 1 x DBH into next loop]. Make sure that you go into the two loops in the middle of the group of three in the previous row. Go into the fabric at the end of the row and come up again to start the next row where the ridge of DBH in that row will lie.
5. Working LR, 1 x DBH into each small loop. Go into the fabric, turn your work over and catch a bit of the fabric. Come up to the top in the same place. Working LR, whip twice into each large loop and once into any smaller loops at the beginning and end. Go into the fabric at the end of

the row and come up again to start the next row where the base of the gap formed in that row will lie.
6. Working LR, [2 x DBH into large loop, needle over and then under the loop that led up to the group. Making sure that the working thread is lying under the needle; pull through to form a buttonhole stitch that lies horizontally below the group of two detached buttonhole stitches. Work two more DBH in the same way. This is called a Two Group Plus Three (2G+3). Move to next large loop]. Repeat [--] to end. Go into the fabric, turn your work over and catch a bit of the fabric. Come up to the top in the same place. Working RL, whip once into each small loop and twice into each large loop. Go into the fabric at the end of the row and come up again to start the next row where the base of the gap formed in that row will lie.
7. Working LR, 1 x DBH into each loop. Go into the fabric, turn your work over and catch a bit of the fabric. Come up to the top in the same place. Working LR, whip twice into each large loop and once into any smaller loops at the beginning and end. Go into the fabric at the end of the row and come up again to start the next row where the base of the gap formed in that row will lie.
8. Working LR, [2 x DBH into large loop, needle over and then under the loop that led up to the group. Making sure that the working thread is lying under the needle; pull through to form a buttonhole stitch that lies horizontally below the group of two detached buttonhole stitches. Work two more DBH in the same way. This is called a Two Group Plus Three (2G+3). Move to next large loop]. Repeat [--] to end. Go into the fabric at the end of the row and come up again to start the next row where the ridge of DBH in that row will lie.
9. Working RL, [2 x DBH, 1 x DBH with picot, 2 x DBH into large loop]. Repeat [--] to end and finish off the thread.
10. Thread 2 mm silk ribbon onto a size 22 (or larger) tapestry needle. Bring the needle up in the middle of the gap created by row 6. Weave the ribbon over and under the bars. Take the needle to the back of the fabric. Come up in the middle of the gap created by row 8. Weave the ribbon over and under the bars. Take the needle to the back of the fabric and end off the ribbon.

NEEDLE LACE EDGING NO. 7 (INSERTION LACE)

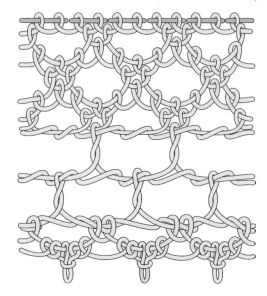

Preparation: BS line along top edge
Top row stitch length: To accommodate 2 x DBH

1. Working LR, 2 x DBH into each BS. Go into the fabric at the end of the row and come up again to start the next row where the ridge of DBH in that row will lie.
2. Working RL, [miss 2 loops, 1 x DBH into next loop, 1 x DBH into next loop]. Repeat [--] to end. Go into the fabric at the end of the row and come up again to start the next row where the ridge of DBH in that row will lie.
3. Working LR, [3 x DBH into large loop, 1 x DBH into small loop]. Repeat [--] to end. Go into the fabric at the end of the row and come up again to start the next row where the ridge of DBH in that row will lie.
4. Working RL, [miss 2 loops, 1 x DBH into next loop, 1 x DBH into next loop]. Make sure that you go into the two loops in the middle of the group of three in the previous row.
5. Working LR, [3 x DBH into large loop, 1 x DBH into small loop]. Repeat [--] to end. Go into the fabric at the end of the row and come up again to start the next row where the ridge of DBH in that row will lie.
6. Working RL, [miss 2 loops, 1 x DBH into next loop, 1 x DBH into next loop]. Make sure that you go into the two loops in the middle of the group of three in the previous row. Repeat [--] to end. Go into the fabric, turn your work

over and catch a bit of the fabric. Come up to the top in the same place. Working LR, whip twice into each large loop. Go into the fabric at the end of the row and end off.
7. Bring your needle up on the left to start the next row where the base of the gap formed in that row will lie. Working LR, take your needle over and under the first loop in the row above, as you would for a DBH. Take the thread under and over the needle to create an additional twist, thereby creating what is referred to in these instructions as a tulle bar (TB). Do a TB into each loop in the row. When you reach the other side, go into the fabric, turn your work over and catch a bit of the fabric. Come up to the top in the same place. Working RL, whip twice into each large loop. Go into the fabric at the end of the row and come up again to start the next row where the base of the gap formed in that row will lie.
8. Working LR, do a TB into each loop in the row. When you reach the other side, go into the fabric, turn your work over and catch a bit of the fabric. Come up to the top in the same place. Working RL, whip twice into each large loop. Go into the fabric at the end of the row and come up again to start the next row where the base of the gap formed in that row will lie.
9. Working RL do 2 x DBH into each large loop. Go into the fabric at the end of the row and come up again to start the next row where the ridge of DBH in that row will lie.
10. Working RL, [2 x DBH, 1 x DBH with picot, 2 x DBH into large loop]. Repeat [--] to end and finish off the thread.
11. Thread 2 mm silk ribbon onto a size 22 (or larger) tapestry needle. Bring the needle up in the middle of the gap created by row 7. Weave the ribbon over and under the bars. Take the needle to the back of the fabric. Come up in the middle of the gap created by row 8. Weave the ribbon over and under the bars. Take the needle to the back of the fabric and end off the ribbon.

NEEDLE LACE EDGING NO. 8

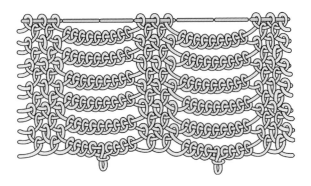

Preparation: BS line along top edge
Top row stitch length: To accommodate 3 x DBH

1. Working LR, [3 x DBH into BS, miss 2 BS]. Repeat [--] to end. Go through the nearest BS down the right hand side that is level with the ridge of the DBH in the row you have just done. Snake down through the next BS.
2. # Working RL, [9 x DBH into large loop, 1 x DBH into small loop, 1 x DBH into small loop]. Repeat [--] to end. Snake down to the next row.
3. Working LR, [1 x DBH into each small loop, i.e. 1 at the end of the group of 9 DBH in the previous row, 1 between the 2 DBH in the middle, and 1 at the beginning of the next group of 9]. Repeat [--] to end. Snake down to the next row.#
4. Keep working the rows from # to # until you have a total of 5 repeats.
5. Working RL, [1 x DBH into each small loop – i.e. 1 at the end of the group of 9 DBH in the previous row, 1 between the 2 DBH in the middle, and 1 at the beginning of the next group of 9 – 4 x DBH, 1 x DBH with picot, 4 x DBH into the large loop]. Repeat [--] to end and finish off the thread.

NEEDLE LACE FILLER NO. I

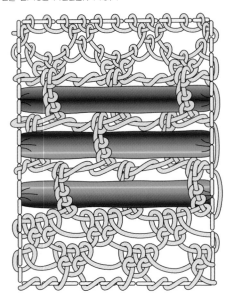

Preparation: BS outline
Top row stitch length: To accommodate 2 x DBH

1. Working LR, 2 x DBH into each BS. Go through the nearest BS down the right hand side that is level with the ridge of the DBH in the row you have just done. Snake down through the next BS.
2. Working RL, [miss 2 loops, 1 x DBH into next loop, 1 x DBH into next loop]. Repeat [--] to end. Snake down to the next row.
3. Working LR, [3 x DBH into large loop, 1 x DBH into small loop]. Repeat [--] to end. Snake down to the next row.
4. Working RL, [miss 2 loops, 1 x DBH into next loop, 1 x DBH into next loop]. Make sure that you go into the two loops in the middle of the group of three in the previous row.
5. Go into the fabric, turn your work over and catch a bit of the fabric. Come up to the top in the same place. Working RL, whip twice into each large loop and once into any smaller loops at the beginning and end. Snake down to start the next row where the base of the gap formed in that row will lie.
6. Working RL, [2 x DBH into the small loop between the 2-DBH group in the previous row, needle over and then under the loop that led up to the group. Making sure that the working thread is lying under the needle; pull through

to form a buttonhole stitch that lies horizontally below the group of two detached buttonhole stitches. Work two more DBH in the same way. This is called a Two Group Plus Three (2G+3)]. Repeat [--] to end.

7. Go into the fabric, turn your work over and catch a bit of the fabric. Come up to the top in the same place. Working LR, whip once into each small loop and twice into each large loop. Snake down to start the next row where the base of the gap formed in that row will lie.

8. Working the 2G+3 into the large loops in the previous row, repeat rows 6 and 7 as many times as you need to for the space that you are working in, bearing in mind that you will want to finish off with a repeat of rows 3 and 4.

9. On the last repeat, do not whip back (row 7).

10. Working into the large loops of the previous row, repeat rows 3 and 4 until you have filled the space.

11. Finish off in the normal way, whipping through any visible back stitches, if necessary.

12. Thread 2 mm silk ribbon onto a size 22 (or larger) tapestry needle. Bring the needle up at the side of the insertion rows. Weave the ribbon over and under the bars in each row. Take the needle to the back of the fabric and end off the ribbon.

Needle Lace Extras

EXTRAS NO. I (PICOT)

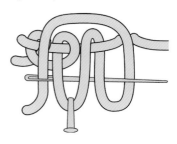

Preparation: BS line along top & bottom edges
Top row stitch length: To accommodate 2 x DBH

1. Take the needle over and under the loop onto which the preceding DBH have been attached, catching the thread under a pin, which you have placed directly below the point where the ridge of the DBH lies.

2. Turning your work to the right, so that you will be pulling towards yourself, work a DBH over the threads that are held by the pin, as indicated in the diagram, and making sure that the needle goes over the free thread, to form a buttonhole stitch.

3. Turning your work upright again, continue straight into the next DBH that will be formed, as usual over the loop.

Note that a picot can be made with additional DBH over the threads that are held by the pin, which case you work those before continuing with the normal stitches that are formed over the loop at the top.

EXTRAS NO. 2 (PICOT BAR EDGE)

Preparation: BS line along top & bottom edges
Top row stitch length: To accommodate 2 x DBH

1. The bar can be worked with a total of either 3 or 5 stitches. Work a line a backstitch to accommodate the relevant number of stitches.

2. Bring the needle up out of the same hole where the backstitch started. Work a DBH over the backstitch (for a 3-stitch bar) of 2 x DBH (for a 5-stitch bar).

3. Referring to the instructions for making a picot above, work a single picot. Work a DBH over the backstitch (for a 3-stitch bar) of 2 x DBH (for a 5-stitch bar) taking the needle back into the fabric where the backstitch ended.

4. Miss the next backstitch and continue by working bars on each alternate backstitch.

5. Return to the beginning and work bars on each of the unfilled backstitches..

EXTRAS NO. 3 (3-ROW ARCH)

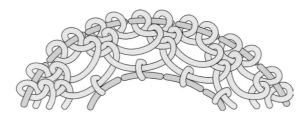

Preparation: BS line along top & bottom edges
Top row stitch length: To accommodate 2 x DBH

1. Working LR, 2 x DBH into each BS. Go into the fabric at the end of the row and come up again to start the next row where the ridge of DBH in that row will lie.
2. Working RL, [1 x DBH each into two loops, miss a loop].]. Repeat [--] to end. Go into the fabric at the end of the row and come up again to start the next row where the ridge of DBH in that row will lie.
3. Working LR, 1 x DBH into each small loop. Go into the fabric at the end of the row and come up again to start the next row where the ridge of DBH in that row will lie.
4. Working RL, come up just below the bottom backstitch adjacent to the centre of the large loop in the third row of needle lace. Catch the loop and go into the fabric, tucking your needle under the backstitch and pulling firmly.

EXTRAS NO. 4 (4-ROW ARCH)

Preparation: BS line along top & bottom edges
Top row stitch length: To accommodate 2 x DBH

1. Working LR, 2 x DBH into each BS. Go into the fabric at the end of the row and come up again to start the next row where the ridge of DBH in that row will lie.
2. Working RL, [1 x DBH each into three loops, miss a loop]. Repeat [--] to end. Go into the fabric at the end of the row and come up again to start the next row where the ridge of DBH in that row will lie.
3. Working LR, [1 x DBH each into two loops, miss a loop]. Repeat [--] to end. Go into the fabric at the end of the row and come up again to start the next row where the ridge of DBH in that row will lie.
4. Working RL, 1 x DBH into each small loop. Go into the fabric at the end of the row and come up again to start the next row where the ridge of DBH in that row will lie.

Working LR, come up just below the bottom backstitch adjacent to the centre of the large loop in the third row of needle lace. Catch the loop and go into the fabric, tucking your needle under the backstitch and pulling firmly.

NEEDLE WEAVING

Single weaving

Warp: Colour 1
Weft: Colour 1 or 2 (pattern repeat
2 rows)

1. O1, U1
2. (U1) O1, U1

Double weaving

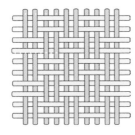

Warp: Colour 1
Weft: Colour 1 or 2
(pattern repeat 4 rows)

1. O2, U2
2. O2, U2
3. U2, O2
4. U2, O2

Checks and stripes no. 1

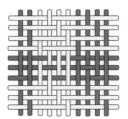

Warp: 4 x colour 1
4 x colour 2
Weft: 4 x colour 2
3 x colour 1
(pattern repeat 7 rows)

COLOUR 2
1. (O2, U1) O3, U1
2. (O1, U1) O3, U1
3. (U1) O3, U1
4. O3, U1

COLOUR 1
5. (U3) O1, U3
6. (U2) O1, U3
7. (U1) O1, U3

Check and stripes no. 2

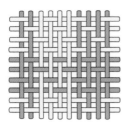

Warp: 4 x colour 1
4 x colour 2
Weft: 4 x colour 1
4 x colour 2
(pattern repeat 8 rows)

COLOUR 2
1. O1, U2
2. (U2) O1, U2
3. (U1) O1, U2
4. O1, U2

COLOUR 1
1. (U2) O1, U2
2. (U1) O1, U2
3. O1, U2
4. U2, O1

Check and stripes no. 3

Warp: 4 x colour 1
        4 x colour 2
Weft: 4 x colour 1
        4 x colour 2
        (pattern repeat 3/4 rows)

1. O1, U2
2. U2, O1
3. (U1) O1, U2

Change colour every fourth row

Check and stripes no. 4

Warp: 4 x colour 1
        4 x colour 2
Weft: 2 x colour 1
        2 x colour 2
        (pattern repeat 4 rows)

COLOUR 1
1. (U2) O1, U2
2. O1, U2

COLOUR 2
3. (U2) O1, U2
4. (U1) O1, U2

Check and stripes no. 5

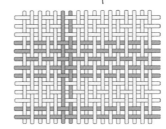

Warp: 10 x colour 1
        2 x colour 2
Weft: 5 x colour 2
        3 x colour 1
        (pattern repeat 8 rows)

COLOUR 1
1. (U1) O1, U2
2. O1, U2
3. (U1) O1, U2

COLOUR 2
4. (U2) O1, U2
5. O1, U1
6. (U1) O1, U1
7. O1, U1
8. (U2) O1, U2

Check and stripes no. 6

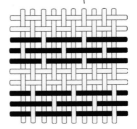

Warp: colour 1
Weft: colour 1
        colour 2
        (pattern repeat 10 rows)

COLOUR 2
1. O1, U1
2. U1, O1

COLOUR 1
3. O3, U1
4. (O1, U1) O3, U1
5. O3, U1

COLOUR 2
6. U1, O1
7. O1, U1

COLOUR 1
8. (U1) O3, U1
9. (O2, U1) O3, U1
10. (U1) O3, U1

Check and stripes no. 7

Warp: 6 x colour 1
   6 x colour 2
Weft: 6 x colour 1
   6 x colour 2
   (pattern repeat 12 rows)

COLOUR 1
1. O2, U2
2. O2, U2
3. (U2) O2, U2
4. (U2) O2, U2
5. O2, U2
6. O2, U2

COLOUR 2
7. (U2) O2, U2
8. (U2) O2, U2
9. O2, U2
10. O2, U2
11. (U2) O2, U2
12. (U2) O2, U2

Check and stripes no. 8

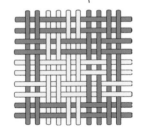

Warp: 4 x colour 1
   4 x colour 2
Weft: 4 x colour 1
   4 x colour 2
   (pattern repeat 8 rows)

COLOUR 1
1. (U2) O2, U2
2. (U2) O2, U2
3. O2, U2
4. O2, U2

COLOUR 2
5. (U2) O2, U2
6. (U2) O2, U2
7. O2, U2
8. O2, U2

Check and stripes no. 9

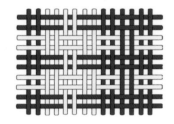

Warp: 6 x colour 1
   6 x colour 2
Weft: 2 x colour 1
   2 x colour 2
   (pattern repeat 4 rows)

COLOUR 1
1. (U2) O2, U2
2. (U2) O2, U2

COLOUR 2
3. O2, U2
4. O2, U2

Check and stripes no. 12

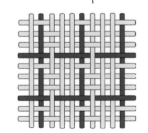

Warp: 1 x colour 1
   3 x colour 2
Weft: 3 x colour 2
   1 x colour 1
   (pattern repeat 4 rows)

COLOUR 2
1. O1, U3
2. (U3) O1, U3
3. (U3) O1, U3

COLOUR 1
4. O3, U1

Check and stripes no. 13

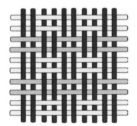

Warp: Colour 1
Weft: Colour 2
   Colour 3
   (pattern repeat 4 rows)

COLOUR 2
1. (U2) O2, U2
2. (U2) O2, U2

COLOUR 3
3. 3. O2, U2
4. 4. O2, U2

Check and stripes no. 14

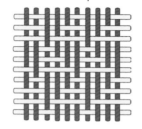

Warp: Colour 1
Weft: Colour 2
(pattern repeat 6 rows)

1. O1, U3
2. O2, U2
3. O3, U1
4. (U3) O1, U3
5. (U2) O2, U2
6. (U1) O3, U1

Check and stripes no. 15

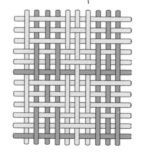

Warp: 3 x colour 1
3 x colour 2
Weft: 5 x colour 2
1 x colour 1
(pattern repeat 6 rows)

COLOUR 2
1. 1.   O3, U3
2. 2.   O1, U1
3. 3.   O3, U3
4. 4.   (U1) O1, U1
5. 5.   (U3) O3, U3

COLOUR 1
6. 6.   (U1) O1, U1

Pattern no. 1

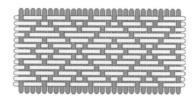

Warp: Colour 1
Weft: Colour 2
(pattern repeat 12 rows)

1. O3, U1
2. (U1) O3, U1, O1, U1
3. (O1 U1) O3,U1
4. (O2, U1) O5, U1
5. O3, U1
6. (U1) O3, U1, O1, U1
7. (O1 U1) O3, U1
8. (U1) O3, U1, O1, U1
9. O3, U1
10. (O2, U1) O5, U1
11. (O1, U1) O3, U1
12. (U1) O3, U1, O1, U1

Pattern no. 2

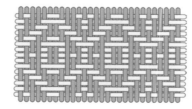

Warp: Colour 1
Weft: Colour 2
(pattern repeat 14 rows)

1. (O1, U3) O1, U1, O1, U3, O2, U3
2. (O2, U3) O1, U3, O4, U3

3. (U1) O2, U2, O1, U2, O2, U2
4. (U2) O2, U3, O2, U4
5. (O1, U2) O2, U1, O2, U2, O2, U2
6. (O2, U2) O3, U2, O4, U2
7. (U1) O1, U3, O1, U3, O1, U2
8. (U1) O1, U1, O1, U1, O1, U1, O1, U1, O1, U2
9. Repeat row 7
10. Repeat row 6
11. Repeat row 5
12. Repeat row 4
13. Repeat row 3
14. Repeat row 2

Pattern no. 3

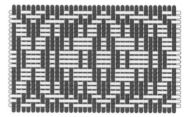

Warp: Colour 1
Weft: Colour 2
(pattern repeat 21 rows)

1. (U1) O2, U4, O1, U1, O4, U2, O1, U2, O4, U1, O1, U4, O2, U1
2. (O2, U2) O1, U1, O4, U1, O1, U2, O3, U2, O1, U1, O4, U1, O1, U2, O3, U2
3. O1, U2, O4, U1, O1, U4, O2, U1, O2, U4, O1, U1, O4, U2
4. *(U2) O2, U1, O1, U4, O1, U1, O2, U3, O2,U1, O1, U4, O1, U1, O2, U3*
5. Repeat * to *
6. Repeat * to *
7. #(U1) O2, U4, O1, U1, O4, U2, O1, U2, O4,U1, O1, U4, O2, U1#
8. Repeat # to #
9. Repeat # to #
10. « (O2, U2) O1, U1, O4, U1, O1, U2, O3, U2, O1, U1, O4, U1, O1, U2,

O3, U2»
11. Repeat « to »
12. Repeat « to »
13. Repeat « to»
14. Repeat row 7 (#)
15. Repeat row 8 (#)
16. Repeat row 9 (#)
17. Repeat row 4 (*)
18. Repeat row 5 (*)
19. Repeat row 6 (*)
20. Repeat row 3
21. Repeat row 2

Pattern no. 4

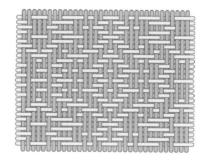

Warp: Colour 1
Weft: Colour 2
        (pattern repeat 22 rows)

1. O3, U3, O4, U1, O1, U2, O3, U2, O1, U1, O4, U3
2. (U4) O4, U5, O2, U1, O2, U5, O4, U5
3. (U3) O2, U5, O1, U1, O2, U3, O2, U1, O1, U5, O2, U3
4. (U4) O4, U5, O2, U1, O2, U5, O4, U5
5. O3, U3, O4, U4, O3, U4, O4, U3
6. (U4) O4, U5, O2, U1, O2, U5, O4, U5
7. (U3) O2, U4, O1, U2, O2, U3, O2, U2, O1, U4, O2, U3
8. (O1, U1) O2, U2, O1, U3, O3, U2, O1, U2, O3, U3, O1, U2, O2, U1

9. O3, U4, O4, U3, O3, U3, O4, U4
10. (U1) O1, U3, O3, U1, O1, U3, O2, U1, O2, U3, O1, U1, O3, U3
11. (U4) O2, U6, O2, U3, O2, U6, O2, U5
12. (U3) O2, U3, O1, U1, O3, U2, O1, U2, O3, U1, O1, U3, O2, U3
13. (U4) O2, U6, O2, U3, O2, U6, O2, U5
14. O3, U2, O3, U1, O1, U3, O2, U1, O2, U3, O1, U1, O3, U2
15. Repeat row 13
16. Repeat row 12
17. Repeat row 11
18. Repeat row 10
19. Repeat row 9
20. Repeat row 8
21. Repeat row 7
22. Repeat row 6

Pattern no. 5

Warp: Colour 1
Weft: Colour 2
        (pattern repeat 6 rows)

1. (U1) O1, U3, O1, U1
2. (U2) O1, U1, O1, U3
3. (U3) O1, U5
4. O1, U5
5. (U3) O1, U5
6. (U2) O1, U1, O1, U3

Pattern no. 6

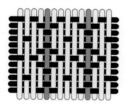

Warp: 5 x Colour 1
        1 x Colour 2
Weft: Colour 3
        (pattern repeat 6 rows)

1. (U1, O1, U1), O1, U3, O1, U1
2. O1, U3, O1, U1
3. (U5) O1, U5
4. (U2) O1, U5
5. (U5) O1, U5
6. O1, U3, O1, U1

Pattern no. 7

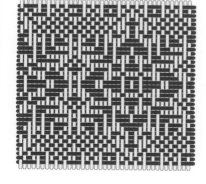

Warp: Colour 1
Weft: Colour 1
        Colour 2

COLOUR 2
1. (O2, U1) O1, U1, O1, U1, O3, U1, O1, U1, O1, U1, O1, U1, O3, U1
2. (U1) O1, U2, O1, U2, O1, U1, O1, U2, O1, U1, O1, U2, O1, U1, O1, U2, O1, U2, O1, U1, O1, U2, O1, U2, O1, U1
3. (O2, U1) O1, U1, O1, U1, O3, U1,

O1, U3, O1, U1, O3, U1, O1, U1, O1,
U1, O3, U1

4. (U2, O1, U1, O1, U1, O1, U3, O1,
U2,) O1, U2, O1, U3, O1, U1, O1, U1,
O1, U3, O1, U1, O1, U1, O1, U3, O1,
U2

5. (U1) O1, U1, O1, U1, O1, U1, O1,
U1, O1, U2, O3, U2, O1, U1, O1, U1,
O1, U1, O1, U1, O1, U1

6. O1, U1, O1, U1, O1, U1, O1, U1,
O1, U4, O1, U4, O1, U1, O1, U1, O1,
U1, O1, U1

COLOUR 1

7. (U1) O1, U1

COLOUR 2

8. O1, U1, O1, U1, O1, U1, O1 U2, O2,
U2, O1, U2, O2, U2, O1, U1, O1, U1,
O1, U1, O1,

9. U1 (O1, U2) O2, U1, O1, U5, O3,
U5, O1, U1, O2, U2, O1, U2

10. (U2) O3, U1, O1, U1, O1, U2, O5,
U2, O1, U1, O1, U1, O3, U3

11. O1, U4, O2, U1, O1, U1, O3, U1,
O3, U1, O1, U1, O2, U4

12. (U2) O5, U1, O1, U1, O3, U1, O3,
U1, O1, U1, O5, U3

13. O1, U6, O2, U1, O1, U2, O1, U2,
O1, U1, O2, U6

14. (U1) O1, U2, O5, U4, O1, U4, O5,
U2, O1, U1

15. O1, U1, O1, U6, O2, U1, O3, U1,
O2, U6, O1, U1

16. U1, O1, U1, O1, U1, O3, U1, O2, U1,
O3, U1, O2, U1, O3, U1, O1, U1, O3

17. O1, U3, O3, U4, O1, U3, O1, U4,
O3, U3

18. (U3) O4, U2, O2, U1, O3, U1, O2,
U2, O4, U5

19. O1, U1, O3, U2, O4, U1, O1, U1,
O1, U1, O4, U2, O3, U1

20. Repeat row 19

21. Repeat row 18
22. Repeat row 17
23. Repeat row 16
24. Repeat row 15
25. Repeat row 14
26. Repeat row 13
27. Repeat row 12
28. Repeat row 11
29. Repeat row 10
30. Repeat row 9
31. Repeat row 8

COLOUR 1

32. Repeat row 7

COLOUR 2

33. Repeat row 6
34. Repeat row 5
35. Repeat row 4
36. Repeat row 3
37. Repeat row 2

Back to row 1

Pattern no. 8

Warp: Colour 1
Weft: Colour 2
    (pattern repeat 17 rows)

1. (U1) O1, U3
2. (U4) O3, U5
3. (U3) O2, U1, O2, U3
4. (O1) U1, O3

5. (O4) U3, O5
6. (U3) O5, U3
7. (U3) O5, U3
8. (O4) U3, O5
9. (O1) U1, O3
10. (U3) O2, U1, O2, U3
11. (U4) O3, U5
12. (U1) O1, O3
13. O3, U5
14. (O1) U1, O2, U3, O2
15. (O1, U1) O3, U1
16. (O1) U1, O2, U3, O2
17. O3, U5

Pattern no. 9
(music staves)

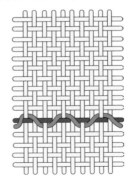

Warp: Colour 1 (perlé no. 12)
Weft: Colour 1 (perlé no. 12)
    Colour 2 (Stranded Cotton)
    (pattern repeat 19 rows)

COLOUR 1

1. U1, O1
2. O1, U1
3. U1, O1
4. O1, U1
5. U1, O1
6. O1, U1
7. U1, O1
8. O1, U1
9. U1, O1
10. O1, U1

COLOUR 2
11. U1, O1
12. U1 (behind) O1 (front)

COLOUR 1
13. O1, U1

COLOUR 2
14. U1, O1
15. U1 (behind) O1 (front)

COLOUR 1
16. O1, U1

COLOUR 2
17. U1, O1
18. U1 (behind) O1 (front)

COLOUR 1
19. O1, U1

COLOUR 2
20. U1, O1
21. U1 (behind) O1 (front)

COLOUR 1
22. O1, U1

COLOUR 2
23. U1, O1
24. U1 (behind) O1 (front)

Return to row 1.

Once you have completed the staves, stitch the music notes using a thread that is a shade darker than the one you used for the lines. Use either French knots or size 15° beads for the dots and straight stitches for the lines. Arrange them artistically, without thought as to whether they actually play a tune.

Braids and edges no. 1

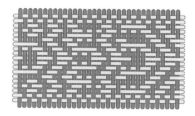

Using perlé no. 12 thread, this weave covers a height of 12 mm with the length being as wide as you need.

Warp: Colour 1 (12 mm stitches)
Weft: 2 x colour 1
15 x colour 2
2 x colour 1

COLOUR 1
1. U1, O1
2. O1, U1

COLOUR 2
3. (U1) O2, U4, O1, U1, O4, U2, O1, U2, O4, U1, O1, U4, O2, U1
4. (O2, U2) O1, U1, O4, U1, O1, U2, O3, U2, O1, U1, O4, U1, O1, U2, O3, U2
5. O1, U2, O4, U1, O1, U4, O2, U1, O2, U4, O1, U1, O4, U2
6. *(U2) O2, U1, O1, U4, O1, U1, O2, U3, O2, U1, O1, U4, O1, U1, O2, U3*
7. Repeat * to *
8. Repeat * to *
9. #(U1) O2, U4, O1, U1, O4, U2, O1, U2, O4, U1, O1, U4, O2, U1#
10. Repeat # to #
11. Repeat # to #
12. « (O2, U2) O1, U1, O4, U1, O1, U2, O3, U2, O1, U1, O4, U1, O1, U2, O3, U2»
13. Repeat « to »
14. Repeat « to »
15. Repeat « to »
16. Repeat row 11 (#)

17. Repeat row 10 (#)
18. Repeat row 9 (#)
19. Repeat row 8 (*)
20. Repeat row 7 (*)
21. Repeat row 6 (*)
22. Repeat row 5
23. Repeat row 4
24. Repeat row 3

COLOUR 1
25. Repeat row 2
26. Repeat row 1

Braids and edges no. 2

Using perlé no. 12 thread, this weave covers a height of 14 mm with the length being as wide as you need.

Warp: Colour 1 (14 mm stitches)
Weft: 2 x colour 1
21 x colour 2
2 x colour 1

COLOUR 1
1. U1, O1
2. O1, U1

COLOUR 2
1. (U1) O2, U4, O1, U1, O4, U2, O1, U2, O4, U1, O1, U4, O2, U1
2. (O2, U2) O1, U1, O4, U1, O1, U2, O3, U2, O1, U1, O4, U1, O1, U2, O3, U2
3. O1, U2, O4, U1, O1, U4, O2, U1,

O2, U4, O1, U1, O4, U2

4. *(U2) O2, U1, O1, U4, O1, U1, O2, U3, O2, U1, O1, U4, O1, U1, O2, U3*

5. Repeat * to *

6. Repeat * to *

7. #(U1) O2, U4, O1, U1, O4, U2, O1, U2, O4, U1, O1, U4, O2, U1#

8. Repeat # to #

9. Repeat # to #

10. « (O2, U2) O1, U1, O4, U1, O1, U2, O3, U2, O1, U1, O4, U1, O1, U2, O3, U2»

11. Repeat « to »

12. Repeat « to »

13. Repeat « to »

14. Repeat row 11 (#)

15. Repeat row 10 (#)

16. Repeat row 9 (#)

17. Repeat row 8 (*)

18. Repeat row 7 (*)

19. Repeat row 6 (*)

20. Repeat row 5

21. Repeat row 4

22. Repeat row 3

COLOUR 1

23. Repeat row 2

24. Repeat row 1

Braids and edges no. 3

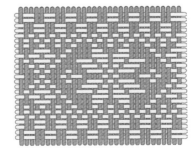

Using perlé no. 12 thread, this weave covers a height of 14 mm with the length being as wide as you need.

Warp: Colour 1 (14 mm stitches)
Weft: 4 x colour 2
2 x colour 1
2 x colour 1

COLOUR 2

1. O2, U2

2. O2, U2

3. (U2) O2, U2

4. (U2) O2, U2

COLOUR 1

5. O1, U1

6. (U1) O1, U1

COLOUR 2

7. O1, U2, O1, US, O1, U3, O1, U2, O1, U2, O1, U3, O1, U2, O1, U2

8. (O2, U3) O1, U4, O2, U3, O2, U4, O1, U3, O3, U3

9. (U1) O2, U1, O1, U5, O3, U1, O3, U5, O1, U1, O2, U1

10. (O2, U1) O1, U3, O3, U1, O2, U1, O2, U1, O3, U3, O1, U1, O3, U1

11. O1, U1, O1, U5, O3, U1, O1, U1, O1, U1, O3, U5, O1, U1

12. (U1) O1, U3, O1, U3, O3, U1, O1, U1, O3, U3, O1, U3, O1, U1

13. O1, U3, O1, U1, O2, U4, O1, U1, O1, U4, O2, U1, O1, U3

14. Repeat row 12

15. Repeat row 11

16. Repeat row 10

17. Repeat row 9

18. Repeat row 8

19. Repeat row 7

20. Repeat row 6

21. Repeat row 6

22. Repeat row 4

23. Repeat row 3

24. Repeat row 2

25. Repeat row 1

Braids and edges no. 4

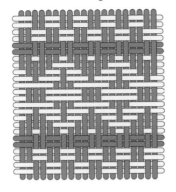

Using perlé no. 12 thread, this weave covers a height of 14 mm with the length being as wide as you need.

Warp: Colour 1 (14 mm stitches)
Weft: Colour 2

1. (U2) O2, U2

2. (U2) O2, U2

3. O2, U2

4. O2, U2

5. (U2) O2, U2

6. (U2) O2, U2

7. (U1) O1, U3

8. (U4) O3, U5

9. (U3) O2, U1, O2, U3

10. (O1) U1, O3

11. (O4) U3, O5

12. (U3) O5, U3

13. (O4) U3, O5

14. (O1) U1, O3

15. (U3) O2, U1, O2, U3

16. (U4) O3, U5

17. (U1) O1, U3

18. (U2) O2, U2

19. (U2) O2, U2

20. O2, U2

21. O2, U2

22. (U2) O2, U2

23. (U2) O2, U2

Braids and edges no. 5

Using perlé no. 12 thread, this weave covers a height of 14 mm with the length being as wide as you need.

Warp: Colour 1 (14 mm stitches)
Weft: Colour 2

1. (U2) O2, U2
2. (U2) O2, U2
3. O2, U2
4. O2, U2
5. (U2) O2, U2
6. (U2) O2, U2
7. (O1) U1, O3
8. (U3) O2, U1, O2, U3
9. (U4) O3, U5
10. (U1) O1, O3
11. O3, U5
12. (O1) U1, O2, U3, O2
13. (O1, U1) O3, U1
14. Repeat Row 12
15. Repeat Row 11
16. Repeat Row 10
17. Repeat Row 9
18. Repeat Row 8
19. Repeat Row 7
20. Repeat Row 6
21. Repeat Row 5
22. Repeat Row 4
23. Repeat Row 3
24. Repeat Row 2
25. Repeat Row 1

Texture no. 1

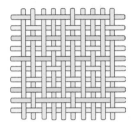

Warp: Colour 1
Weft: Colour 1
    (pattern repeat 8 rows)

1. (U1) O3, U1
2. O1, U3
3. O1, U1
4. (U2) O1, U3
5. (U1) O1, U1
6. (U2) O1, U3
7. O1, U3
8. O1, U1

Texture no. 2

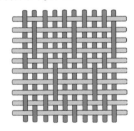

Warp: Colour 1
Weft: Colour 2
    (pattern repeat 8 rows)

1. O1, U1
2. *(U1) O3, U1*
3. Repeat * to *
4. Repeat * to *
5. O1, U1
6. #(O2, U1) O3, U1#
7. Repeat # to #
8. Repeat # to #

Texture no. 3

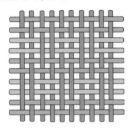

Warp: Colour 1
Weft: Colour 1
    Colour 2
    (pattern repeat 8 rows)

COLOUR 1

1. O1, U1
2. (U1) O1, U1

COLOUR 2

3. O2, U2
4. O2, U2

COLOUR 1

5. O1, U1
6. (U1) O1, U1

COLOUR 2

7. (U2) O2, U2
8. (U2) O2, U2

Texture no. 4

Warp: Colour 1
Weft: Colour 2
    (pattern repeat 11 rows)

1. *O1, U3*
2. Repeat * to *
3. #(U1) O3, U1#
4. Repeat # to #
5. Repeat # to #
6. Repeat * to *
7. Repeat * to *
8. Repeat * to *
9. Repeat # to #
10. Repeat # to #
11. Repeat # to #

Texture No. 5

Warp: colour 1
Weft: colour 2
        (pattern repeat 4 rows)

1. (O1, U2) O2, U2
2. (U2) O2, U2
3. (U1) O2, U2
4. O2, U2

Texture no. 6

Warp: Colour 1
Weft: Colour 2
        (pattern repeat 16 rows)

1. (O1, U2) O2, U2
2. O2, U2
3. (U1) O2, U2
4. (U2) O2, U2
5. (O1, U2) O2, U2
6. O2, U2
7. (U1) O2, U2
8. (U2) O2, U2
9. (O1, U2) O2, U2
10. (U2) O2, U2
11. (U1) O2, U2
12. O2, U2
13. (O1, U2) O2, U2
14. (U2) O2, U2
15. (U1) O2, U2
16. O2, U2

Texture no. 7

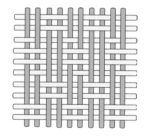

Warp: Colour 1
Weft: Colour 2
        (pattern repeat 6 rows)

1. (U2) O2, U2
2. (U2) O2, U2
3. (U1) O1, U3
4. O2, U2
5. O2, U2
6. O1, U3

Texture no. 8

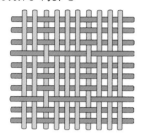

Warp: colour 1
Weft: colour 1
        (pattern repeat 4 rows)

1. (U3) O1, U3
2. (U3) O1, U3
3. (U3) O1, U3
4. O3, U1

Texture no. 9

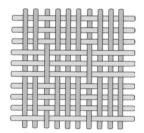

Warp: colour 1
Weft: colour 1 or 2
        (pattern repeat 6 rows)

1. (U3) O1, U3
2. (U3) O1, U3
3. (U3) O1, U3
4. O3, U1
5. O3, U1
6. O3, U1

BEAD EMBROIDERY STITCHES

Using beads In your embroidery

When attaching beads to your embroidery you should use a small, short needle that will be able to go through even the smallest bead. Size 10 or 12 Bead Embroidery needles are suitable, as are size 10, 11 or 12 Quilting needles. Long beading needles are cumbersome and should be avoided.

You can use a double strand of fine beading thread but, as the available colours are limited, it is often best to use matching embroidery cotton. Thread a long, single strand into the needle, double it over and tie a knot at the end so that, in effect, you are working with a double strand.

Attaching a single bead

Bring your needle up through the fabric and pick up a bead. Pull the bead down the thread until it touches the fabric. Slide the needle down between the two threads until it touches the bead and go back into the fabric at that point. This will ensure that the length of the stitch holding the bead is correct and is a particularly useful way to attach bugle beads.

Attaching a bead with a bead

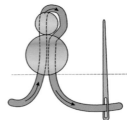

Bring your needle up through the fabric at the correct point. Pick up the larger and then the smaller bead. Return down through the larger bead and tighten the thread. The smaller bead holds the larger bead in place.

Bead circles

Bring the needle up through the fabric. Pick up as many beads as your require to make the size of circle that you need. From the beginning of the line of beads, take the needle through the first three beads for a second time, making sure that you do not snag the thread with the needle. Go into the fabric, having left enough space to accommodate the three beads that have a double string of thread. Pull through, manipulating the beads so that they form a circle.

With the same thread, work a small couching stitch between each bead, over the circle of thread that holds the bead circle. If you pull that circle of thread out a little as you stitch, the bead circle will form more perfectly.

Bead couching

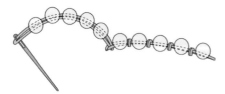

Come up through the fabric at the beginning of the line. Pick up not less than 2 and not more than 5 beads. Lay them along the line that you need to follow and, leaving approximately the width of a bead after the end of the beads, go into the fabric. Push the beads back to the beginning of the line and couch over the thread between each bead, pulling the line into place as you go. Bring the needle up between the two threads, and scraping the last bead in the line. Pick up the next group of beads. Continue in this way. When you reach the end of the line, go through the fabric, catch the thread in the voile backing fabric and return through the same hole. Run the needle and thread through the whole line of beads, going into the fabric when you exit the first bead you picked up at the beginning of the line. Tug the thread slightly to tighten it. This pulls the line of beads neatly into place. End off the thread securely.

Bead picot

Bring the needle up through the fabric. Pick up 4 beads and allow them to drop down to touch the fabric. Take the needle down through the first bead and through the fabric. If you would like the picot to lie flat against the fabric, come up a little way up to catch the top bead with a small stitch that goes through the bead and back into the fabric.

Bead stem stitch

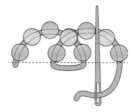

Pick up 5 or 7 beads (always an odd number). Go through the fabric making sure that the line of beads forms a slight loop. Come up halfway back and pick up 5 (or 7) beads. Go into the fabric halfway further and before you tighten, come up halfway back — just past the end of the first loop. Tighten the thread. Continue in this way, making sure that you always come up on the same side of the loop.

Beaded fly stitch

Start at the tip with a straight stitch. Come up on the left and go down on the right of the straight stitch, leaving a loop. Come up at the bottom of the straight stitch, catching the loop before you tighten. Pick up a bead and go into the fabric below it, leaving enough room for the bead to sit happily. Leave a space of about 1 mm on the left side, start the next fly stitch.

Beaded Palestrina stitch

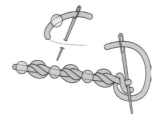

Working from left to right, or along the edge that you wish to embellish, come up at the beginning of the line. Pick up a bead and leaving sufficient space for that bead, go into the fabric slightly above the line, coming out below the line. Pull through. Go over and under the thread, pulling towards the bead. Go over and under the thread again in the space below where you previously went under the thread. Make sure the loop of thread is under the needle. Pull through and tighten the knot that forms. Repeat as required. End off with a knot and take your thread to the back to end off.

Caged flat back crystal

Hold the flat back crystal in place on the circle drawn for its placement.

- Use a waste thread that is a completely different colour from the thread you will use to stitch the black cage that holds the flat back crystal in place.
- Come through the fabric at the top of the crystal. Go into the fabric at the bottom thus forming a straight stitch that goes down the mid-line of the crystal.
- Now work three more stitches to form a star that holds the crystal in place. The first should go over the horizontal mid- line. The last two go from top right to bottom left and then from top left to bottom right. When working the last two stitches whip under the intersection of the first two stitches. This holds them all together and stops them from sliding off the crystal.
- Finish off by coming up one more time and making a knot over the intersection. This will make it easy to pull these stitches out.

- Using two strands of stranded cotton or a perlé thread, do a circle of backstitch around and adjacent to the crystal.

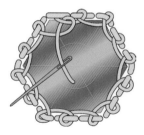

- Using the same thread, continue by working a detached buttonhole stitch under each backstitch.

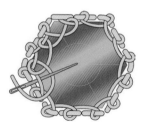

- When you get back around to the first buttonhole stitch, take your needle through the loop of that stitch to secure the end of the row and continue in the opposite direction working into each of the loops created in the first row.
- Work a third row in the same way. When you reach the end of that row, continue in the same direction, whipping through each of the loops.
- When you get back to where you started the whipping stitches, pull the thread to tighten the last row and to make sure that it fits snugly against the crystal.

Ease the needle under the detached buttonhole stitches and take it through the fabric to end off.

Don't pull the thread too tightly, as this will create a kink in the last row of the cage you have created.

Simple bead flowers and leaves

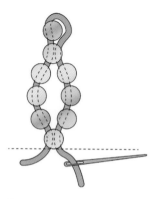

Bring the needle up through the fabric and pick up 6* beads. Go down the 5th bead, pick up 3* beads and go down the 1st bead and through the fabric. *Vary the size of the flower or leaf by adjusting the number of beads picked up.

BEADING TECHNIQUES

General tips and basic knowledge

- Abbreviations:
  - PU means pick up;
  - GT means go through.
- Work the techniques in this gallery with fine beading thread.
- Because you are attaching the beaded items to fabric, it is vital to check that the thread is colour fast.
  - Wind a small amount onto a plastic floss card;
  - Plunge the card into very hot – almost boiling – water;
  - Remove it and pat it dry on a light coloured towel;
  - If there is no colour left on the towel it is safe to use.
- Use a size 11 or 12 beading or bead embroidery needle.
- The tension of your work must be tight. Very tight, otherwise the beadwork will be floppy.
- To start these bead items, PU 1 bead. GT it a second time without snagging the thread. Pull it down towards the end of the thread, leaving a tail of approximately 6" (150 mm). This will act as a stopper bead and you will remove it eventually.

Peyote-stitch flowers and leaves

FOUR-BEAD FLOWER

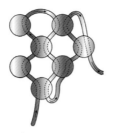

1. With approximately 1 yd (1 m) of thread on your needle, PU 4 beads.

2. Changing direction so that you are working from the top to the bottom, PU 1 bead and GT the 5th bead in the line of 4.

3. PU 1 bead and GT the 1st bead in the line of 4. Not including the stopper bead, this is the first bead that you picked up.

4. Changing direction so that you are working from the bottom to the top, GT the last bead that you added in the previous row.

5. PU 1 bead and GT the top bead.

6. Changing direction so that you are working from the top to bottom, GT the last bead that you added in the previous row.

7. Take the needle and thread down the remaining beads on the side of the petal coming out of the bottom bead.

8. Turn the petal over and, working bottom to top, GT the first prominent bead.

9. PU 1 bead and GT the top bead.

10. Changing direction so that you are working from the top to bottom, GT the last bead that you added in the previous row.

11. Continue taking your needle down the side of the petal exiting the 1st bead.

12. PU 1 bead. Take the needle down bead #1 at the bottom of the previous petal and back up the bead you have just added.

13. PU 1 bead. Take the needle down bead #2 on the side of the previous petal and back up the bead you have just added.

14. PU 2 beads.

15. Changing direction so that you are working from the top to the bottom, PU 1 bead and GT the 3rd bead in the line of 4.

16. PU 1 bead and GT the 1st bead in the line of 4 beads.

17. Changing direction, take the needle up through bead #2 which is already attached to bead #2 of the previous petal.

18. PU 1 bead and GT the bead at the top.

19. Changing direction, GT the prominent bead that is the last bead you added in the previous row continuing down the rest of the beads that form the side of this half of the petal, coming out of the bead at the bottom.

Complete the other side of the petal by adding the missing bead, as indicated above. Bring the thread down the side beads, exiting the bottom bead.

20. When you have added the last bead to the 5th petal, GT the prominent bead.

21. Take your needle up through the adjacent, 2nd bead, on the left side of the first petal, down through the 2nd bead and through the 1st bead of the 5th petal.

22. Take your needle up through the bottom bead of the 1st petal and down through the bottom bead of the 5th petal.

(See *Attaching Flowers And Leaves To The Fabric* on page 71 complete the flower).

SIX-BEAD FLOWER

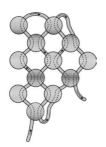

1. With approximately 1 yd (1 m) of thread on your needle, PU 6 beads.

2. Changing direction so that you are working from the top to the bottom, PU 1 bead and GT the 5th bead in the line of 6. PU 1 bead and GT the 3rd bead in the line of 6 beads.

3. PU 1 bead and GT the 1st bead in the line of 6. Not including the stopper bead, this is the first bead that you picked up.

4. Changing direction so that you are working from the bottom to the top, GT the last bead that you added in the previous row.

5. PU 1 bead and GT the next prominent bead.

6. PU 1 bead and GT the top bead.

7. Changing direction so that you are working from the top to bottom, GT the last bead that you added in the previous row.

8. PU 1 bead and GT the prominent bead below.

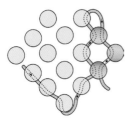

9. Take the needle and thread down the remaining beads on the side of the petal coming out of the bottom bead.

10. Turn the petal over and, working bottom to top, GT the first prominent bead.

11. PU 1 bead and GT the next prominent bead.

12. PU 1 bead and GT the top bead.

13. Changing direction so that you are working from the top to bottom, GT the last bead that you added in the previous row.

14. PU 1 bead and GT the prominent bead below. Continue taking your needle down the side of the petal exiting the 1st bead.

15. PU 1 bead. Take the needle down bead #1 at the bottom of the previous petal and back up the bead you have just added. PU 1 bead. Take the needle down bead #2 on the side of the previous petal and back up the bead you have just added.

16. PU 4 beads.

17. Changing direction so that you are working from the top to the bottom, PU 1 bead and GT the 5th bead in the line of 6.

18. PU 1 bead and GT the 3rd bead in the line of 6 beads.

19. PU 1 bead and GT the 1st bead in the line of 6.

20. Changing direction, take the needle up through bead #2 which is already attached to bead #2 of the previous petal.

21. PU 1 bead. Take the needle down bead #3 on the side of the previous petal and back up the bead you have just added. GT the next prominent bead.

22. PU 1 bead and GT the bead at the top.

23. Changing direction, GT the prominent bead that is the last bead you added in the previous row.

24. PU 1 bead, GT the next prominent bead, continuing down the rest of the beads that form the side of this half of the petal, coming out of the bead at the bottom.

Complete the second half of this petal in the same way as you did the first petal.

Continue adding petals until you have a total of 5 petals.

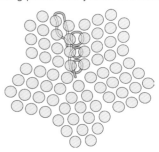

25. When you have added the last bead to the 5th petal, GT the prominent bead.

26. Take your needle up through the adjacent, 3rd bead, on the left side of the first petal, down through the 3rd bead and through the 2nd bead of the 5th petal.

27. Take your needle up through the adjacent, 2nd bead, on the left side of the first petal, down through the 2nd bead and through the bottom bead of the 5th petal.

28. Take your needle up through the bottom bead of the 1st petal and down through the bottom bead of the 5th petal.

(See *Attaching Flowers And Leaves To The Fabric* on page 71 to complete the flower.)

EIGHT-BEAD FLOWER

1. With approximately 1 yd (1 m) of thread on your needle, PU 8 beads.

2. Changing direction so that you are working from the top to the bottom, PU 1 bead and GT the 7th bead in the line of 8.

3. PU 1 bead and GT the 5th bead in the line of 8 beads.

4. PU 1 bead and GT the 3rd bead in the line of 8 beads.

5. PU 1 bead and GT the 1st bead in the line of 8. Not including the stopper bead, this is the first bead that you picked up. Changing direction so that you are working from the bottom to the top, GT the last bead that you added in the previous row.

6. PU 1 bead and GT the next prominent bead.

7. PU 1 bead and GT the next prominent bead.

8. PU 1 bead and GT the top bead.

9. Changing direction so that you are working from the top to bottom, PU 1 bead and GT the last bead that you added in the previous row.

10. PU 1 bead and GT the prominent bead below.

11. PU 1 bead and GT the last prominent bead at the bottom of the row.

12. Changing direction and working bottom to top, GT the last bead in the previous row.

13. PU 1 bead and GT the next prominent bead.

14. PU 1 bead and GT the top bead.

15. Changing direction, GT the last bead that you added in the previous row.

16. PU 1 bead and GT the next prominent bead.

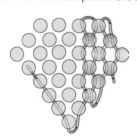

17. Take the needle and thread down the remaining beads on the side of the petal coming out of the bottom bead.

18. Turn the petal over and, working bottom to top, GT the first prominent bead.

19. PU 1 bead and GT the next prominent bead.

20. PU 1 bead and GT the next prominent bead.

21. PU 1 bead and GT the top bead.

22. Changing direction so that you are working from the top to bottom, PU 1 bead and GT the last bead that you added in the previous row.

23. PU 1 bead and GT the prominent bead below.

24. PU 1 bead and GT the last prominent bead at the bottom of the row.

25. Changing direction and working bottom to top, GT the

last bead in the previous row.

26. PU 1 bead and GT the next prominent bead.

27. PU 1 bead and GT the top bead. Changing direction, GT the last bead that you added in the previous row.

28. PU 1 bead and GT the next prominent bead. Continue taking your needle down the side of the petal exiting the 1st bead.

29. PU 1 bead. Take the needle down bead #1 at the bottom of the previous petal and back up the bead you have just added.

30. PU 1 bead. Take the needle down bead #2 on the side of the previous petal and back up the bead you have just added.

31. PU 6 beads.

32. Changing direction so that you are working from the top to the bottom, PU 1 bead and GT the 7th bead in the line of 8.

33. PU 1 bead and GT the 5th bead in the line of 8.

34. PU 1 bead and GT the 3rd bead in the line of 8 beads.

35. PU 1 bead and GT the 1st bead in the line of 8.

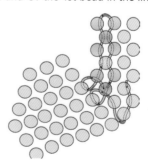

36. Changing direction, take the needle up through bead #2 which is already attached to bead #2 of the previous petal.

37. PU 1 bead. Take the needle down bead #3 on the side of the previous petal and back up the bead you have just added. GT the next prominent bead.

38. PU 1 bead and GT the next prominent bead.

39. PU 1 bead and GT the bead at the top.

40. Changing direction, PU 1 bead and GT the prominent bead that is the last bead you added in the previous row.

41. PU 1 bead and GT the next prominent bead. PU 1 bead. Go up bead #4 on the side of the previous petal and down the bead you have just added.

42. GT the next prominent bead.

43. Changing direction, take the needle up through bead #4 which is already attached to bead #4 of the previous petal.

44. PU 1 bead. Take the needle down bead #5 on the side of the previous petal and back up the bead you have just added. GT the next prominent bead.

45. PU 1 bead and GT the bead at the top.

46. Changing direction, PU 1 bead and GT the prominent bead that is the last bead you added in the previous row. GT the next prominent bead, continuing down the rest of the beads that form the side of this half of the petal, coming out of the bead at the bottom.

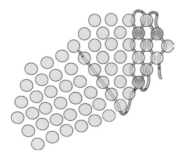

Complete the second half of this petal in the same way as you did the first petal and continue adding petals until you have a total of 5 petals.

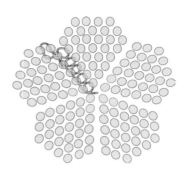

47. When you have added the last bead to the 5th petal, GT the prominent bead.

48. Take your needle up through the adjacent, 5th bead, on the left side of the first petal, down through the 5th bead and through the 4th bead of the 5th petal.

49. Take your needle up through the adjacent, 4th bead, on the left side of the first petal, down through the 4th bead and through the 3rd bead of the 5th petal.

50. Take your needle up through the adjacent, 3rd bead, on the left side of the first petal, down through the 3rd bead and through the 2nd bead of the 5th petal.

51. Take your needle up through the adjacent, 2nd bead, on the left side of the first petal, down through the 2nd bead and through the bottom bead of the 5th petal.

52. Take your needle up through the bottom bead of the 1st petal and down through the bottom bead of the 5th petal.

(See *Attaching Flowers And Leaves To The Fabric* on page 71 to complete the flower.)

TEN-BEAD FLOWER

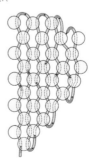

1. With approximately 2 yd (1½ m) of thread on your needle, PU 10 beads.

2. Changing direction so that you are working from the top to the bottom, PU 1 bead and GT the 9th bead in the line of 10.

3. Changing direction so that you are working from the top to the bottom, PU 1 bead and GT the 7th bead in the line of 10.

4. PU 1 bead and GT the 5th bead in the line of 10 beads.

5. PU 1 bead and GT the 3rd bead in the line of 10 beads. PU 1 bead and GT the 1st bead in the line of 10. Not including the stopper bead, this is the first bead that you picked up.

6. Changing direction so that you are working from the bottom to the top, GT the last bead that you added in the previous row.

7. PU 1 bead and GT the next prominent bead.

8. PU 1 bead and GT the next prominent bead.

9. PU 1 bead and GT the next prominent bead.

10. PU 1 bead and GT the top bead.

11. Changing direction so that you are working from the top to bottom, PU 1 bead and GT the last bead that you added in the previous row.

12. PU 1 bead and GT the prominent bead below.

13. PU 1 bead and GT the prominent bead below.

14. PU 1 bead and GT the last prominent bead at the bottom of the row.

15. Changing direction and working bottom to top, GT the last bead in the previous row.

16. PU 1 bead and GT the next prominent bead.

17. PU 1 bead and GT the next prominent bead

18. PU 1 bead and GT the top bead.

19. Changing direction, GT the last bead that you added in the previous row.

20. PU 1 bead and GT the next prominent bead.

21. PU 1 bead and GT the last prominent bead at the bottom of the row.

22. Changing direction and working bottom to top, GT the last bead in the previous row.

23. PU 1 bead and GT the next prominent bead.

24. PU 1 bead.

THE DISCOMBOBULATION:

(So-called because the initial reaction to this manipulation is one of shock and confusion. Take it step-by-step and you will see it is do-able)

1. Referring to the diagram above, having picked up a bead as instructed in (25.) above, take the needle down and through the top bead of the previous row, on the left, and the bead diagonally below that.

2. Changing direction, take the needle up the bead immediately to the right of the bead you have just come down, and through the bead diagonally above that (the bead you went down in (1.) above).

3. Changing direction again, take the needle down the bead you have just exited (the bead you added at the beginning of this process).

4. PU 1 bead and GT the prominent bead below that and the beads that follow, exiting bead #1 at the bottom.

I will refer to the discombobulation again, as we move further into the instructions for this flower.

5. Turn the petal over and continue working on the right hand side. GT the first prominent bead at the bottom.

6. Working bottom to top, PU 1 bead and GT the next prominent bead.

7. PU 1 bead and GT the next prominent bead.

8. PU 1 bead and GT the next prominent bead.

9. PU 1 bead and GT the top prominent bead.

10. Changing direction, PU 1 bead and GT the next prominent bead.

11. PU 1 bead and GT the next prominent bead.

12. PU 1 bead and GT the next prominent bead.

13. PU 1 bead and GT the bottom prominent bead.

14. Changing direction, GT the first prominent bead at the bottom.

15. PU 1 bead and GT the next prominent bead.

16. PU 1 bead and GT the next prominent bead.

17. PU 1 bead and GT the top prominent bead.

18. Changing direction, GT the first prominent bead at the top.

19. PU 1 bead and GT the next prominent bead.

20. PU 1 bead and GT the bottom prominent bead.

21. Changing direction, GT the first prominent bead at the bottom. PU 1 bead and GT the next prominent bead.

22. PU 1 bead.

23. Repeat the discombobulation described previously to finish the petal.

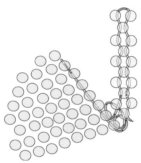

24. PU 1 bead. Take the needle down bead #1 at the bottom of the previous petal and back up the bead you have just added.

25. PU 1 bead. Take the needle down bead #2 on the side of the previous petal and back up the bead you have just added.

26. PU 8 beads.

27. Changing direction so that you are working from the top to the bottom, PU 1 bead and GT the 9th bead in the line of 10.

28. Changing direction so that you are working from the top to the bottom, PU 1 bead and GT the 7th bead in the line of 10.

29. PU 1 bead and GT the 5th bead in the row of 10.

30. PU 1 bead and GT the 3rd bead in the row of 10 beads.

31. PU 1 bead and GT the 1st bead in the row of 10.

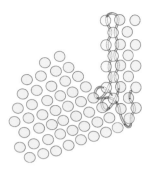

32. Changing direction, take the needle up through bead #2 which is already attached to bead #2 of the previous petal.

33. PU 1 bead. Take the needle down bead #3 on the side of the previous petal and back up the bead you have just added. GT the next prominent bead.

34. PU 1 bead and GT the next prominent bead.

35. PU 1 bead and GT the next prominent bead.

36. PU 1 bead and GT the bead at the top.

37. Changing direction, PU 1 bead and GT the prominent bead that is the last bead you added in the previous row.

38. PU 1 bead and GT the next prominent bead.

39. PU 1 bead and GT the next prominent bead.

40. PU 1 bead. Go up bead #4 on the side of the previous petal and down the bead you have just added.

41. GT the next prominent bead.

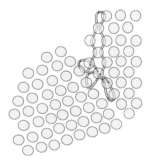

42. Changing direction, take the needle up through bead #4 which is already attached to bead #4 of the previous petal.

43. PU 1 bead. Take the needle down bead #5 on the side of the previous petal and back up the bead you have just added. GT the next prominent bead.

44. PU 1 bead and GT the next prominent bead.

45. PU 1 bead and GT the bead at the top.

46. Changing direction, GT the prominent bead that is the last bead you added in the previous row.

47. PU 1 bead and GT the next prominent bead.

48. PU 1 bead. Go up bead #6 on the side of the previous petal and down the bead you have just added.

49. GT the next prominent bead.

50. Changing direction, take the needle up through bead #6 which is already attached to bead #6 of the previous petal.

To complete this side of the petal, follow instructions 1 – 4 in the discombobulation.

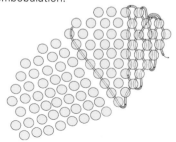

51. Continue working on the right hand side. GT the first prominent bead at the bottom.

52. Working bottom to top, PU 1 bead and GT the next prominent bead.

53. PU 1 bead and GT the next prominent bead.

54. PU 1 bead and GT the next prominent bead.

55. PU 1 bead and GT the top prominent bead.

56. Changing direction, PU 1 bead and GT the next prominent bead.

57. PU 1 bead and GT the next prominent bead.

58. PU 1 bead and GT the next prominent bead.

59. PU 1 bead and GT the bottom prominent bead.

60. Changing direction, GT the first prominent bead at the bottom.

61. PU 1 bead and GT the next prominent bead.

62. PU 1 bead and GT the next prominent bead.

63. PU 1 bead and GT the top prominent bead.

64. Changing direction, GT the first prominent bead at the top.

65. PU 1 bead and GT the next prominent bead.

66. PU 1 bead and GT the bottom prominent bead.

67. Changing direction, GT the first prominent bead at the bottom.

68. PU 1 bead and GT the next prominent bead.

69. PU 1 bead.

70. Repeat the discombobulation described on page 67 to finish the petal.

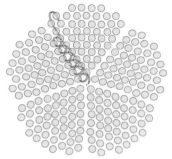

71. When you have added the last bead to the 5th petal, GT the prominent bead and the bead that follows that one.

72. Take your needle up through the adjacent, 6th bead, on the left side of the first petal, down through the 6th bead and through the 4th bead of the 5th petal.

73. Take your needle up through the adjacent, 5th bead, on the left side of the first petal, down through the 5th bead and through the 4th bead of the 5th petal.

74. Take your needle up through the adjacent, 4th bead, on the left side of the first petal, down through the 4th bead and through the 3rd bead of the 5th petal.

75. Take your needle up through the adjacent, 3rd bead, on the left side of the first petal, down through the 3rd bead and through the 2nd bead of the 5th petal.

76. Take your needle up through the adjacent, 2nd bead, on the left side of the first petal, down through the 2nd bead and through the bottom bead of the 5th petal.

77. Take your needle up through the bottom bead of the 1st petal and down through the bottom bead of the 5th petal.

(See *Attaching Flowers And Leaves To The Fabric* on page 71 to complete the flower.)

LEAVES

- Peyote stitch leaves are worked with an even number of beads.
- To create a leaf shape, work each side until you have 2 prominent beads with a space in between them in the final row. If you fill that space with a bead the leaf will have a pointed edge, which is not what you want. It should be ovate.
- The smallest leaf that you could make with these instructions would have 8 beads in the first row.
- Within reason, you can make this leaf any size you want to by picking up additional pairs of beads in the first row.
- The instructions below are for a 10-bead leaf.

(See *Attaching Flowers And Leaves To The Fabric* on page 71 to complete the flower.)

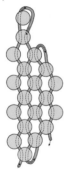

1. With 12" (300 mm) of thread on the needle, pull the stopper bead that you have picked up to the centre of the length of thread.

2. PU 10 beads.

3. Changing direction, take the needle down through the 9th bead.

4. PU 1 bead and GT the 7th bead.

5. PU 1 bead and GT the 5th bead.

6. PU 1 bead and GT the 3rd bead.

7. PU 1 bead and GT the bead at the bottom.

8. Changing direction, take the needle up through the first prominent bead, which is the last bead you added on the way down.

9. PU 1 bead and GT the next prominent bead.

10. PU 1 bead and GT the next prominent bead.

11. PU 1 bead and GT the top prominent bead.

12. Changing direction, take the needle down through the first prominent bead, which is the last bead you added on the way up.

13. PU 1 bead and GT the next prominent bead.

14. PU 1 bead and GT the bottom prominent bead.

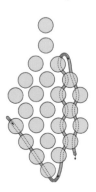

15. Take your needle down the rest of the beads that form the side of this half of the leaf, coming out of the bead at the bottom. (Depending on how many beads you have picked up in your first row, you may finish the final row at the top. If so, change direction and go down all of the beads that form the side of the leaf, still coming out of the bottom bead).

16. Thread the needle onto the other half of the thread.

17. Changing direction, take the needle up through the first prominent bead.

18. PU 1 bead and GT the next prominent bead.

19. PU 1 bead and GT the next prominent bead.

20. PU 1 bead and GT the top prominent bead.

21. Changing direction, take the needle down through the first prominent bead, which is the last bead you added on the way up.

22. PU 1 bead and GT the next prominent bead.

23. PU 1 bead and GT the bottom prominent bead.

24. Take your needle down the rest of the beads that form the side of this half of the leaf, coming out of the bead at the bottom.

Remove the needle from the thread and tie both of the thread tails tightly together with a double knot. Pull very hard as you do the first part of the knot so that the sides of the leaf curl in slightly. This makes the leaf look more natural and more interesting.

ATTACHING FLOWERS AND LEAVES TO THE FABRIC

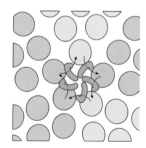

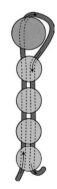

The diagram above depicts the centre of the flower.

1. There should be two tails of thread at the base of the completed flower. Thread the longest tail on a beading needle.
2. Take the needle through the fabric at the point where you would like to place the flower.
3. Bring the needle up in the small gap in the centre of the flower at approximately the place where two petals abut one another.
4. Work a small couching stitch over the thread, or threads, that run from the bottom bead of the one petal to the bottom bead of the adjacent petal.
5. Work the same stitch over the threads at the meeting points of the remaining petals.
6. Come up through the fabric behind one of the petals approximately level with the second or third bead up from the base of the flower.
7. Take the needle through the closest bead and back into the fabric.
8. Attach a second petal through a bead, at the back, on the opposite side of the flower.
9. If you have sufficient thread left on the needle, come up in the centre of the flower. (If not, end off that thread and use the remaining tail.)

10. Pick up as many beads as you need to make a stamen in the centre of the flower. Consider a different, often larger bead at the top.
11. Change direction, bringing the needle back down all of the beads, except for the top one that acts as a stopper bead.
12. Go back into the fabric and either end off or come back up a few more times to make additional stamens as needed.
13. Once you have your flowers in place arrange the leaves where you would like them to be, using the same method.
14. There should be two tails of thread at the base of the completed leaf. Thread the longest tail on a beading needle.
15. Take the needle through the fabric at the point where you would like to place the leaf, tucking the bottom end under the petal of a flower.
16. Come up through the fabric adjacent to the second or third bead on one side of the leaf.
17. Take the needle through that bead and back into fabric.
18. End off that thread and do the same with the second thread, attaching a bead on the opposite side of the leaf.
19. When you have placed all of the leaves, complete the arrangement by placing twigs and small branches around the flowers and leaves.
20. These are worked in the same way as the stamens using small beads for the stalk and larger beads for the tip.
21. Bring the needle up through the fabric from underneath the petals of the flowers so that these twigs radiate from the flowers. Make a variety of lengths.
22. If the twigs won't lie the way you want them to, place a small couching stitch between two of the beads in the stalk, two or three beads up from the base.

Beaded braids

These are derived from jewellery-making techniques and are useful for the intersections between fabric patches.

LINKED DAISY CHAIN

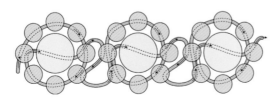

The number of beads in the circle of the daisy chain is always an even number and will vary according to the size of the bead in the centre.

1. PU 8 small beads. Pull them down until they are touching the stopper bead at the bottom.
2. GT the first bead again and pull the beads together to make a circle.
3. PU a large bead.
4. Go up the 4th bead away from where you came out of the circle.
5. Pull the thread tightly, making sure that the circle sits nicely around the big bead.
6. PU 1 small bead.
7. Go down the bead below the one that you have just come out of.
8. PU 1 small bead and go up the bead you picked up in (5.) above.
9. You should now have a filled circle with two small beads sitting one above the other to the right of that circle. Those two beads are the start of the next circle.
10. [PU 6 small beads.
11. Go up the lower bead of the two that are described in (9.) above. Pull the beads together to make a circle.
12. PU a large bead.
13. Go up the 4th bead away from where you came out of the circle.
14. Pull the thread tightly, making sure that the circle sits nicely around the big bead.
15. PU 1 small bead.
16. Go down the bead below the one that you have just come out of.

17. PU 1 small bead and go up the bead you picked up in (5.) above.
18. You should now have a filled circle with two small beads sitting one above the other to the right of that circle. Those two beads are the start of the next circle.]
19. Repeat from [to] (10 to 18 above) until the daisy chain is the required length.
20. Remove the stopper bead that you added to the start and thread that end on a needle.
21. Take the needle through the fabric at the beginning of the line where you wish to place the daisy chain.
22. Thread the other end onto another needle and take the needle through the fabric at the end of the line where you wish to place the daisy chain.
23. Working from both ends alternately, work a couching stitch over the thread between the beads on either side of the circle as well as a stitch or two over the thread at the point where the circles meet one another.

CHEVRON VARIATION

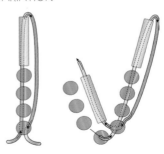

PU 1 x 15° bead. GT it one more time, so that it will be a stopper bead. Ignore it from now on.

1. PU 4 x 15° beads and 1 x #1 bugle bead.
2. Go down the 1st bead that you picked up and pull tight so that the bugle turns around and lies adjacent to the top 3 x 15° beads.
3. PU 4 x 15° beads and 1 x #1 bugle bead.
4. Go down the 1st bead that you picked up and pull tight so that the bugle turns around and lies adjacent to the top 3 x 15° beads.
5. Go up the bugle of the first set.

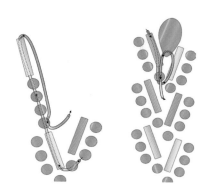

3. GT the next bead in the circle.

4. Repeat steps 2 and 3 until there is a 15° and fire polished bead circle coming out of each of the 5 beads in the centre circle.

6. Keep adding sets in this way until the chain you are making reaches the required length. Make sure that the sets lie alternately to the left and right. It is easier to turn it over as you work on each new set.

7. The Christmas branch needed for the project in this book requires 11 sets (or 5½ pairs).

8. At the end, having gone through the 15° bead at the bottom of the last set, PU 1 x drop bead, go back down the 15° bead and, not depicted in the diagram above so that it remains easy to read, GT the drop bead and the 15° bead a second time. End off.

9. Using the tails of thread, attach it to the fabric by taking the bottom tail into the fabric on the edge of the block. Come up through the fabric all the way along the branch, couching beads in the middle of the branch and on both sides. Use the end tail if necessary, doing the same, making sure the branch is secure

SNOWFLAKE NO. 1

1. PU 5 x 15° beads and GT the first two beads again to close the circle.

2. PU 1 x 15° bead, 1 x 3 mm fire polished bead, 1 x 15° bead, 1 x 3 mm fire polished bead, 1 x 15° bead, 1 x 3 mm fire polished bead, 1 x 15° bead. GT the bead that you exited in the circle, entering on the opposite side.

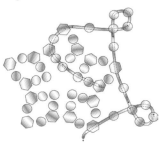

5. GT the next bead in the centre circle and work up the 1 x 15° bead, 1 x 3 mm fire polished bead, 1 x 15° bead and 1 x 3 mm fire polished bead on the left side of the circle depicted above, exiting on the right of the fire polished bead.

6. PU 5 x 15° beads. Go down the second bead, PU 1 x 15° bead and GT the 3 mm fire polished bead at the top of the next radiating circle.

7. Repeat step 6 between every radiating circle.

8. Work the thread through the beads until you exit one of the beads in the centre circle. Cut off the thread leaving a long tail.

9. Using the tail, attach the snowflake to the fabric. Couch between the beads in the centre circle.

10. Thereafter place a couching stitch on each side of the fire polished bead at the top of each radiating circle.

11. Come through the fabric to the right of the bead at the tip of the picot between each radiating circle. GT that bead and go back through the fabric.

12. This should secure the snowflake, but if you feel you would like to add more couching stitches, you can do so, making sure that they are evenly spaced over the whole snowflake.

SNOWFLAKE NO. 2

1. PU 10 x 15° beads and GT all of the beads again to close the circle.
2. PU 1 x 15° bead, 1 x 3 mm fire polished bead, 1 x 15° bead, 1 x 3 mm fire polished bead, 1 x 15° bead, 1 x 3 mm fire polished bead, 1 x 15° bead. GT the bead that you exited in the circle, entering on the opposite side.

3. GT the next 2 beads in the circle.
4. Repeat steps 2 and 3 until there is a 15° and fire polished bead circle coming out of every second bead in the centre circle. There should be 5 of these radiating circles with a single bead between each on at the bottom.
5. GT the next 2 beads in the centre circle and work up the 1 x 15° bead, 1 x 3 mm fire polished bead, 1 x 15° bead and 1 x 3 mm fire polished bead on the left side of the circle depicted above, exiting on the right of the fire polished bead.
6. PU 1 x 15° bead, 1 x 3 mm fire polished bead and 1 x 15° bead. Go down the fire polished bead, PU 1 x 15° bead and GT the 3 mm fire polished bead at the top of the next radiating circle.
7. Exiting on the far side of the bead, PU 6 x 15° beads. Go down the third bead, PU 2 x 15° beads and GT the 3 mm fire polished bead at the top of the next radiating circle.

8. Repeat steps 6 and 7 between every radiating circle.

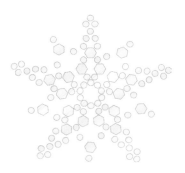

9. Work the thread through the beads until you exit one of the beads in the centre circle. Cut off the thread leaving a long tail.
10. Using the tail, attach the snowflake to the fabric. Couch between every second bead in the centre circle.
11. Thereafter place a couching stitch on each side of the fire polished bead at the top of each radiating circle.
12. Come through the fabric to the right of the bead at the tip of the picot between and at the tip of each radiating circle. GT that bead and go back through the fabric.
13. This should secure the snowflake, but if you feel you would like to add more couching stitches, you can do so, making sure that they are evenly spaced over the whole snowflake.

SNOWFLAKE NO. 3

1. PU 10 x 15° beads and GT all of the beads again to close the circle.
2. PU 1 x 15° bead, 3 x 3 mm fire polished bead, 1 x 15° bead. GT the bead that you exited in the circle, entering on the opposite side.
3. GT the next 2 beads in the circle.
4. Repeat steps 2 and 3 until there is a 15° and fire polished bead circle coming out of every second bead in the centre circle. There should be 5 of these radiating circles with a single bead between each at the bottom.

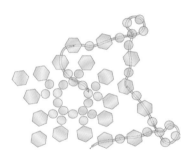

5. GT the next 2 beads in the centre circle and work up the 1 x 15° bead and 2 x 3 mm fire polished beads on the left side of the circle depicted above, exiting on the right of the fire polished bead.

6. PU 1 x 15° bead, 1 x 3 mm fire polished bead and 5 x 15° beads. Go down the second bead, PU 1 x 15° bead, 1 x 3 mm fire polished bead, 1 x 15° bead and GT the 3 mm fire polished bead at the top of the next radiating circle.

7. Repeat steps 6 and 7 between every radiating circle.

8. Work the thread through the beads until you exit one of the beads in the centre circle. Cut off the thread leaving a long tail.

9. Using the tail, attach the snowflake to the fabric. Couch between every second bead in the centre circle.

10. Thereafter place a couching stitch on each side of the fire polished bead at the top of each radiating circle.

11. Come through the fabric to the right of the bead at the tip of the picot between and at the tip of each radiating circle. GT that bead and go back through the fabric.

This should secure the snowflake, but if you feel you would like to add more couching stitches, you can do so, making sure that they are evenly spaced over the whole snowflake.

SIMPLE TATTING TECHNIQUES

Tatting consists of a double knot formed over a circle of thread in two stages. This is called the double stitch (ds). It is how you arrange the knots, often interspersing them with spaces to form picots (p), which creates this knotted lace.

The technique

Load the shuttle with thread: depending on the type of shuttle you are using, you will either wind the thread directly onto the shuttle or, alternatively, fill the shuttle bobbin with thread and insert that bobbin into the space provided in the shuttle.

DOUBLE STITCHES (DS)

1. Hold the shuttle in your right hand;

2. Leaving a tail at the overlap, form a loose loop by winding the thread over four fingers of your left hand, allowing the thread to overlap at the top of your index finger;

3. Hold the overlap together by placing the thumb of that hand on the top of the overlap.

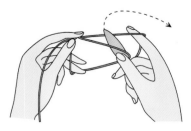

4. Guide the shuttle through the loop from the front to the back.

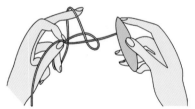

5. Return by guiding the shuttle from the back to the front, going over the loop that lies over the fingers of your other hand and under the thread that leads to the shuttle.

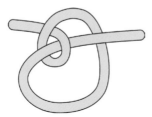

6. Tighten the stitch by holding the thread that goes to the shuttle firmly with the right hand and pulling the thread that forms the loop around the fingers of the left hand (often called the click and flip). You do this by continuing to hold the overlap together with your thumb and index finger, using the lower fingers of your left hand to pull the loop up and away from you until the thread has tightened to form a loop, similar to a buttonhole stitch, around the circle that goes around the finger of your left hand.

7. Before you go any further, check that the shuttle thread will still slide by tugging on that thread. This is very important. It has to slide.

8. If it won't slide you have (a) tightened the loop in the wrong way and (b) won't be able to continue lengthening the thread you are using because additional thread comes from the shuttle. If it won't slide, loosen the completed stitch and try again.

9. When you are starting out, check that your thread will slide every time you tighten a stitch. Once you get better and more practised, you will find that you don't need to because, somehow, you know when you've got it wrong. Even then, you should still check from time to time to make sure that the shuttle thread is sliding.

10. Take the shuttle to the back by moving over the circle on your left hand.

11. Bring it to the front by going under the loop around the hand and over the thread leading to the shuttle.

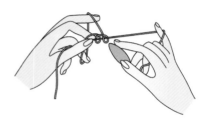

12. Tighten the thread by holding the thread that goes to the shuttle firmly with the right hand and pulling the thread that forms the circle around the fingers of the left hand (the click and flip).

13. You have just completed your first double stitch (ds).

14. Continue by adding double stitches to the loop in this way, following the pattern that you have in front of you.

CLOSING (CLOSE)

15. When you have added the required number of double stitches (ds), hold them in place with your thumbnail and index finger.

16. Pull the thread that goes to the shuttle.

17. If you have tightened each stitch correctly, and carefully checked that the shuttle thread continues to slide, you should be able to pull through until the last double stitch touches the first. This is called closing.

TO CONTINUE

18. Push the tatting you have just completed to the left, form a loose loop by winding the thread over the four fingers of your left hand, allowing the thread to overlap on the top of your index finger.

19. Hold the overlap together by placing the thumb of that hand on top of the overlap.

20. Start the next double stitch.

21. When tightening, pull the stitch to where you want it to be*, hold it tightly between the thumb and index finger of your left hand, complete the second half of the stitch.

*More often than not, you will want the tightened stitch to hug the closed petal that you have just done. In some cases, however, you will want to leave a gap of ⅛ to ¼" (3 to 5 mm) so that the tatting will form a braid-like line.

ADDING A PICOT (P)

22. Instead of tightening the double stitch so that it lies against the previous double stitch, leave a gap of ⅛ to ¼" (3 to 5 mm).

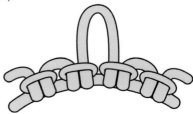

23. After completion of the subsequent double stitch, slide it back so that it touches the double stitch before the gap.

24. This will allow a picot to form.

JOINING PICOT TO PICOT

25. Using the hook at the top of the shuttle (or a fine crochet hook) pull the thread of the circle around your hand through the picot to which you want to join the current work, allowing a loop to form.

26. Pass the shuttle through that loop.

27. Draw the loop in – making sure that the thread still slides.

28. Continue making double stitches around the circle.

The patterns

SPIRAL TATTED FLOWER AND LEAF

Leave a 6" (150 mm) tail at the beginning. This will be used to stitch the flower onto the embroidery or patchwork.

VARIATION 1

7 (9; 11) ds, p, 7 (9; 11) ds. Close.
Repeat x 3 leaving no space between these identical petals.
Continue by adding: 5 (7; 9) ds, p, 5 (7; 9)ds. Close.
Repeat x 2 leaving no space between these identical petals.
Leave a 6" (150 mm) tail and cut off.

VARIATION 2

13 ds, p, 13 ds. Close.
Repeat x 4 leaving no space between these identical petals.
Continue by adding: 11 ds, p, 11 ds. Close.
Repeat x 3 leaving no space between these identical petals.
Continue by adding: 9 ds, p, 9 ds. Close.
Repeat x 2 leaving no space between these identical petals.
Leave a 6" (150 mm) tail and cut off.

LEAF

Leave a 6" (150 mm) tail to stitch the leaf onto the fabric.

5 (7; 9; 11; 13) ds, p, 5 (7; 9; 11; 13) ds. Close. Leave a 6" (150 mm) tail and cut off.

- Attach the flower to a fabric base by threading the long tail onto a needle and going into the fabric from the top.
- Come up to catch the first (larger) petal with a small stitch over the threads at the point where the double stitches meet at the bottom.

- Nudge and stitch each petal into place, so that they form the shape of a four (or 5) petal flower, leaving a small empty circle in the centre.
- Continue stitching in a spiral placing the smaller petals on top of the circle of larger petals that form the first layer of the flower.
- When you reach the end, thread the short tail onto another needle, take it to the back and end off.
- Returning to the working needle, come up in the centre, pick up a large bead and go back down, making sure that the bead forms the centre of the flower.
- Attach leaves, in a variety of sizes, by threading one of the tails onto the needle. Lift the petals of the flower at the point where you want to add the leaf.
- Going underneath the petal, take the needle in from the top. Come up to catch the leaf with a small stitch over the threads at the point where the double stitches meet at the bottom.
- End off and thread the other tail on the needle.
- Take it into the fabric and come up again low down on the side of the leaf. Catch the leaf by going through one of the double stitch gaps. Do the same on the other side.
- Continue to add leaves, that come out from under the petals, here and there.

TREFOIL FLOWER

Leave a 6" (150 mm) tail at the beginning. This will be used to stitch the flower onto the embroidery or patchwork.

VARIATION 1

3 ds, 5p, 3 ds. Close.
5 ds, 5p, 5 ds. Close.
3 ds, 5p, 3 ds. Close.

VARIATION 2

5 ds, 5p, 5 ds. Close.
7 ds, 5p, 7 ds. Close.
5 ds, 5p, 7 ds. Close.
Leave a 6" (150 mm) tail and cut off.

- Attach the flower to a fabric base by threading the starting tail onto a needle and going into the fabric from the top at the relevant spot. At this stage nudge the three petals of the flower into place and secure each with a pin. Make sure that you leave a small centre area in which to stitch a single bead.
- Come up to catch the base of each petal with a small stitch over the threads at the point where the double stitches meet at the close.
- End off that thread.
- Now using the other tail, catch every picot of each petal with a small couching stitch, pulling the petals out so that they sit flat and evenly spaced.
- Using the same thread, stitch a bead in the centre of the flower.

SHELL BORDER

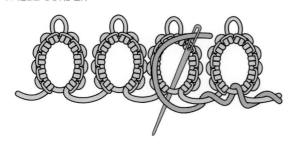

Leave a tail of 6" (150 mm) at the beginning and the end of the border. This will be used to stitch it to the patchwork.

VARIATION 1

5 ds, 1 p, 5 ds. Close.
Leaving about 4 mm of cotton, repeat above until required length.

VARIATION 2

7 ds, 1 p, 7 ds. Close.
Leaving about ⅛" (4 mm) of cotton, repeat above until required length.

VARIATION 3

7 ds, 3 p, 7 ds. Close.
Leaving about 4 mm of cotton, repeat above until required length.

VARIATION 4

5 ds, 3 p, 5 ds. Close.
Leaving about 4 mm of cotton, repeat above until required length.

- Thread the tails onto two needles and go into the fabric at the start and the end of where you wish to place the border. On each end you should pull the thread through until it stretches evenly over the area you wish to cover.
- Come back, alternately placing a stitch over the base of each where the shell has closed, working towards the middle.
- With either the same threads, or a completely new thread, catch each picot with a couching stitch.
- Still using the same thread, whip over the thread that runs between each shell and through the close where the two sides of the shell meet.
- Finally, stitch a single drop bead into the centre of each shell.

TATTED DAISY CHAIN

Leave a tail of 4" (100 mm) at the beginning and the end of each daisy. These will be woven into the adjacent petals once 4 are completed, to both join and to lose those tail threads.

- 7 ds, 1 p, 1 ds, 1 p, 1 ds, 1 p#, 1 ds, 1 p, 1 ds, 1 p, 7 ds. Close.
- Repeat the above sequence for 3 more petals, leaving as little thread as possible between each petal.
- Join the the first petal to the last and end off the threads.
- 7 ds, 1 p, 1 ds, 1 p, 1 ds, 1 p*, 1 ds, 1 p, 1 ds, 1 p, 7 ds. Close.

- Repeat the above sequence for 2 more petals, leaving as little thread as possible between each petal.
- Start the 4th petal as usual. When you reach the picot marked *, join it to the picot marked # above following the instructions for Joining Picot To Picot in the basic Tatting instructions.
- Complete the petal following the pattern that you have been working.
- Join the first petal to the last and end off the threads.

Continue to add daisies in the same way until the daisy chain reaches the required length. Stitch the chain to the patchwork using the same thread that you have used for the tatting. Work a small couching stitch over the close at the base of each petal. Couch each picot onto the fabric and, if necessary, work a small stitch approximately halfway up each side of each petal, coming up through the fabric and going down between two of the tatting threads.

TATTED CLOVER

Leave a tail of 4" (100 mm) at the beginning and the end of each daisy. These will be woven into the adjacent petals once 4 are completed, to both join and to lose those tail threads.

VARIATION 1
[7 ds, 1 p, 1 ds, 1 p, 1 ds, 1 p, 1 ds, 1 p, 7 ds. Close.
5 ds, 1 p, 1 ds, 1 p, 1 ds, 1 p, 1 ds, 1 p, 5 ds. Close.]
Repeat from [to] leaving as little thread as possible between each petal.

VARIATION 2
[7 ds, 1 p, 1 ds, 1 p, 1 ds, 1 p, 1 ds, 1 p, 7 ds. Close.
6 ds, 1 p, 1 ds, 1 p, 1 ds, 1 p, 1 ds, 1 p, 6 ds. Close.]
Repeat from [to] leaving as little thread as possible between each petal.

- Join the the first petal to the last and end off the threads.
- Stitch the clover flower into place using the tail that you left at the beginning.
- Add leaves as directed by the project pattern following the instructions for the leaf under Spiral Tatted Flower , see page 78.

RAMBLING VINE TATTED FLOWERS

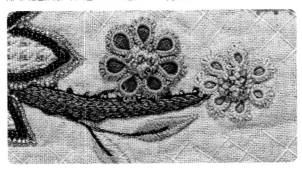

Leave a tail of 2¾" (70 mm) at the beginning and the end of each flower. These will be used to attach the flower to fabric.

VARIATION 1
9 ds, 5 p, 9 ds. Close.
[Leave a gap of ¼" (5 mm) before starting the next petal.]
Repeat [to] 6 times making a total of 7 petals.

VARIATION 2
7 ds, 5 p, 7 ds. Close.
[Leave a gap of ¼" (5 mm) before starting the next petal.]
Repeat [to] 6 times making a total of 7 petals.

Attaching the flower to the fabric:
- Thread one of the tails onto a sharp needle and take it into the fabric on the circle that depicts the position of the flower. Pull through until the tatted petal touches the fabric. Come up and catch the base of the first petal with a couching stitch.
- Thread the other tail onto another sharp needle and take it into the circle in the same hole that you went into when you pulled the other tail through the fabric. Estimating where the petal on that end will sit on the circle, pull the thread through leaving thread equal to the length of the

thread between each petal. Come up and catch the base of the last petal with a couching stitch.

- Working alternately with both needles, catch the base of each petal, making sure that you are more-or-less following the line of the circle (it doesn't have to be exactly on the line as you will be filling the centre with knots).
- Once you have secured the base of each petal, using what is left of the tails (or threading up more of the same thread, if you need to) work round the outside of each flower securing each and every picot.
- Refer to the notes of the project for the centre of the flower.

FINISHING TECHNIQUES

Stabilising your crazy patchwork

Where traditional Crazy Patchwork techniques form part, or all, of a project in this book they have been finished with quilt batting and hand quilting techniques.

SANDWICHING YOUR PROJECT

1. Cut pieces of cotton voile and batting as directed for the individual project.
2. On a large, flat surface place the voile, followed by the batting and then the crazy patchwork/embroidery project.
3. Place a few pins, here and there, all over the project, pinning the three layers together. Replace the pins with large tacking stitches, as the sandwiched layers will need to stretch when you place them in an embroidery frame or hoop.
4. Pin and tack all the way around the outer four edges.
5. Now place the three layers in a quilting hoop or onto a large embroidery frame, stretching (or lacing with an unbreakable thread, like a 2-ply beading thread,) as you go. It is important to make sure that all the layers are stretched evenly and as tightly as possible.
6. Once you are certain that this is the case, start your hand quilting techniques.

HAND STITCHING TECHNIQUES

Securing the beads

Using a single strand of stranded cotton that is, in most cases, the same colour as the thread with which the beads were stitched onto the project and threaded on a small (size 11 or 12) bead embroidery needle, come up through the 3 layers of the sandwiched project:

- Where single beads are stitched onto the fabric, go through each and every single bead again. This will include any beads that have been placed within any of the tatting techniques, the combination embroidery stitch borders and at the base of the simple bead flowers.
- Where beads have been secured with bead couching, place an additional couching stitch after approximately every second or third bead in a line. If the bead couched line consists of only two or three beads, come up at the beginning, go through the beads and go back into the fabric at the end of the bead line.
- Where you have used bead stem stitch, place small running stitches along the line, slightly beneath the bead stem stitch, making sure that those running stitches are invisible. Use a thread that is close to the colour of the fabric patch.
- Where a bead has been attached with a smaller bead, repeat the process by attaching it a second time in the same way, but going through the three layers of textiles again.

Beads have been spread evenly throughout the projects in this book, so if you are careful about re-securing all of the beads, and if your sandwiched project has been well stretched in the hoop or frame, this will go much of the way towards stabilizing the project. But you have a way to go yet.

Working the block intersections

Following the guidelines for running stitch in the Embroidery Techniques gallery and using a single strand of stranded cotton that is closest in colour to the fabric of the block, work running stitches around block intersections. If it is possible to do so, you should stitch in the ditch. If this is not possible because of stitching over the intersections, try to hide your running stitches under the existing embroidery stitches, making them all but invisible. If you have already stitched along a line while securing the beads, you do not need stitch along that edge again.

USEFUL EMBROIDERY STITCHES

Meandered running stitch

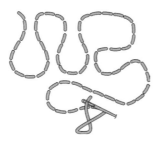

Usually done free hand on a sewing machine, hand-stitched meandering involves working running stitch, as described in the embroidery techniques, stitched in swirls and paths that do not cross over each other. Because the fabric is stretched tightly in a frame, you cannot take the needle in and out of the sandwiched layers in one action. Rather take the needle down, pull through, then return to the top by taking the needle up in a separate action. Keep the tension tight so that the sandwiched layers are pulled together.

Trellis couching

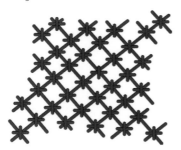

Referring to the instructions for Trellis Couching in the embroidery techniques gallery, trellis couching, or variations thereof, is useful in larger unembellished areas. Start by laying your diagonal trellis stitches. These will be long and will be placed further apart than they would be in conventional embroidery. As depicted in the diagram above, vary the length of these stitches to suit the shape of the area you wish to cover, not necessarily taking them all the way to the edge. Stitch either a couching stitch or, as above, a cross-stitch over each intersection. Make sure that all of the trellis stitches have been secured sufficiently, laying extra stitches if necessary.

BUTT JOINTS

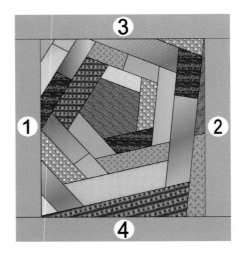

The easiest way to put a border around a crazy patch panel is with the butt-joint method:

- Decide on the width of the border.
- Add at least ⅝" (15 mm) to allow for a seam allowance on each side.
- Cut four strips (1 for each side) that are the correct width and at least ⅝" (15 mm) longer than each side.
- With right sides together, pin and stitch a strip to sides 1 and 2.
- Flip the strips back, press with an iron and trim the length on each side to the upper and lower edge of the panel.
- With right sides together, pin and stitch a strip to sides 3 and 4, taking in the strips already added on sides 1 and 2.
- Flip the strips back, press with an iron and trim the length on each side to correspond with sides 1 and 2.

CONTINUOUS BINDING

Cut a 2½" (65 mm) strip of fabric, on the straight grain of the fabric, that is long enough to go all the way around the bordered edge of the project, with room to spare for the corners. This will vary according to the size of the project.

If you are working on a large project, it is unlikely that you will have a piece of fabric long enough for a continuous strip, so make sure that you join on the diagonal.

> ## TOP TIP
> **The best tools for cutting strips are a rotary cutter, a quilters' ruler and a self-healing cutting mat.**

Fold the strip in half and press it with an iron, so that you end up with a long strip that is 1¼" (30 mm) wide.

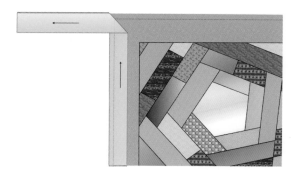

- With the raw edge of the strip facing the outer edge and starting in the middle of the bottom border of the project, pin and stitch the strip to the end of that side. (Leave 2¾" (70 mm) to accommodate working a diagonal join when you get back to where you started.)
- Referring to the diagram above, fold the strip to the left to create a 45° angle at the corner.

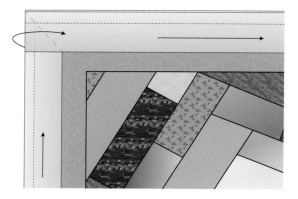

- With the 45° angle neatly underneath, fold the fabric, at a 90° angle to the right. Pin and stitch it, with raw edges to the outside, to the corresponding edge.
- Work the remaining 3 corners in this way.
- When you meet up with where you started on the bottom edge, unfold the binding, work a diagonal join, fold it in half again and complete the stitching along that edge.

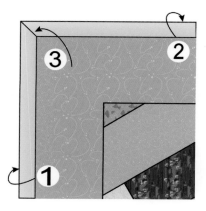

- Referring to arrows (1) and (2) in the diagram above, turn the binding to the back of the project so that the folded edge meets up with the stitching line. Pin and hand stitch the binding on the back, making sure your stitching corresponds to the back stitching line.
- A mitre will have formed on each corner (3). Slip stitch the two sides together.

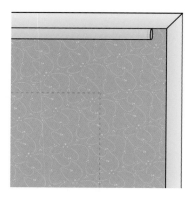

- If your project is required to hang on a wall, hem each short end of a strip of fabric that will be wide enough to encircle a dowel rod, with two seam allowances. Fold the raw edges together to make a tube.
- When stitching the back of the binding closed, incorporate that tube, as indicated in the diagram above.

STRETCHING YOUR EMBROIDERY

There are many different ways to stretch you embroidery. I am giving you instructions for what works best for me.

Raised round item

1. Referring specifically to the project, Gussy Up, the shaker box comes with a cardboard circle that fits in the lid. This circle is too pliable for stretching embroidery and you will need to replace it with either a piece of foam core board or, alternatively, a circle of ⅛" (3 mm) wood. MDF works well and if you take the circle of cardboard into your local timber merchants, they should be able to cut the wood using the cardboard as a template.

2. After you have left the timber merchants with the wooden circle, go to your local foam shop and get them to cut you a circle of ⅝" (15 mm) medium density foam. Glue the foam to the wooden or foam core board circle.

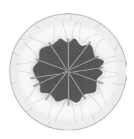

3. Trim and overlock the embroidery back to about 3" (70 mm) larger than the board and foam lid-inner.

4. With the embroidered area over the foam side of the lid inner, take the extra fabric around to the back and, using an unbreakable thread (2-ply beading thread is good) start the lacing.

- Working with about 5 yd (5 m) of thread so that, if you're lucky, you will be able to do all the lacing with a continuous thread, make a huge knot on the end and come up at the top.
- Go in at the bottom and pull through loosely.
- Go in slightly to the left of – about ¼" (10 mm) – where you came out at the top.
- Come up slightly to the right of – about ¼" (10 mm) – where you last went in at the bottom.

- When you have completed about a quarter of the circle, checking that the edge of the embroidered area is level with the edge of the lid-inner, tighten the lacing threads – very tight, so that they hurt your fingers, and continue to lace in the same way.
- Tighten at the halfway point, three-quarter point and again when you meet up with where you started, checking every time that your embroidered edge hugs the edge of the lid-inner.
- End off with another huge knot, making sure that the thread won't slip through, so that the lacing doesn't loosen.

5. When you have used the lacing method to stretch a piece of embroidery, it creates an uneven surface on the back – the side that needs to be glued into the lid. This makes it difficult to glue and it is therefore a good idea to back the lid-inner with a piece of stable fabric.

- Cut this piece of fabric 1¼" (30 mm) larger than the diameter of the lid-inner.
- Work a gathering stitch all the way around the edge.
- Place it over the back of the inner and pull the gathering thread, so that it sits tightly over the inner.
- Slowly ease the fabric that is on the front of the lid-inner to the back, pinning it to the edge of the back of the lid-inner.
- Stitch it to the edge of the lid-inner with small, barely visible stitches.

Square and rectangular items

Every now and then somebody invents a product that makes your life a whole lot easier. Grip n Frame makes the stretching of embroidery over square or rectangular shapes a simple task. It works well over wood or, for smaller projects, foam core board.

CALCULATE THE SIZE OF YOUR BOARD AS FOLLOWS

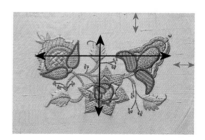

- Decide if you want the picture mounted and how wide you want the mounting to be.
- Measure the outside width of the embroidery, add ⅛" (5 mm) for a slight edge before the mounting starts, then add the mounting measurement x 2 (because the mounting will be on two sides, left and right). The total is the width of the board.
- Measure the outside height of the embroidery and do the same calculation. The total is the height of the board.

- Cut the Grip n Frame strips to fit the board and fit them to each side of the rectangle.

- Making sure that the embroidery is facing upwards and in the centre, stretch the fabric over the board, catching the fabric in the teeth of the Grip n Frame strip on all sides.
- Measure the widest/highest part of the embroidery on each side to make sure that it is centered and, if it isn't (this is the best part about Grip n Frame), loosen the fabric and reposition it, until you are happy.

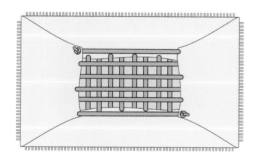

- Turn the stretched embroidery over and lightly lace the excess fabric so that it doesn't flap around, and also to make sure that it stays there. Having taken the time to make sure it's done properly you don't want it to work loose.

And now deliver it to be framed.

Gussy up

This 7½" (190 mm) diameter project has been designed specifically to fit into the lid of a wooden box which can be used to store your needlework or other trinkets. Aside from the weaving that makes up some of the blocks, all of the techniques can be used by quilters in the embellishment of traditional patchwork. Should you wish to mount your embroidery in an identical box, purchasing details and mounting guidelines are at the end of these instructions.

Materials

FABRIC

15¾ x 15¾" (400 x 400 mm) linen cotton blend fabric,
  colour 'natural';
15¾ x 15¾" (400 x 400 mm) cotton voile backing fabric,
  colour white or Ecru.

NEEDLES

Size 7	embroidery needle
Size 9	embroidery needle
Size 10	embroidery needle
Size 10	bead embroidery needle
Size 12	bead embroidery needle
Size 22	chenille needle
Size 28	tapestry needle
Size 26	tapestry needle

Unless otherwise instructed use:
- two strands of thread when working with stranded cotton;
- one strand of thread when working with perlé cotton, Lizbeth tatting cotton and Diamant thread;
- one strand of stranded cotton, doubled over and threaded onto a bead embroidery needle for the bead embroidery;
- one strand of beading thread for the beadwork.

THREADS

DMC STRANDED COTTON

0052	Variegated Violet
0319	Very Dark Pistachio Green
0340	Medium Blue Violet
0367	Dark Pistachio Green
0368	Light Pistachio Green
0369	Very Light Pistachio Green
0500	Very Dark Blue Green
0550	Very Dark Violet
0552	Dark Violet
0554	Light Violet
0597	Turquoise
0598	Light Turquoise
0743	Medium Yellow
0744	Pale Yellow
0745	Light Pale Yellow
0746	Off White
0777	Very Dark Raspberry
0796	Dark Royal Blue
0798	Dark Delft Blue
0799	Medium Delft Blue
0800	Pale Delft Blue
0934	Black Avocado Green
0958	Dark Sea Green
0959	Medium Sea Green
3032	Medium Mocha Brown
3033	Very Light Mocha Brown
3688	Medium Mauve
3689	Light Mauve
3782	Light Mocha Brown
3790	Ultra Dark Beige Grey
3809	Very Dark Turquoise
3810	Dark Turquoise
3812	Very Dark Sea Green
3823	Ultra Pale Yellow
3831	Very Dark Dusty Rose
3832	Medium Raspberry
3833	Light Raspberry

DMC PERLÉ COTTON #12

0814	Dark Garnet
0644	Medium Beige Grey
3813	Light Blue Green
Ecru	Ecru

CHAMELEON THREADS PERLÉ NO. 12

033	Forest Shade
113	Artichoke (x2)

DI VAN NIEKERK'S HAND PAINTED SILK RIBBON

2 mm:

59	Orchid
100	Deep Shade
115	Copper Rose
133	Azure Blue

4mm:

19	Fern Green
25	Dark Pine
41	Mixed Berry
49	Salsa Orange

7 mm:

112	Snap Dragons
114	Rose

DMC DIAMANT METALLIC THREAD

D3821	Light Gold

METTLER METALLIC MACHINE EMBROIDERY THREAD

2108	Gold

LIZBETH TATTING COTTON #80

652	Royal Blue
622	Pink Medium
603	Ecru
631	Country Purple Light

SAJOU FILS DENTELLE AU CHINOIS

6942	Pear Drop
6951	Tenderness

SUPERLON BEADING THREAD

SLAA-TE	Teal
SLAA-CB	Capri Blue
SLAA-BU	Burgundy
SLAA-CR	Cream
SLAA-PU	Purple
SLAA-LO	Light Orchid
SLAA-OL	Olive

BEADS

MIYUKI BEADS
Round Rocailles

15°	140FR	Matte Transparent Red Orange AB
15°	143FR	Matte Transparent Chartreuse AB
15°	257	Transparent Topaz AB
15°	264	Raspberry Lined Crystal AB
15°	516	Light Daffodil Yellow
15°	524	Sky Blue Ceylon
15°	1424	Silver Lined Teal
15°	1627	Frosted Silver Lined Light Cranberry
15°	1653	Frosted Silver Lined Dusk Blue
15°	1890	Transparent Emerald Gold Luster
15°	2442	Crystal Ivory Gold Luster
11°	19F	Matte Silver Lined Sapphire
11°	312	Cranberry
11°	554	Pale Yellow Silver Lined Alabaster
11°	571	Sea Green Silver Lined Alabaster
11°	577	Butter Cream Gold Lined Alabaster
11°	645	Dark Rose Silver Lined Alabaster
8°	2405FR	Matte Transparent Teal AB

TILA BEADS

TL 2005	Matte Metallic Dark Raspberry

3.4 MM DROP BEADS

DPMix11	Heather

DELICA BEADS

DB11-109	Crystal Ivory Gold Lustre
DB11-117	Violet Gold Lustre
DB11-624	Light Rose Silver Lined Alabaster

INSTRUCTIONS

The blocks in this design are numbered. Each block is described in detail below. The techniques that form the borders of the blocks are described in the instructions for each block. It is however wise to only work them once you have completed the surrounding blocks.

Block I

1. Referring to the embroidery stitches gallery, add texture to the block by filling in the background with trellis couching with cross stitch filling. Use stranded cotton 3032 for the trellis and 3033 for the cross stitch filling. Don't stitch over the areas covered by the flower and leaf as you work this filling, but make sure that you go up to the edge of these motifs.

2. Pad each petal of the flower with horizontal satin stitch using 2 strands of 745. Thereafter work long and short stitch shading over the padding, starting at the base with 1 strand of 744, working through 745 to 3823 at the tip. Using 1 strand of 743, work 3 long stitches of differing lengths from the base towards the tip of each petal, to provide shadow.

- Work an outline stitch along one side of each petal, starting at the centre and working to just past the halfway point at the rounded tip. Use 1 strand of 3782.
- Fill the centre of the flower with a double layer of French knots using 2 strands of 744 and 1 strand of 3032 threaded onto the needle at the same time. Stitch an odd number of beads 15° 257 between the knots.

3. Following the directions for twisted stitches in the embroidery stitch gallery, fill each half of the leaf with diagonal twisted long and short stitch. Use stranded cotton 369 for the top and 368 for the bottom half. Using the colour image as your guide, work intermittent outline stitch on the edge of the leaf using 1 strand of 367.

4. Using 819, work a line of twisted couching down the vein of the leaf and up the stem.

- The three tendrils on the right are also worked with twisted couching using 368. Work a line of fine stem stitch on the bottom edge of each tendril using 1 strand of 819.

Block 2

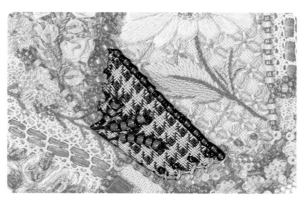

1. Fill the block with needle weaving checks and stripes 1. Use Lisbeth #80.652 for colour 1 and 603 for colour 2.

2. Referring to the line drawing at the back of the book to guide you, work 3 stalks of beaded fly stitch using stranded cotton 777 and bead 11° 645. You will need to tie these stalks up with the featherstitch edge referred to in block 11.

3. Stitch a line of bead couching on the border between blocks 1 and 2 using beads 11°19F alternating with bead 15°1653. Use 1 strand of 796.

Blocks 3 and 4

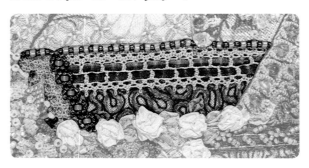

1. Referring to the needle lace gallery work backstitch around block 3 and thereafter work needle lace numbered stitch 8 over the entire block. Use Sajou 6951.

2. Referring to the embroidery techniques gallery, fill block 4 with two tone vermicelli stitch using first, 2 strands of variegated stranded cotton 52 and then a single strand of 550.

TOP TIP

Always start weaving a block at the widest point. As the block narrows, continue to count in the warp threads that you have eliminated. If you don't, the pattern will be lost..

---

3. Referring to the needle lace gallery and using Lisbeth #80.603, work needle lace edging 3 laying it over the existing vermicelli couching. Catch the loop of each picot with a single strand of Ecru, stretching the lace down so that it lies straight and even. Weave 2 mm silk ribbon 133 through the two rows that require it.

4. Referring to the linked daisy chain in the beading techniques gallery and using beads 8 x 15° 1424, 1 x 11° 571 and teal beading thread, work a 5-circle daisy chain. Stitch it firmly along the border between blocks 3 and 4.

5. Bead couch a line of alternating beads 15° 1424 and 11° 571 using stranded cotton 500. When you have completed block 7 the bead couched edge will continue along that border.

Block 5

1. Fill the block with weaving checks and stripes 2. Use perlé #12.814 for colour 1 and perlé #12.Ecru for colour 2.

2. Once you have completed block 7, work a line of featherstitch along the common edge using stranded cotton 934. Referring to the line drawing at the back of the book to guide you, work 3 stalks of beaded fly stitch using stranded cotton 934 and bead 11° 577. You will need to tie these stalks up with the featherstitch edge.

3. Following the instructions for variation 2 of the shell border in the tatting techniques gallery, work 14 shells with perlé #12.644.

When you have completed blocks 6 and 10, stitch the tatted border over the weaving in this block, continuing along the top of block 10 where these two blocks abut blocks 1 and 6. Place beads DPMix 11 in the centre of each shell.

Block 6

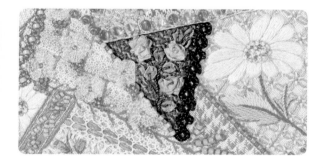

1. Following the instructions for woven trellis in the embroidery stitches gallery, fill block 6 using stranded cotton 958

for shade 1, 3812 for shade 2 and 959 for shades 3 and 4.

2. Referring to twisted couching in the embroidery gallery and using the line drawing at the back of the book as your guide, work the stem of the rose branch with stranded cotton 3790.

- Each of the leaves is a ribbon stitch worked with 4 mm ribbon 19. Work a straight stitch vein over the ribbon stitch with 3790. Extend the stitch down to go under the twisted couching branch.
- Each of the flowers is a French knot ribbon rose which is to be found in the silk ribbon embroidery gallery. Use 7 mm ribbon 114 and stranded cotton 3689 for the stab stitches.

3. Using beads 1 x 11°19F, 8 x 15°1653 and Capri blue beading thread, work a 9-circle daisy chain. Stitch it firmly along the border that runs between block 6 and blocks 1 and 2.

Block 7

1. Fill this block with needle weaving texture 6 using perlé #12.3813 for colour 1 and perlé #12.Ecru for colour 2.

2. Turning to the peyote-stitch flowers and leaves in the beading gallery, make the following:

- 1 x 6-bead flower using bead DB11-117 with purple beading thread;
- 2 x 4-bead flowers using bead DB11-109 with cream beading thread;
- 2 x 8-bead leaves and 3 x 10-bead leaves using bead 15° 1890 with olive beading thread.

Following the instructions for attaching flowers and leaves on page 71, attach the flowers and leaves, using the tail ends of the flower and leaf threads, beads 15H257 for the stalks and 11° 554 for the tips of the stamens and twigs.

Block 8

1. Following the guidelines for layered buttonhole stitch in the embroidery techniques gallery, cover the block using stranded cotton 777, 3831, 3832 and 3833. Started with the darkest of the 4 colours, moving through the shades to the lightest in about the middle of the block and back to the darkest on the other end.

2. Make the following peyote-stitch flowers and leaves:
- 1 x 6-bead and 2 x 4-bead flowers using DB11-109 with cream beading thread;
- 1 x 4-bead and 1 x 6-bead flowers using DB11-624 and light orchid beading thread;
- 1 x 8-bead and 2 x 10-bead leaves using bead 15° 1631 with olive beading thread;
- 3 x 8-bead and 4 x 10-bead leaves using bead 15° 1890 with olive beading thread;
- Following the instructions for attaching flowers and leaves at the end of the that section of beading gallery, attach the flowers and leaves, stitching through the weaving base, using the tail ends of the flower and leaf threads, beads 15H257 for the stalks and 11° 554 for the tips of the stamens and twigs.

3. When you have filled block 17, work a straight cretan stitch border along the edge that abuts blocks 2, 1, 3 and 17. Use stranded cotton 800. Stitch beads 15° 1627 with stranded cotton 3833 to the tips of the cretan stitch that run into block 8. Stitch beads 15° 1653 with stranded cotton 796 to the tips on the other side.

Block 9

1. Using the colour image as your guide, fill alternate blocks with needle lace numbered stitch 8 using Sajou 6942. Work a whipped backstitch along the edge of each block, not including any lines that form the main outer edges. Use stranded cotton 3831.

2. Bead couch a line of alternating beads 15° 1424 and 11° 571 using stranded cotton 500 along the border between blocks 9 and 6.

3. When you have completed block 11, using stranded cotton 3831, work featherstitch starting at the corner where block 11 intersects with block 12, continuing to the point where block 9 intersects with blocks 24 and 25. Remember that you need to tie this stitch up with the beaded fly stitch branches in block 2 (2) above. Stitch a single bead 15° 1627 to the tips of the featherstitches, on both sides.

4. When you have completed block 24, using beads 8 x 15° 1424 and 1 x 11° 571 with teal beading thread, work a 7-circle daisy chain. Stitch it firmly along the border between blocks 9 and 24.

5. Each vacant space in block 9 needs a 4-bead peyote stitch flower worked with bead 15° 2442 using cream beading thread and an 8-bead leaf working with bead 15° 1424 and teal beading thread. Use the tails to attach the beads and leaves, stitching a single bead 15° 257 in the centre of each flower.

Block 10

1. Using stranded cotton 3032, cover the block with basic trellis couching. Work a small couching stitch over each intersection using 368. In the middle of each square of the trellis work a small French knot using stranded cotton 340.

2. When you have completed block 24, using beads 8 x 15° 198 and 11° 312 with burgundy beading thread, work a 3-circle daisy chain. Stitch it firmly along the border between blocks 5 and 10.

Block 11

1. Fill block 11 with two tone vermicelli stitch using first 2 strands of stranded cotton 3033 and then a single strand of 3032.

2. Using Lizbeth #80.603, work needle lace edging 5 facing into the block along the border that abuts blocks 9 and 11. Thread 2 mm silk ribbon 59 into the gaps created by rows 6 and 8.

3. Using the line drawing at the back of the book as your guide, work the branches with twisted couching using stranded cotton 3790.

- Each of the leaves is a ribbon stitch worked with 4 mm ribbon 25. Work a straight stitch vein over the ribbon stitch with stranded cotton 500. Extend the stitch down to go under the twisted couching branch or into a leaf stem.

- Each of the buds is also a ribbon stitch, overlapping the bottom of the insertion lace, if necessary. Use 4 mm ribbon 49. With stranded cotton 500, work a straight stitch down the middle of each ribbon stitch and a fly stitch around the base to form the calyx. Extend the leg of the fly stitch down to join a stem or branch.

4. Now complete the featherstitch border explained in block 9 (3) above.

Blocks 12, 13 and 14

1. Referring to the needle weaving gallery, fill block 12 with texture 5 using Lizbeth #80.603 for colour 1 and Lizbeth #80.613 for colour 2.

2. Referring to the instructions for variation 1 of the spiral tatted flower in the tatting techniques gallery, work 3 of the smallest of those flowers using Chameleon perlé #12.113.

- Using the line drawing at the back of the book as your guide, stitch a Tila bead TL 2005 onto each of the rectangles depicted for block 12 using 3790.
- With 2 strands of the same thread, work a line of whipped backstitch for each stem and stitch the tatted spiral flower into place on the small circle, following the guidelines for attaching the flower in the tatting techniques gallery.
- Finally, stitch a single drop bead, DPMix 11 into the centre of each flower.

3. Referring to the needle lace gallery work needle lace numbered stitch 8 over the entire block. Use Sajou 6951.

4. Fill block 14 with weaving checks and stripes 2. Use perlé #12.814 for colour 1 and perlé #12.Ecru for colour 2.

5. Using beads 8 x 15° 198 and 11° 312 with burgundy beading thread, work a 3-circle daisy chain. Stitch it firmly along the border between blocks 12 and 13.

6. Starting in the corner that forms the intersection of blocks 11, 12 and 28, bead couch a line of of alternating beads 15° 198 and 11° 312 using stranded cotton 777. When you reach the end of that bottom edge, turn the corner and continue up the side of block 12 that is adjacent to blocks 2 and 8, up the side of block 13 where it is adjacent to block 8, between block 13 and 14, up to the intersection of 31, 33 and 14.

7. When you have completed blocks 30 and 31, starting in the corner that is the intersection of blocks 30, 13 and 14, work wheatear stitch down the sides of blocks 13 and 14 that are adjacent to blocks 30 and 28. Use stranded cotton 777 and stitch a single bead 11° 312 into the centre of each stitch.

8. When you have completed blocks 8, 15 and 34, referring to the instructions for attaching a bead with a bead in the bead embroidery gallery, work the remaining two edges of block 14. At small intervals attach bead 8° 2405FR with bead 15° 1424. Use stranded cotton 500.

Block 15

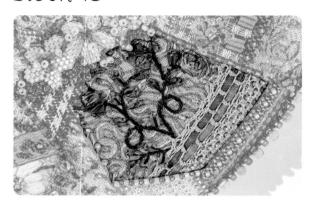

1. Fill block 15 with two-tone vermicelli stitch using first 2 strands of stranded cotton 3033 and then a single strand of 3032.

2. Using Lizbeth #80.603 and bead 15° 2442, do needle lace edging 4, facing into the block. Thread 2 mm silk ribbon 100 into the gaps created by rows 6 and 8.

3. Referring to the line drawing at the back of the book as your guide, work the branches in the block with stranded cotton 319.

- Each of the leaves is a ribbon stitch worked with 4 mm ribbon 25. Work a straight stitch vein over the ribbon stitch with stranded cotton 319. Extend the stitch down to go under the twisted couching branch or into a leaf stem.
- Each of the flowers is a French knot ribbon rose which is to be found in the silk ribbon embroidery gallery. Use 7 mm ribbon 112 and stranded cotton 3832 for the stab stitches.

Block 16

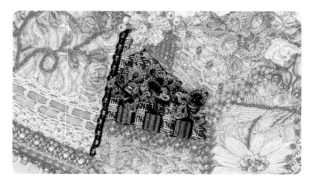

1. Referring to the needle weaving gallery, fill block 16 with checks and stripes 1 using Lizbeth #80.603 for colour 1 and Lizbeth #80.652 for colour 2.

2. Referring to the instructions for block 12 (2), work 3 identical spiral tatted flowers on stems in Tila bead plant pots.

3. Stitch a line of bead couching on the border between blocks 15 and 16 using beads 11°19F alternating with bead 15°1653. Use 1 strand of 796 and continue the line until you reach the corner where block 15 intersects with blocks 36 and 37.

Block 17

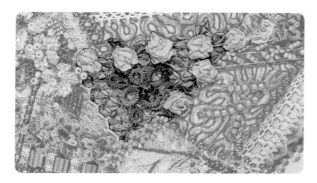

1. Referring to the embroidery stitches gallery, fill the block with trellis couching with triangular filling. Use stranded cotton 3033 for the trellis, 3032 for the couching stitches. Continue with 3032 for the long, horizontal stitches described in the third stage.

2. Turning to the tatting gallery, work a tatted clover variation 1, using Chameleon perlé #12.113.

- Using Chameleon perlé #12.33 and the colour image as your guide, work the leaves. You will need a 9 ds leaf, a 7 ds leaf and a 5 ds leaf, placing them radiating out from between the petals into the spaces that allow for the various sizes.

3. Once you have completed blocks 39 and 40, work the rose border.

- Each leaf is a silk ribbon stitch worked with 4 mm ribbon 19. Secure each ribbon stitch with a straight stitch vein using 3790.
- Work a French knot ribbon rose on each of the small circles with 7 mm ribbon 114 secured with 1 strand of 3689.

Blocks 18 and 19

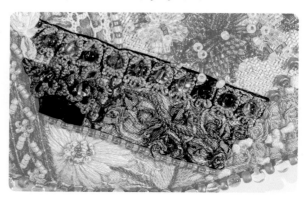

1. Fill block 18 with needle weaving checks and stripes 9 using Lizbeth #80.603 for colour 1 and Lizbeth #80.622 for colour 2.

2. Referring to the instructions for variation 1 of the spiral tatted flower in the tatting gallery, work 2 of the smallest spiral tatted flowers using Chameleon perlé #12.113.

- Referring to the instructions for block 12 (2), work 2 identical spiral tatted flowers on stems in Tila bead plant pots.

3. Fill block 19 with two tone vermicelli stitch using first 2 strands of stranded cotton 3033 and then a single strand of 3032.

- Using the line drawing at the back of the book as your guide, work the vine with twisted couching using stranded cotton 3790.
- Each of the leaves is a ribbon stitch worked with 4 mm ribbon 25. Work a straight stitch vein over the ribbon stitch with stranded cotton 3790. Extend the stitch down to go under the twisted couching branch.
- Work a French knot ribbon rose on each of the small circles with 4 mm ribbon 41 secured with bead 15° 264 and stranded cotton 3688.

4. Work a short line of featherstitch on the border between blocks 18 and 19 using stranded cotton 777.

5. Using DMC perlé #12.3813 and following the instructions for the shell border in the tatting techniques gallery, work a border of 10 shells. Secure along the top edge of block 19 and most of block 18, stretching it to where it will meet up with the corner ribbon rose. Place a bead DP mix11 in the centre of each shell. Work outline stitch using 1 strand of 500 along top edge of the shell border to create definition.

Block 20

1. Fill block 20 with satin stitch using 2 strands DMC 554. Referring to the embroidery stitches gallery, work trellis couching with cross stitch filling over the satin stitch using a single strand of 552.

2. After you have worked block 21 and using the line drawing at the back of the book as your guide, work the vine with twisted couching using stranded cotton 3790.

- The flowers and leaves encroach slightly into block 19. Each flower is a drizzle stitch worked with 3823. Vary the cast-ons from 5 to 9, creating differing sizes. Stitch a bead 15° 516 into the bottom centre of each flower.
- Each of the leaves is a lazy daisy stitch worked with stranded cotton 958.

Blocks 21, 22 and 23

1. Referring to the instructions in the embroidery stitches gallery, fill block 21 with battlement couching. Start by using stranded cotton 796, moving through 798 and 799 to 800, which is also used for the final stage, the couching of the top layer intersections.

- Working from the needle lace gallery, using Lizbeth #80.603, work edging no. 1 facing into block 21, theading 2 mm silk ribbon 115 through the row 6 gap.
- Turning to the bead embroidery techniques and referring to the instructions for attaching a bead with a bead, stitch bead 8° 2405FR held in place with bead 15° 1424 using stranded cotton 3809. Place them slightly apart. When you reach the edge that intersects with blocks 9 and 10, and using the colour image as your guide, continue these beads in the available space on the border.

2. Fill block 22 with needle lace number stitch 8 using Sajou 6942.

3. Following the instructions for block 1, work block 23 in the same way, using the same threads.

4. Using stranded cotton 3832 and bead 15° 1627, do feather stitch along the bottom edge of block 21 encroaching onto blocks 22 and 23. Place a bead on each tip.

5. On the border between blocks 22 and 23, as well as that between 23 and 24, work a line of up and down buttonhole stitch. Pick up a bead as you work the first stage of the buttonhole, so that it will lie on the ridge of the stitch. Use stranded cotton 3831 and bead 15° 1627.

Blocks 24 and 25

1. Fill block 24 with needle weaving texture 6 using perlé #12.3813 for colour 1 and perlé #12.Ecru for colour 2.

2. Once you have completed the weaving, referring to the line drawing at the back of the book to guide you, work the 3-stalk branch of beaded fly stitch using stranded cotton 777 and bead 11° 645.

3. Following the instructions for block 1, work block 25 in the same way, using the same threads.

4. Referring to the linked daisy chain in the beaded braids section of the beading techniques gallery and using beads

8 x 15° 1424, 1 x 11° 571 and teal beading thread, work a 7-circle daisy chain. Stitch it firmly. along the border between blocks 9 and 24.

5. Attach bead 8° 2405FR with bead 15° 1424 using stranded cotton 3809 on the border between 24 and 25. Place them slightly apart.

Block 26

1. Create a solid background of blue by working rows of compacted stem (or outline) stitch using 1 strand of 798. Work backwards and forwards making sure that each row is up against, touching the previous row of stitches.

- Outline each long side with outline stitch using 1 strand of 796.
- The width of the blue background will measure approximately ⅓" (10 mm).
- Determine that mid-line and, with a washout pen, draw a line down the centre.
- Starting from the end that is closest to block 9, mark a dot of about ⅛" (5 mm) down the mid- line. Mark two more dots, each just under ⅔" (15 mm) apart.

TOP TIP

I have provided imperial conversions for metric measurements. The braid measurements should be exact, so if you're still on imperial, get yourself a metric ruler for this task.

- Rule two more lines each ³/₆₄" (1 mm) in from the edge of the block on each side. Couch a line of light gold DMC Diamant D3821 with Mettler 2108 along each of these lines.
- Using the same thread, couch down the centre line, leaving about a ⅛" (5 mm) gap at each dot, with the dot in the middle of that gap.
- Using 798, stitch a bead 15° 516 to each of the dots in the gaps down the mid-line.
- Stitch 5 beads 15° 140FR in a circle around the yellow bead to resemble a small flower.
- Using the colour image as your guide, bead couch 2-3 diagonal bead stalks coming off the centre gold line. Use bead 15° 143FR.

Block 27

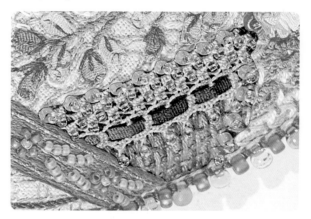

1. Following the guidelines for layered buttonhole stitch in the embroidery techniques gallery, cover the block using variegated stranded cotton 52.

2. Referring to edging no. 4 in the needle lace gallery, work the border at the top of the block, eliminating row 9 of the pattern so that you are left with just one insertion row for the ribbon. Catch each picot at the bottom edge with a single bead stitched through the loop, pulling the lace down and stretching it as you work along. Use Lizbeth #80.603 and bead 15° 2442, inserted with 2 mm ribbon 100.

3. When you have completed block 29 attach beads 11° 577 with beads 15° 2442 at intervals along the common edge using stranded cotton 3033.

Block 28

1. Referring to the instructions in the embroidery stitches gallery, fill block 28 with battlement couching. Start by using stranded cotton 3809, moving through 3810 and 597 to 598, which is also used for the final stage, the couching of the top layer intersections.
2. Once you have completed blocks 29, 30 and 31, work the rose border.
- Each leaf is a silk ribbon stitch worked with 4 mm ribbon 19. Secure each ribbon stitch with a straight stitch vein using 3790.
- Work a French knot ribbon rose on each of the small circles with 7 mm ribbon 114 secured with 1 strand of 3689.
3. Attach beads 8° 2405FR with beads 15° 1424 at intervals along the common edge with block 11, using stranded cotton 3809.

Block 29

1. Referring to block 17 above, fill the background of block 29 in the same way using the same threads.
2. Turning to the tatting section of the techniques gallery, work a tatted clover variation 2, using Chameleon perlé #12.113.
3. Using Chameleon perlé #12.33 and the colour image as your guide work 4 ds leaves and stems. Work the stem in buttonhole stitch and attach 3 of the leaves where they need to be. The fourth leaf radiates from the top of the flower.

TOP TIP

When stitching multiple colour beads to a background of a single colour it is usually best to use a thread that is the same colour as the background.

Block 30

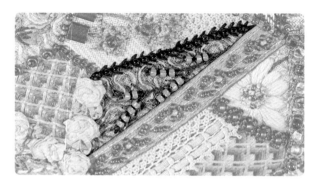

1. Fill the background of block 30 with two-tone vermicelli stitch using first 2 strands of stranded cotton 3033 and then a single strand of 3032.
2. Using the drawing of the pattern at the back of this book as your reference, work the branch in beaded fly stitch with stranded cotton 368 and bead 11° 577. Where the stalks narrow from the fly stitch into a single line, switch to stem stitch.

Block 31

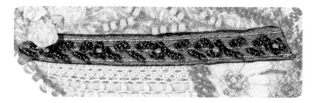

1. Following the instructions for block 26, create an identical 'braid' using the following threads and beads:
- Compacted stem stitch background: stranded cotton 3833;
- Stem stitch outline on each side of the block: stranded cotton 777;

- Couched gold lines: Diamant D3821 and Mettler 2108.
- Bead flower centre: 15° 516;
- Bead flower circle: 15° 1653;
- Bead line stalks: 15° 1890.
- Stitch the beads on with 3833.

Blocks 32 and 33

1. Referring to the instructions in the embroidery stitches gallery, fill block 31 with battlement couching. Start by using stranded cotton 796, moving through 798 and 799 to 800, which is also used for the final stage, the couching of the top layer intersections.
- Working from the needle lace techniques gallery, work edging no. 2 along the top edge of block 31 using Lizbeth #80.603 and threading 2 mm silk ribbon 115 through the insertion gaps.

2. Refer back to the instructions for block 1 to work the background, the flower and the stem in block 33.

3. Using beads 1 x 11°19F, 8 x 15°1653 and Capri blue beading thread, work a 5-circle daisy chain. Stitch it firmly along the border that runs between block 32 and 33.

Blocks 34 and 35

1. Fill block 34 with needle weaving texture 6 using perlé #12.3813 for colour 1 and perlé #12.Ecru for colour 2.
- Once you have completed the weaving, referring to twisted couching in the working with twisted thread section at the end of the embroidery gallery and using the line drawing at the back of the book as your guide, work the vine with stranded cotton 3790.
- Each of the flowers is a drizzle stitch worked with 554. Vary the cast-ons from 5 to 9, creating differing sizes. Stitch a bead 15° 264 into the bottom centre of each flower.
- Each of the leaves is a lazy daisy worked with stranded cotton 500.

2. Following the instructions for variation 2 of the shell border in the tatting techniques gallery, work 9 shells with Chameleon perlé #12.113. Stitch the tatted border over the weaving on the side adjacent to blocks 32 and 33. Place beads DPMix 11 in the centre of each shell.

3. Fill block 35 with needle lace number stitch 8 using Sajou 6942.

4. Using stranded cotton 3832 and bead 15° 1627, do featherstitch between blocks 34 and 35, continuing up between 34 and 15 until you reach the t-juntion at the top. Place a bead on each tip.

5. When you have completed block 36, work a line of up and down buttonhole stitch. Pick up a bead as you work the first stage of the buttonhole, so that it will lie on the ridge of the stitch. Use stranded cotton 3831 and bead 15° 1627.

Block 36

1. Following the guidelines for layered buttonhole stitch (woven) in the embroidery stitches gallery, fill block 36. Use stranded cotton 3810 and 3809 alternately and weave with 597.

2. Referring to the linked daisy chain in the beading gallery and using beads 8 x 15° 1424, 1 x 11° 571 and teal beading thread, work a 8-circle daisy chain. Stitch it firmly to the edge adjacent to block 15.

Block 37

1. Referring to the needle weaving gallery, fill block 37 with texture 5 using Lizbeth #80.603 for colour 1 and Lizbeth #80.613 for colour 2.

- Once you have completed the weaving, and using the line drawing at the back of the book as your guide, work the vine with twisted couching using stranded cotton 3790.
- Each of the flowers is a drizzle stitch worked with 3688. Vary the cast-ons from 5 to 9, creating differing sizes. Stitch a bead 15° 264 into the bottom centre of each flower.
- Each of the leaves is a lazy daisy worked with stranded cotton 3812.

2. Work a 6-circle daisy chain using beads 1 x 11°19F, 8 x 15°1653 and Capri blue beading thread. Stitch it firmly along the border that runs between blocks 16 and 37.

Blocks 38 and 39

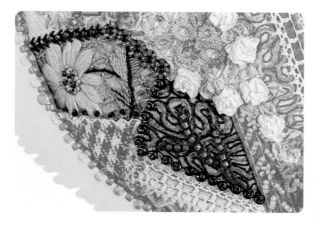

1. Following the instructions for block 1, work block 38 in the same way, using the same threads and beads.

2. Work wheatear stitch down the side of the block adjacent to blocks 16 and 37. Use stranded cotton 777 and stitch a single bead 11° 312 into the centre of each stitch.

3. Using beads 8 x 15° 198 and 11° 312 with burgundy beading thread, work a 5-circle daisy chain. Stitch it firmly along the border adjacent to block 17, meeting up with the silk ribbon roses.

4. Fill block 39 with 2-tone vermicelli stitch variation using 2 strands of 598 for the larger, first layer of swirls and 1 strand of 3809 for those that lie in between.

- Once you have completed the weaving, referring to the line drawing at the back of the book to guide you, work the 3-stalk branch of beaded fly stitch using stranded cotton 777 and bead 11° 645.

5. When you have completed block 42, attach bead 8° 2405FR with bead 15° 1424 using stranded cotton 3809 on the borders between 39, 43 and 42. Place them slightly apart and encroach on the blocks on either side in all cases.

Block 40

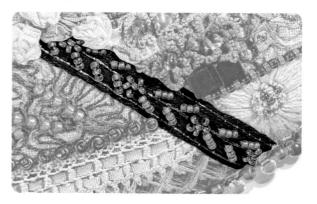

1. Following the instructions for block 26, create an identical 'braid' using the following threads and beads:

- Compacted stem stitch background: stranded cotton 777;
- This braid does not need an additional outline, the thread colour is dark enough;
- Couched gold lines: Diamant D3821 and Mettler 2108.
- Bead flower centre: 15° 516;
- Bead flower circle: 15° 524;
- Bead line stalks: 15° 143FR.
- Stitch the beads on with 777.

Block 41

1. Following the instructions for block 1, work block 41 in the same way, using the same threads and beads.

2. Bead couch a line of beads, alternating 15° 198 and 11° 312 and using stranded cotton 777, on the top edge of the block adjacent to blocks 18 and 19.

Blocks 42 and 43

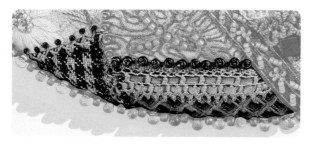

1. Following the instructions for block 32, work block 42 including the needle lace edge, in the same way, using the same threads, ribbons and beads.

2. Fill block 43 with weaving checks and stripes 2. Use perlé #12.814 for colour 1 and perlé #12.Ecru for colour 2.

3. Work a straight cretan stitch border along the edges that abut blocks 38, 39 and 43. Use stranded cotton 800. Stitch beads 5° 1653 with stranded cotton 796 to the tips of each side of the cretan stitch.

FINISHING OFF

The original of this project has been mounted in a wooden box which can be purchased online from http://www.australianneedlearts.com.au/shaker-boxes-round.

- You will need to stretch your embroidery before mounting and guidelines for stretching a round item can be found in the Finishing Techniques gallery under the stretching your embroidery section.
- Once your embroidery has been stretched, finish off the edge with beaded palestrina stitch, found in the bead embroidery gallery using 3 strand of 3809 threaded onto a size 9 embroidery needle, stitching along the side edge all the way around and alternating beads 8° 2405 with DPMix 11.

- Thereafter fix it into the lid of the box using either double sided tape or a hot glue gun. My preference is usually for a hot glue gun.
- Working quickly, inject a generous amount of hot glue around the edge of the base of the indent in the lid, as indicated by the arrow in the diagram above.

Before the glue cools — you don't have much time here — press the bottom side of the lid- inner into the glue, making sure that you press it down — hard — all the way around (a second pair of hands is useful here) until the glue has cooled.

Nightshade

The original of this design measures 9⅞ x 7⅞"
(250 x 175 mm) and has been mounted in the
lid of a box that holds the many remote controls
that the world now requires to operate their
entertainment systems.

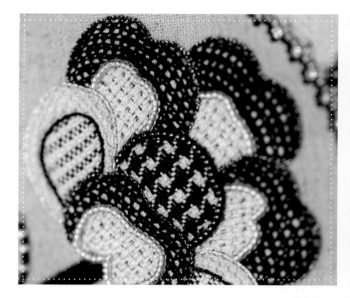

Below: A colourful version of this
project created by Pat van Wyk using
applique techniques.

Materials

FABRIC

15¾ x 17¾" (400 x 450 mm) natural colour linen cotton
  blend fabric
15¾ x 17¾" (400 x 450 mm) cotton voile backing fabric

NEEDLES

Size 7 embroidery needles for the weaving warp stitches;
Size 10 embroidery needles for the stranded cotton
  embroidery stitches;
Size 26 tapestry needles for the weaving weft stitches,
  the needle lace techniques and the whipping;
Size 12 bead embroidery needles for all the bead embroidery.

Unless otherwise instructed use:
- two strands of thread when working with stranded cotton;
- one strand of thread when working with perlé cotton, special
  dentelles and Diamant thread;
- one strand of stranded cotton, doubled over and threaded
  onto a bead embroidery needle for the bead embroidery;
- one strand of beading thread for the beadwork.

The design is divided into sections. Each section has been
described in detail.

THREADS

DMC STRANDED COTTON
Ecru	Ecru
310	Black

DMC PERLÉ COTTON #12
Ecru	Ecru
310	Black

DMC SPECIAL DENTELLES #80
Ecru	Ecru
310	Black

DMC DIAMANT METALLIC THREAD
D140	Black and gold
D3821	Light gold

C-LON BEADING THREAD
SLAA-BL	Black

BEADS

MIYUKI BEADS
15° 401F	2g	Matte black
15° 458	8g	Metallic brown iris
15° 2442	8g	Crystal ivory gold lustre
11° 401F	2g	Matte black
11° 577	2g	Cream gold lined alabaster
8° 401F	2g	Matte black
#1-401	2g	Opaque black
SB1.8-234	8g	Sparkle gold lined crystal

PRECIOSA GLASS PEARLS
2mm	1g	Cream

SWAROVSKI 34SS 2028 FLATBACK RHINESTONES
34ss	1	Jet

INSTRUCTIONS

Starting in the middle of the design and working from the
top left flower:

1. Fill the top section with weaving checks and stripes 1. Use
perlé #12.310 for colour 1 and perlé #12. Ecru for colour 2.
2. When you have completed all the surrounding embroidery, outline the outer edge with bead couching using bead
15° 458 and 310 stranded cotton.
3. Pad the middle section with stem stitch using stranded
cotton Ecru. Cover the padding with vertical satin stitch that
fans around the shape using 1 strand of the same thread.

4. Outline the satin stitch with backstitch using special dentelles 310.

5. Working horizontally with the same thread, do needle lace numbered stitch 7 over the satin stitch using the back stitches to anchor the detached buttonhole stitches.

6. When you have completed all the surrounding embroidery, outline the outer edge with couching using Diamant D140.

7. Fill the bottom section of the flower centre and the middle of the upper petals with weaving texture 7 using perlé #12. Ecru for both warp and weft. When you have completed the weaving work an additional weft row below rows 3 and 6. Follow the sequence of the row above and use Diamant D140.

8. When you have completed all the surrounding embroidery, outline the outer edges with bead couching using bead 15°2442 and Ecru stranded cotton.

9. Fill the centre of each of these petals following instructions 7 and 8 above.

10. Fill the outer section of each of these petals following instructions 3 to 6 above.

11. Fill the centre section of each of these petals with weaving checks and stripes 6. Use perlé #12.Ecru for colour 1 and perlé #12. 310 for colour 2.

12. Pad the outer section with stem stitch using stranded cotton Ecru. Cover the padding with vertical satin stitch that fans around the shape using 1 strand of the same thread.

13. Outline the satin stitch with backstitch using special dentelles Ecru.

14. Working horizontally with the same thread, do needle lace numbered stitch 2 over the satin stitch using the back stitches to anchor the detached buttonhole stitches.

15. Couch a line of Diamant 3821 around the outer edge of this section and work a line of whipped back stitch in the ditch between the two sections of the petal using stranded cotton 310.

Moving to the large leaf in the centre:

16. The right hand side of the leaf is filled with weaving checks and stripes 5 using perlé #12.Ecru for colour 1 and perlé #12. 310 for colour 2.

17. Outline the entire section with whipped chain stitch using stranded cotton 310.

18. Couch a line of Diamant 3821 in the ditch between the black outline and the weaving.

19. Fill the left section of this leaf with weaving pattern 2 using perlé #12.Ecru for colour 1 and perlé #12. 310 for colour 2.

20. Couch a line of Diamant D140 around the outer edge.

21. Work the vein of the leaf starting at the tip of the section by bead couching 5 x 15° 458 beads, followed by 3 x 11° 401F beads each secured with a 15° 458 bead. Continue by adding 20 x 401F beads each secured with a 15° 458 bead. Add further 6 x 11° 401F beads each secured with a 15° 458 bead and complete the line to the bottom of the section on the right by bead couching 15° 458 beads to the end.

22. Outline the left edge of the beads with a line of whipped chain stitch that is worked through the existing weaving, keeping your line consistent to create the left edge of the vein.

23. The middle of this flower is filled with weaving stripes and checks 4 using perlé #12.Ecru for colour 1 and perlé #12. 310 for colour 2.

24. When you have completed all the surrounding embroidery, outline the outer edge with bead couching using bead 15° 458 and 310 stranded cotton.

25. Pad the oval shape section with horizontal satin stitch using stranded cotton Ecru.

26. Cover the padding with vertical satin stitch using 1 strand of the same thread.

27. Outline the satin stitch with backstitch using special dentelles 310.

28. Working horizontally with the same thread, do needle lace numbered stitch 7 over the satin stitch using the back stitches to anchor the detached buttonhole stitches.

29. When you have completed all the surrounding embroidery, outline the upper edge by bead couching a semi circle of 2 mm cream glass pearls in a semi-circle using stranded cotton Ecru. The lower half is a bead couched line of 15° 458 beads using stranded cotton 310.

30. Work these petals with weaving texture 3. Use perlé #12.310 for colour 1 and perlé #12. Ecru for colour 2 for the middle petal on each side and perlé #12.Ecru for colour 1 and perlé #12. 310 for colour 2 for the others.

31. Couch an outline with Diamant D3821 around each petal.

32. Fill the wedge shape at the top of the flower following instructions 25 to 28 above. Outline the top edge with a line of couching using Diamant D140.

33. Pad each of the four petals with satin stitch using stranded cotton Ecru. Cover the padding with vertical satin stitch that fans slightly using 1 strand of the same thread.

34. Outline the satin stitch with backstitch using special dentelles Ecru.

35. Working horizontally with the same thread, do needle lace numbered stitch 2 over the satin stitch using the back stitches to anchor the detached buttonhole stitches.

36. Outline the outer edge of each petal with couching using Diamant D140.

37. Using the colour image as your guide and starting at the base of each stamen, bead couch 3 to 5 15° 458 beads, followed by alternating 11°577 and 15° 458 beads, ending each line with a 2 mm cream glass pearl and using stranded cotton 310.

43. Start in the middle of this flower by encasing a Jet 208 Swarovski flat back crystal in a detached buttonhole cage.

Follow the instructions in the Bead Embroidery techniques gallery and use stranded cotton 310.

44. When you have completed the surrounding embroidery bead couch a circle of 2 mm cream glass pearls around and adjacent to the crystal.

45. The large petals that form the main part of the flower are worked with weaving texture 2 using perlé #12.310 for colour 1 and perlé #12. Ecru for colour 2 for petals 1, 3 and 5. Use perlé #12.Ecru for colour 1 and perlé #12.310 for colour 2 for the remaining petals.

46. Couch an outline around the petals. Use Diamant D3821 for petals 1, 3 and 5 and Diamant D140 for petals 2 and 4.

47. The two petals that form the calyx are needle lace over satin stitch worked in the same way as those described in 33. to 36.

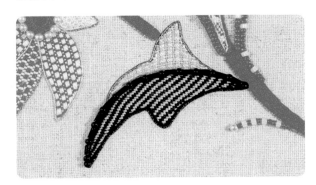

38. Fill the top section of this leaf with weaving texture 8 using perlé #12.Ecru.

39. Outline the outer edge with couching using Diamant D3821.

40. Fill the bottom section of the leaf with weaving texture 5 using perlé #12.310 for colour 1 and perlé #12. Ecru for colour 2.

41. Outline the outer edge with whipped backstitch using stranded cotton 310. Couch a line of Diamant D140 adjacent to and touching the whipped backstitch.

42. Starting at the base of the vein with bead 15° 458, bead couch a line alternating that bead and bead #1.401 bugle to the tip, finishing with at least one or more 15° 458 beads.

48. All of the branches are worked with vertical lines of chain stitch using stranded cotton 310.

49. Outline the outer-side curve of each branch with couching using Diamant D140.

50. The bead stems coming out of each branch are worked following instruction 37. for the stamens that come out of the tip of the right hand flower.

Now move onto creating the 'crazy patch' blocks that form the border of the design by weaving each block to resemble a patch of fabric. Each block is numbered in the pattern at the back of the book and the relevant weaving stitch along with the threads used are listed below. Start in the top left corner.

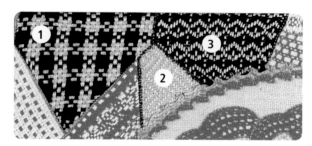

Block 1

CHECKS AND STRIPES 7
Colour 1: perlé #12.Ecru
Colour 2: perlé #12.310

Block 2

TEXTURE 6
Colour 1: perlé #12.Ecru
Colour 2: perlé #12.Ecru

Block 3

PATTERN 8
Colour 1: perlé #12.Ecru
Colour 2: perlé #12.310

Block 4

TEXTURE 2
Colour 1: perlé #12.310
Colour 2: perlé #12.Ecru

Block 5

CHECKS AND STRIPES 5
WARP:
Colour 1: perlé #12.Ecru
Colour 2: Diamant D140

WEFT (REPEATS):
Colour 1: perlé #12.Ecru
Colour 2: Row 1: perlé #12.310
           Row 2: Diamant D140
           Row 3: perlé #12.310
           Row 4: Diamant D140
           Row 5: perlé #12.310

Block 6

TEXTURE 8
WARP (REPEATS):
3 x perlé #12.Ecru
1 x Diamante D3821

WEFT:
perlé #12.Ecru

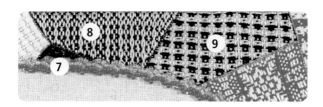

Block 7

CHECKS AND STRIPES 14
Colour 1: perlé #12.Ecru
Colour 2: Diamant D140

Block 8

PATTERN 5
Colour 1: perlé #12.Ecru
Colour 2: perlé #12.310

Block 9

CHECKS AND STRIPES 15
Colour 1: perlé #12.Ecru
Colour 2: perlé #12.310

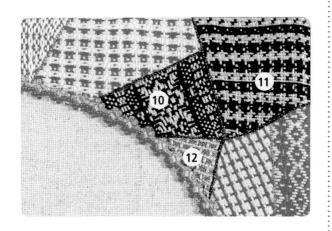

Block 10

PATTERN 7
Colour 1: perlé #12.310
Colour 2: perlé #12.Ecru

Block 11

CHECKS AND STRIPES 4
Colour 1: perlé #12.Ecru
Colour 2: perlé #12.310

Block 12

TEXTURE 2
Colour 1: perlé #12.Ecru
Colour 2: Diamant 3821

Block 13

CHECKS AND STRIPES 12
Colour 1: perlé #12.310
Colour 2: perlé #12.Ecru

Block 14

PATTERN 8
Colour 1: perlé #12.Ecru
Colour 2: perlé #12.310

Block 15

SINGLE WEAVING
WARP AND WEFT (REPEATS):
2 x perlé #12.310
4 x perlé #12.Ecru
1 x Diamant 3281
1 x perlé #12.310
1 x Diamant 3281

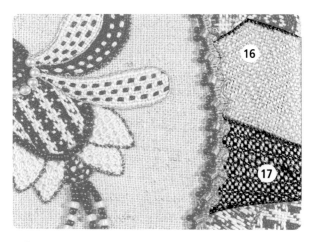

Block 16

TEXTURE 6
Colour 1:   perlé #12.Ecru
Colour 2:   perlé #12.Ecru

Block 17

SINGLE WEAVING
WARP:
perlé #12.Ecru

WEFT (REPEATS):
Row 1:   perlé #12.310
Row 2:   perlé #12.310
Row 3:   Diamant D140
Row 4:   Diamant D140
Row 5:   Diamant D140

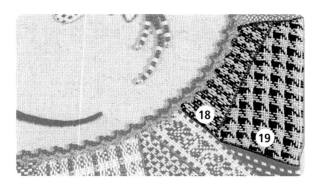

Block 18

PATTERN 6
Colour 1:   perlé #12.Ecru
Colour 2:   Diamant 3821
Colour 3:   perlé #12.310

Block 19

CHECKS AND STRIPES 1
Colour 1:   perlé #12.310
Colour 2:   perlé #12.Ecru

Block 20

TEXTURE 3
Colour 1:   perlé #12.310
Colour 2:   perlé #12.Ecru

Block 21

BRAIDS AND EDGES 3
Colour 1:   perlé #12.Ecru
Colour 2:   perlé #12.310

Block 22

CHECKS AND STRIPES 14
Colour 1:   perlé #12.310
Colour 2:   perlé #12.Ecru

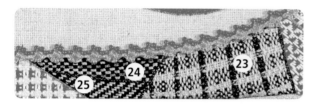

Block 23

CHECKS AND STRIPES 5
WARP:
Colour 1:   perlé #12.Ecru
Colour 2:   Diamant D140

WEFT (REPEATS):
Colour 1:   perlé #12.Ecru
Colour 2:   Row 1: perlé #12.310
                 Row 2: Diamant D140
                 Row 3: perlé #12.310
                 Row 4: Diamant D140
                 Row 5: perlé #12.310

Block 24

CHECKS AND STRIPES 13
Colour 1:   perlé #12.Ecru
Colour 2:   perlé #12.310
Colour 3:   Diamant 3821

Block 25

TEXTURE 5
Colour 1:   perlé #12.310
Colour 2:   perlé #12.Ecru

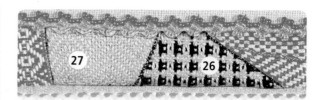

Block 26

CHECKS AND STRIPES 15
Colour 1:   perlé #12.Ecru
Colour 2:   perlé #12.310

Block 27

TEXTURE 6
Colour 1:   perlé #12.Ecru
Colour 2:   perlé #12.Ecru

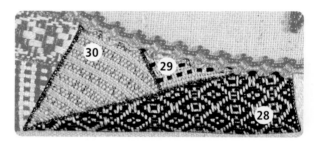

Block 28

PATTERN 2
Colour 1:   perlé #12.310
Colour 2:   perlé #12.Ecru

Block 29

TEXTURE 3
Colour 1:   perlé #12.Ecru
Colour 2:   perlé #12.310

Block 30

CHECKS AND STRIPES 6
Colour 1: perlé #12.Ecru
Colour 2: Diamant 3821

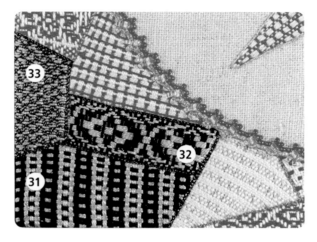

Block 31

CHECKS AND STRIPES 9
Colour 1: perlé #12.Ecru
Colour 2: perlé #12.310

Block 32

BRAIDS AND EDGES 2
Colour 1: perlé #12.310
Colour 2: perlé #12.Ecru

Block 33

CHECKS AND STRIPES 14
Colour 1: perlé #12.Ecru
Colour 2: Diamant D140

Block 34

CHECKS AND STRIPES 12
Colour 1: perlé #12.310
Colour 2: perlé #12.Ecru

Block 35

PATTERN 7
Colour 1: perlé #12.Ecru
Colour 2: perlé #12.310

Block 36

TEXTURE 2
Colour 1: perlé #12.Ecru
Colour 2: Diamant 3821

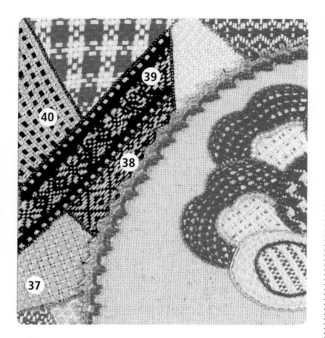

Block 37

TEXTURE 8
Colour 1: perlé #12.Ecru

Block 38

PATTERN 1
Colour 1: perlé #12.310
Colour 2: perlé #12.Ecru

Block 39

BRAIDS AND EDGES 3
Colour 1: perlé #12.310
Colour 2: perlé #12.Ecru

Block 40

TEXTURE 3
Colour 1: perlé #12.Ecru
Colour 2: perlé #12.310

When you have completed all of the blocks they should be outlined with long couched stitches that stretch from corner to corner. Use Diamant D140, couching evenly along each line. Do not outline on the circular side of blocks that are on the inner edge of the border. These are covered with bead work.

To create a link between the two design elements and referring to the instructions for the linked daisy chain in the beaded braids section of the beading techniques gallery, make a beaded chain that measures about 24" (61 cm) long. The length will depend on the tension of your work, which should be tight.

Use bead SB1.8-234 for the central, larger bead along with 4 x 15° 458 and 4 x 15° 2442 round beads for the 8 bead circle which goes around the cube. Use black beading thread.

Attach the bead chain to the circular edge of the border with the same beading thread working small, barely visible couching stitches that go over at least once on each side of the circle and once where the circles link. It is best to start in the centre of the chain, working to each side, estimating the correct placement as you go as pinning it down first tends to distort the line. Provided you don't tangle your thread it is easy enough to undo the couching stitches if you need to adjust the line.

FINISHING INSTRUCTIONS

This design has been mounted in a box that was made by my picture framer. Other than suggesting you might like to stretch it yourself, following the instructions for stretching rectangular embroidery, there are no additional finishing instructions.

Waiting for Santa

The original of the cuff of the Christmas stocking measures 14⅛ x 4⅓" (360 x 110 mm). The completed stocking is 16⅛" (410 mm) high x 10¼" (260 mm) wide at its widest points.

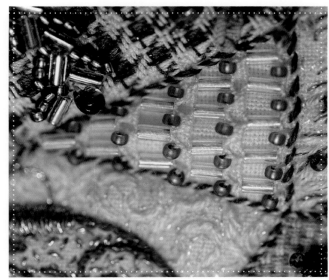

Materials

FABRIC AND BATTING

20 x 12" (500 x 300 mm) stable white cotton fabric (quilting
fabric is good);
1⅓ yd (1¼ m) cotton voile;
1⅓ yd (1¼ m) lightweight polyester batting.

100% COTTON QUILTING FABRICS

20" (½ m) Royal Blue Gingham

EXTRAS

- White Sewing Machine Thread
- 20" (½ m) white bias binding (narrow)
- The royal blue gingham used for the stocking was quilted on a
  long arm quilting machine. You can, however quilt if yourself
  following the instructions for the base of the basket cover in
  Savannah winter.
- A 24" scroll frame was used to embroider the cuff of the
  Christmas Stocking.

HAND STITCHING NEEDLES

Size 7	Embroidery Needle
Size 10	Embroidery Needle
Size 10	Bead Embroidery Needle
Size 12	Bead Embroidery Needle
Size 26	Tapestry Needle

Unless otherwise instructed use:
- A standard good quality white machine sewing thread, a size
  70 needle and the standard foot for making up the stocking.
  (We don't supply these in our kits.)
- two strands of thread when working with stranded cotton;
- one strand of thread when working with Lizbeth #80 and
  Diamant thread;
- one strand of stranded cotton, doubled over and threaded
  onto a bead embroidery needle for the bead embroidery;
- one strand of beading thread for the beadwork.

THREADS AND RIBBONS

DMC STRANDED COTTON

1 skein each:

318	Light Steel Grey
797	Royal Blue
799	Medium Delft Blue
800	Pale Delft Blue
3812	Very Dark Sea Green

2 skeins:

B5200	Snow White

DMC DIAMANT METALLIC THREAD

D168	Light Silver

MADEIRA GLAMOUR #12 THREAD

3038	Sapphire
3057	Emerald
3000	Prism Snow White

LIZBETH TATTING COTTON #80

601	White
605	Silver
651	Blue Medium
652	Royal Blue
688	Sea Green Dark

DI VAN NIEKERK'S HAND PAINTED SILK RIBBON

2mm:

66	Light Indigo

4 mm:

31	Marine
66	Light Indigo

7 mm:

103	White

BEADS

MIYUKI BEADS
Round Rocailles:

15° 1	2 g	Silver Lined Crystal
15° 19F	2 g	Matte Silver Lined Sapphire
15° 250	6 g	Crystal AB
15° 1424	2 g	Silver Lined Teal
11° 1	10 g	Silver Lined Crystal
8° 1	2 g	Silver Lined Crystal

TILA BEADS

TL 250	2 g	Crystal AB

3 MM BUGLE BEADS #1

#1 1	2 g	Silver Lined Crystal
#1 250	4 g	Crystal AB

2.8 MM DROP BEADS

DP28.19	10 g	Silver Lined Sapphire
DP28.20	10 g	Silver Lined Cobalt
DP28.2425	2 g	Silver Lined Teal

3.4 MM DROP BEADS

DP 250	6 g	Crystal AB
DPF 31	10 g	Mint Green Lined Sapphire

DELICA BEADS

DB11-257	4 g	Sky Blue Ceylon

CZECH BEADS

150 x 3 mm Fire Polished Crystal AB
60 x 35 mm Twisted Bugle Silver Lined Crystal

SUPERLON BEADING THREAD

C-Lon AA	Teal
C-Lon AA	Grey
C-Lon AA	White
C-Lon AA	Light Blue

INSTRUCTIONS

- If you are tracing the cuff design onto fabric from the drawings at the back of the book, make sure that you leave at least 6" (150 mm) of fabric below the bottom edge of the cuff. This is needed when you make the stocking.
- Each block on the front of the cuff is outlined with backstitch using Lizbeth #80 601 whipped with 2 strands of 797. Do this after completion of the embroidery that is inside the block but before working anything that breaks the boundaries of any particular block. Outline a few blocks at a time so that, where you are able to, you will be able to work continuous lines.
- Attach the 3-dimensional bead flowers, leaves and snowflakes when you have completed all the other work, as the threads tend to catch on them, creating a bit of a nuisance for you.

Blocks 1 and 2

1. Referring to the needle weaving techniques, fill block 1 with texture 3. Use Lizbeth #80 652 for colour 1 and 601 for colour 2.

2. Fill block 2 with double weaving using Use Lizbeth #80 601 for colour 1 and 605 for colour 2

- Using bead 15° 1424 and teal beading thread, work 2 x 8-bead leaves following the instructions in the beading techniques gallery. Referring to the image above, attach them to the weaving leaving a small space between the two.
- Using grey beading thread and coming up in the centre space work three separate twigs that consist of 3 x 15° 250 with a 15° 19F bead at the tip.
- Place 3 x drop beads DP28.19 in a triangle around the twigs.

Block 3

1. Working on the lines that are drawn in this block, work fly stitch with 1 strand of B5200 and 1 strand of 3057 Glamour #12 threaded onto the needle at the same time.

- Once you have completed the fly stitch on the lines and using the colour image as your guide, work a branch between each of those lines to fill it up a bit. They are not drawn because to have done so would have made the line drawing a little messy, so use your discretion.
- Using stranded cotton 799 and bead 15° 19F, stitch single beads here and there over the branches, using the colour image as your guide.

2. With 1 strand of 3000 Glamour #12, do seeding in the empty spaces surrounding the branches.

3. Following the instructions for shell border, variation 4, in the tatting gallery, work a border of 7 shells using Lizbeth #80 652. Attach the border on the edge adjacent to block 2, placing a drop bead DP28.19 in the centre of each shell.

Block 4

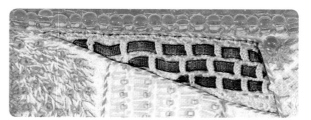

1. Using Lizbeth #80 601, work backstitch on the 4 lines that surround the block.

2. Referring to the instructions for Filler 1 in the needle lace techniques gallery, and using the same thread, fill block 4 using the colour image as your guide.

3. Thread 2 mm silk ribbon 66 into the gaps created by the repeats of rows 6 and 7.

Block 5

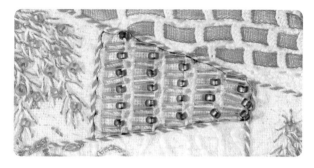

1. Using Lizbeth #80 601, work backstitch on the 4 lines that surround the block.

2. Referring to the instructions for beaded stitch 2 in the needle lace gallery, using the same thread, and beads #1 250 and 15° 19F, fill block 5 using the colour image as your guide.

Block 6

1. Referring to the embroidery stitch gallery, fill block 6 with woven trellis using stranded cotton 800 for shade 1, 3038 Glamour #12 for shade 2 and stranded cotton B5200 for both shades 3 and 4.

2. Referring to the instructions for variation 3 of the shell border in the tatting gallery, work 3 separated, individual shells using Lizbeth #80.652. Attach one each into the top left, top right and bottom left corners and stitch a drop bead DP28.19 into the centre of each shell.

3. Referring to the instructions for snowflake 1 in the beading gallery, make a snowflake using beads 15° 250 and 3 mm fire polished beads, crystal AB. Use white beading thread. Attach the snowflake when you have completed all of the embroidery.

Block 7

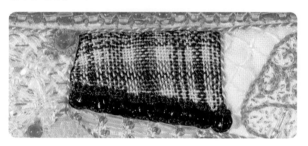

1. Referring to the needle weaving gallery, fill block 7 with single weaving. Starting in the middle of the block, working vertically to the right, use the following Lizbeth #80 threads:
- Warp Stitches: 2 x 652, [3 x 651, 5 x 601, 4 x 688, 2 x 601, 2 x 652, 2 x 601, 4 x 688]. Return to the middle and working to the left repeat from [to]. If you have filled the block before you have used all of the colours in the sequence, do not worry. It is not vital that they are all there to create the feel of tartan. Provided you have used all of the colours at least once.
- Weft Stitches: Starting in the middle of the block, working horizontally to the bottom of the block, follow the sequence of the warp stitches, returning to the middle and working to the top.

2. Following the instructions for shell border, variation 4, in the tatting techniques gallery, work a border of 9 shells using Lizeth #80 652. Attach the border on the edge adjacent to block 10 and 11, placing a drop bead DP28.19 in the centre of each shell.

Block 8

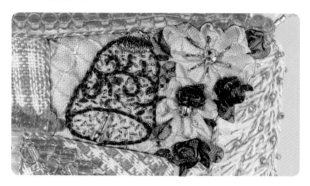

1. Using Diamant D168, pad the silver oval at the top of the bell with horizontal satin stitch. With the same thread, work vertical satin stitch over the padding and couch a line over the 'hanging wire'.

- The lines that form the outline of the bell and, also, the swirl pattern within are worked with backstitch using stranded cotton 799. Whip the backstitch with 3038 Glamour #12.
- The small leaf shapes that radiate from the swirl pattern are lazy daisy stitches worked with 799. Using 3038 Glamour #12, place a small straight stitch within each lazy daisy stitch.
- Using white beading thread, bead couch 1 x 15° 1, 1 x #1 1 and 1 x 8° 1 beads to make the clapper.
- Using Diamant D168, work seeding stitches in all the available space left within both sections of the bell.

2. When you have completed blocks 9, 10, 11 and 16 work the outlines of these blocks, as mentioned at the very beginning of these instructions.

3. Thereafter, return to the silk ribbon flowers that overlap blocks 8 and 9.

- Referring to the colour image as your guide, using 7 mm silk ribbon 103, the larger flower at the top of the arrangement is made with 7 silk ribbon stitches that radiate from the circle in the centre. Secure each petal with a straight stitch down the centre using Diamant D168.
- The smaller flower below that is made with 5 silk ribbon stitches in the same way and using the same ribbon and silver thread.
- Each of the blue flowers is a French knot ribbon rose made with 4 mm silk ribbon 66, secured with 1 strand of 797.

- The leaves are silk ribbon stitches made with 4 mm silk ribbon 31, secured with a straight stitch that runs down the vein of the leaf and done with 1 strand each of 3812 and 3057 Glamour #12 threaded on the needle at the same time.
- Using the same thread combination, work a few lazy daisy leaves which radiate out from the arrangement of flowers and leaves.
- Using white beading thread, place a bead 8° 1 in the centre of each flower and beads 15° 1 here and there between the elements of the arrangement.

4. Fill whatever is still blank in block 8 (mostly to the left of the bell), with white trellis couching using 2 strands of B5200. Using 3000 Glamour #12, work a cross stitch over each intersection.

Block 9

1. With stranded cotton 318, work whipped chain stitch up the centre line to create the trunk of the tree.

- With Diamant D168, create the star at the top of the tree. Work 6 straight stitches from the outside, all going into the same central point.
- Following the instructions for block 3 (1), create the branches of the tree.
- Following the instructions for block 3 (2), fill the blank space in the block with seeding.

Block 10

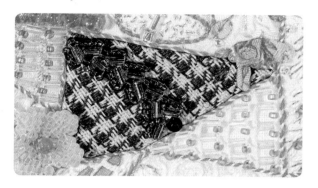

1. Referring to the needle weaving gallery, fill block 11 with checks and stripes 1. Use Lizbeth # 80 601 for colour 1 and 652 for colour 2.
2. Referring to the chevron variation in the beading instructions, work the branch using beads 15° 1424 and bugle #1 colour 1 with grey beading thread. Stitch it in place according to the instructions and using the colour image as your guide.

Block 11

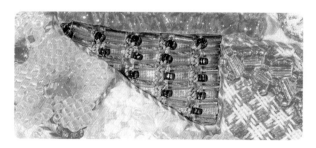

1. Using Lizbeth #80 605, work backstitch on the 4 lines that surround the block.
2. Referring to the instructions for beaded stitch 2 in the needle lace gallery, using the same thread and bead 15° 1424, fill block 11 using the colour image as your guide.

Block 12

Referring to the instructions for block 9, work this tree in the same way, save for the star at the top of the tree.

Block 13

1. Using Diamant D168, pad the silver oval at the top of the decoration with horizontal satin stitch. With the same thread, work vertical satin stitch over the padding and couch a line over the 'hanging wire'.
• The lines that form the outline of the decoration and, also, the swirl pattern within are worked with backstitch using stranded cotton 3812. Whip the backstitch with 3057 Glamour #12.

- The small leaf shapes that radiate from the swirl pattern are lazy daisy stitches worked with 3812. Using 3057 Glamour #12, place a small straight stitch within each lazy daisy stitch.
- Using Diamant D168, work seeding stitches in all the available space left within the decoration.

2. Bearing in mind that you will still add an arrangement of silk ribbon flowers on the left, work two-tone vermicelli stitch over the rest of the block that is not filled with either the decoration or the flowers. Use B5200 for the first layer of swirls, followed by 3000 Glamour #12 for the second layer of smaller swirls.

3. When you have completed blocks 14, 20, and 21 work the outlines of these blocks, as mentioned at the very beginning of these instructions.

4. Thereafter, return to the silk ribbon flowers that overlap blocks 1, 2, 3, 13, 14 and 20 following the guidelines set out for block 8 (3).

Block 14

1. Referring to the needle weaving gallery, fill block 7 with single weaving. Turn your work sideways and starting in the middle of the block, working vertically to the right, use the following Lizbeth #80 threads:

- Warp Stitches: 2 x 652, [2 x 651, 3 x 601, 4 x 688, 1 x 601, 2 x 651, 2 x 652, 3 x 601, 4 x 688]. Return to the middle and working to the left repeat from [to]. If you have filled the block before you have used all of the colours in the sequence, do not worry. It is not vital that they are all there to create the feel of tartan. Provided you have used all of the colours at least once.

- Weft Stitches: Starting in the middle of the block, working horizontally to the bottom of the block, follow the sequence of the warp stitches, returning to the middle and working to the top.

Block 15

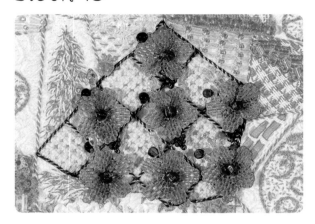

1. Referring to numbered stitch 34 in the needle lace techniques gallery and referring to the colour image as your guide, fill alternate blocks using Lizbeth #80 601.

2. Outline each block with backstitch using Lizbeth #80 601 whipped with 2 strands of 797. This is the same combination that you will use for the outlining of each and every block. You will need to outline block 15 as well, once you have completed the surrounding blocks.

3. The empty blocks are filled with a bead flower arrangement which you will attach once you have finished the rest of the embroidery so as to prevent snagging. Referring to the beading gallery, make:

- 7 x 6-bead flowers using Delica beads DB11-257 and light blue beading thread.
- 7 x 8-bead leaves using beads 15° 1424 and teal beading thread.
- Using the tails of the flowers and leaves, attach each flower to the centre of the block. Once it is secure, stitch a drop bead, DPF 31 in the centre.
- Attach the leaf coming out from under the flower, making sure that the angle is the same for every block.
- Making sure that, likewise they sit at the same angle throughout, use the remaining threads to make a twig

with a 3 mm fire polished Crystal AB bead at the tip and
6 x 15° 250 beads for the stalk and 1 x 15° 250 bead for
the stopper at the top.
- Still using the remaining threads make a second stalk with
  a drop bead DP28.2425 at the tip and 5 x 15° 250 beads
  in the stalk. This twig does not need a stopper bead, just
  go through the drop bead from right to left and down the
  beads in the stalk into the fabric.

Block 16

Fill this block following the instructions for block 5, using
the same threads and beads.

Block 17

Fill this block following the instructions for block 4, using
the same threads and beads.

Block 18

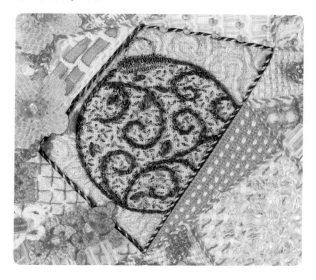

1. Referring to block 13 (1), work the decoration in the same
way using the same threads.
2. Referring to block 13 (2), fill the background of block 18
with two-tone vermicelli stitching using the same threads.

Block 19

Referring to block 2, fill block 19 in the same way using the
same threads and beads.

Block 20

1. Referring to block 6 (1), fill the block with woven trellis using the same threads.
2. Referring to block 6 (2), work 3 tatting shells. Attach one each into the top left, top right and bottom left corners and stitch a drop bead DP28.19 into the centre of each shell.
3. Referring to the instructions for snowflake 3 in the beading techniques gallery, make a snowflake using beads 15° 250 and 3 mm fire polished beads, crystal AB. Use white beading thread. Attach the snowflake when you have completed all of the embroidery to avoid snagging as you continue.

Block 21

Referring to the embroidery techniques' gallery, fill block 21 with trellis couching with cross stitch filling. Use stranded cotton 3812 for the trellis and 3057 Glamour #12 for the straight stitches that form the cross.

1. Referring to the original line drawing at the back of the book, place and stitch 3 x Tila beads TL 250.
• Referring to the tatting gallery, make 5 spiral tatted flowers variation 1, using the 7ds-p-7 ds combination. Use Lizbeth # 80 601 for 1 flower, 651 for 2 flowers and 652 for a further 2 flowers. Using the colour image as your guide place and stitch them into position, placing a drop bead DPF 31 in the centre of each flower.
• Still using the colour image as your guide, work a few leaves with drizzle stitch using Lizbeth #80 688.

Block 22

Referring to block 3, work block 22 in the same way, using the same threads and beads.

Block 23

Referring to block 1, work block 23 in the same way, using the same threads.

Block 24

Referring to block 21, work block 24 in the same way. You will only need 3 flowers for this block, 1 each in Lizbeth #80 601, 651 and 652.

Blocks 25, 26, and 27

1. Referring to beaded stitch 1 in the needle lace gallery, fill block 25 using Lizbeth # 80 605 and bead 15° 1424.
2. Referring to the instructions for block 4, fill block 26 in the same way using the same threads and beads.
3. Referring to needle weaving in the techniques galleries, fill block 27 with checks and stripes 1. Use Lizbeth # 80 601 for colour 1 and 652 for colour 2.
• Following the instructions for shell border, variation 4, in the tatting techniques gallery, work a border of 8 shells using Lizbeth #80 652. Attach the border on the

edge adjacent to blocks 25 and 26, placing a drop bead DP28.19 in the centre of each shell.

Block 28

Referring to the instructions for block 9, work this tree in the same way, save for the star at the top of the tree.

Block 29

Referring to the instructions for block 8, work the bauble in the same way using the same threads and beads. The silk ribbon flowers are identical to those that lie between blocks 8 and 9 and the trellis couched background of the block is also the same, all using the same threads, ribbons and beads.

Blocks 30 and 31

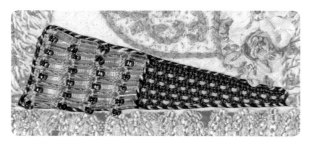

1. Referring back to block 11, fill block 30 in the same way, using the same threads and beads.
2. Referring back to block one, fill block 31 in the same way, using the same thread.

Block 32

Referring to the instructions for block 9, work this tree in the same way, save for the star at the top of the tree.

Blocks 33, 34 and 35

1. Referring to the embroidery techniques' gallery, fill block 33 with trellis couching with cross-stitch filling. Use stranded cotton 800 for the trellis and 3038 Glamour #12 for the straight stitches that form the cross stitch.
- Referring to the original line drawing at the back of the book, place and stitch the 3 x Tila beads TL 250.
- Referring to the tatting gallery, make 5 spiral tatted flowers variation 1, using the 7ds-p-7 ds combination. Use Lizbeth # 80 601 for 1 flower, 651 for another flowers and 652 for 3 flowers. Using the colour image as your guide, place and stitch them into position, placing a drop bead DPF 31 in the centre of each flower.
- Still using the colour image as your guide, work a few leaves with drizzle stitch using Lizbeth #80 688.

2. Fill block 34 following the instructions for block 5, using the same threads and beads.

3. Referring to the needle weaving gallery, fill block 35 with single weaving. Starting on the left of the block, working vertically to the right, use the following Lizbeth #80 threads:
- Warp Stitches: 3 x 688, 2 x 601, 2 x 651, 2 x 652, 2 x 651, 3 x 601, 2 x 688, 2 x 601, 4 x 652, 2 x 651. If you have filled the block before you have used all of the colours in the sequence, do not worry. It is not vital that they are all there to create the feel of checked fabric. Provided you have used all of the colours at least once.
- Weft Stitches: Starting on the top of the block, use the following Lizbeth #80 threads: 2 x 688, 3 x 601, 2 x 651, 2 x 652, 2 x 651, 2 x 601, 2 x 688, 2 x 601, 3 x 652, 2 x 601, 2 x 688, 2 x 601, 2 x 651, 2 x 652, 2 x 651, 2 x 601, 2 x 688.

Block 36, 37 and 38

1. Fill block 36 following the instructions for block 2, using the same threads and beads.

2. Fill block 37 with woven trellis following the instructions referred to in block 6(1).

- Referring to block 6 (2), make a single tatted shell and place it in the bottom right hand corner of block 37.
- Referring back to block 6 (3), using the same threads and beads, make a snowflake following the instructions for snowflake 3, placing and stitching it to the project when you have completed the embroidery to avoid snagging.

3. Referring to the instructions for block 3, work block 38 in the same way. The shell border will require 13 shells and will be placed on the edge adjacent to blocks 36 and 37. All threads and beads are the same as those used for block 3.

The back of the cuff

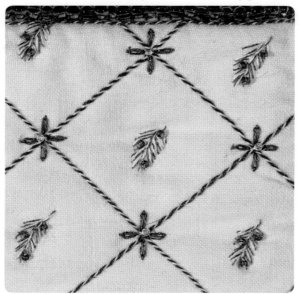

1. As you did for the edge of each block on the front of the cuff, work backstitch using Lizbeth #80 601 whipped with 2 strands of 797 along all the lines of the trellis and including the top and bottom outside lines. You do not need to stitch the left outside line, as this will go into the seam that joins the cuff. Stitch the diagonal lines to that point, though.

2. At each intersection, work 4 lazy daisy stitches using 1 strand each of 3812 and 3057 Glamour #12 threaded onto the same needle. With white beading thread, stitch a single bead 15°250 over the intersection, at the meeting point of the lazy daisy stitches.

3. Each of the small branches is a short line of fly stitch using 1 strand each of B5200 and 3057 Glamour #12 threaded onto the same needle. With 1 strand of 799, stitch 3 beads 15°19F spread over each small branch.

FINISHING INSTRUCTIONS

Referring to the finishing instructions in the techniques galleries, cut a piece each of batting and voile that are slightly larger than the embroidered area.

- Pin and tack the batting and the voile to the back of the embroidered cuff, making sure that all the embroidery is covered.
- Return your work to the hoop, making sure that it is well stretched.
- Following the hand stitching techniques in the finishing instructions, secure all of the beads.
- Using 1 strand of B5200 and following the instructions for working the block intersections, work small, barely visible running stitches adjacent to (even slightly underneath, if you can) all of the whipped backstitches that form the outlines of the blocks. This includes the trellis on the back of the cuff. You should also work these running stitches around the entire perimeter. On the left edge of the back of the cuff, work running stitches on the dotted line. Use a separate length of thread for these so that you can unpick them later if they show when you have assembled the cuff.
- With a sharp pair of scissors, cut away the excess batting and voile on the back, i.e. anything on the outside of the running stitches.

To assemble the stocking

1. The white fabric that you left below the embroidered area of the cuff should be folded to the back of the embroidered area, leaving ⅛" (2 mm) of white showing at the bottom. This will accommodate the bead fringe later.

2. Trim back to ½" (10 mm) on the left, top and right, as indicated in the diagram above. Place some pins at the top and bottom to keep it stable.

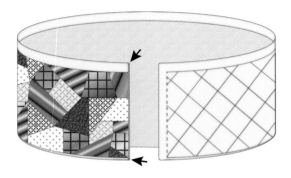

3. To make a tube, fold the"crazy patch" end under from the whipped backstitch, so that no white fabric is exposed.

4. Slip the raw edge of the trellised back into the"crazy patch" side until the ends of the trellis meet the whipped backstitch. Pin and hand stitch along the top side and the underside with white sewing thread, so that the cuff is firmly joined with invisible stitches.

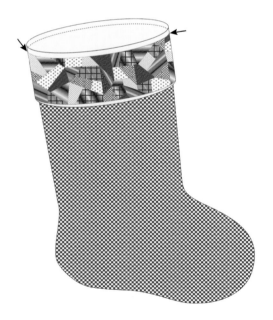

5. Using the stocking pattern at the back of the book, cut out both sides of the stocking – remember that the back is a mirror image of the front.

6. Before stitching, check that it will fit by pinning and sliding into the cuff. Adjust the size of the seams if necessary and, with right sides together, stitch around the sides and the bottom. Work a zig-zag stitch close to the seam to neaten and trim off any excess fabric. Turn out the right way.

7. Slide the cuff over the stocking top, matching up the side seams. Pin and tack along the top line as indicated by the arrow in the diagram above.

8. Starting at the centre back, pin the white bias binding along the same line, making sure that the join at the back is diagonal. Machine stitch into place.

9. Trim off any excess fabric from both the cuff and the stocking. Turn the bias binding to the back, pin and hand stitch on the back.

Bead trimming

1. Following the instructions for beaded Palestrina stitch in the bead embroidery gallery, using 3 strands of 797, attach drop beads DPF 31 all the way around the top of the cuff, stitch over the line that forms the seam which attached the bias binding.

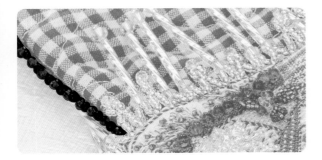

2. Starting just above the point where the cuff lays over the stocking, using the same thread, attach drop beads DP28.19 and DP28.20, alternately and going around to just under the cuff on the other side.

3. Returning to the narrow border of white fabric that you left exposed at the base of the cuff, and using the blue washout pen, place a small dot every ¼" (5 mm).

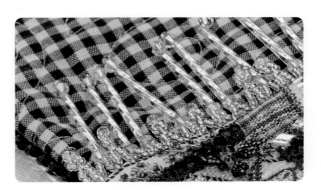

- Using white beading thread, secure it with a small knot on the back of the cuff, coming out through the point of the fold on the left side seam. Following the pattern below work the bead fringe using size 11° 1 beads for the small circles, a 3 mm fire polished, crystal AB bead for the hexagon shapes and a drop bead DP 250 for the oval shape.
- At the end of each dangle, go back into the fabric, bringing the needle out on the next marked dot.
- The pattern below is one set and you repeat this set as many times as you need to, working either backwards of forwards, and eventually meeting up with where you started.

Rambling vine

The original of this design measures 15½ x 15¾"
(395 x 400 mm) and has been made into a wall
hanging which measures 20¾ x 20¾" (530 x
530 mm). Instructions on how to make up the
wall hanging are at the end of the embroidery
instructions. For extra inspiration, Margie Breetzke
has worked up the embroidery design, using
applique and bead embroidery techniques. Find it
on pages 6 and 7.

Materials

FOUNDATION FABRIC AND BATTING

23½ x 23½" (600 x 600 mm) linen/cotton blend fabric,
 colour natural;
2 x 23½ x 23½" (600 x 600 mm) cotton voile;
23½ x 23½" (600 x 600 mm) lightweight polyester batting.

100% COTTON QUILTING FABRICS

Fabric 1
6 in² (250 mm²)
- Block 1
- Block 11b
- Block 12b
- Block 17
- Block 25

Fabric 2
6 in² (250 mm²)
- Block 2
- Block 10a
- Block 13b
- Block 18
- Block 35

Fabric 3
6 in² (250 mm²)
- Block 6a
- Block 22
- Block 31

Fabric 4
6 in² (250 mm²)
- Block 6b
- Block 8a
- Block 19
- Block 23b
- Block 26
- Block 34

Fabric 5
6 in² (250 mm²)
- Block 5
- Block 11a
- Block 23a
- Block 30

Fabric 6
6 in² (250 mm²)
- Block 4
- Block 9b
- Block 16
- Block 21b
- Block 33

Fabric 7
6 in² (250 mm²)
- Block 3
- Block 13d
- Block 14
- Block 32

Fabric 8
6 in² (250 mm²)
- Block 7a
- Block 29

Fabric 9
6 in² (250 mm²)
- Block 7b
- Block 20b

Fabric 10
6 in² (250 mm²)
- Block 8b
- Block 15
- Block 27

Fabric 11
6 in² (250 mm²)
- Block 9a
- Block 12a
- Block 24
- Block 21a

Fabric 12
6 in² (250 mm²)
- Block 10b
- Block 13c
- Block 28

Fabric 13
6 in² (250 mm²)
- Block 13a
- Block 20a

Fabric 14
1¼ yd (1 m)
- Border and Backing

Fabric 15
- A Fat Quarter
- Continuous Binding

A 30" heavy duty scroll frame set was used to work the Rambling Vine project.

The design is divided into sections. Each section has been described in detail.

HAND STITCHING NEEDLES

Size 7	Embroidery Needle
Size 10	Embroidery Needle
Size 10	Bead Embroidery Needle
Size 12	Bead Embroidery Needle
Size 22	Chenille Needle
Size 26	Tapestry Needle

THREADS AND RIBBONS

MADEIRA GLAMOUR #12 THREAD
3000	Prism Snow White

DMC SATIN THREAD
S469	Avocado Green
S3685	Very Dark Mauve

DMC STRANDED COTTON
1 skein each:
316	Medium Antique Mauve
451	Dark Shell Grey
452	Medium Shell Grey
640	Very Dark Beige Grey
642	Dark Beige Grey
644	Medium Beige Grey
778	Very Light Antique Mauve
779	Dark Cocoa
822	Light Beige Grey
902	Very Dark Garnet
934	Black Avocado Green
3021	Very Dark Brown Grey

3051	Dark Green Grey	
3052	Medium Green Grey	
3053	Green Grey	
3371	Black Brown	
3726	Dark Antique Mauve	
3727	Light Antique Mauve	
3802	Very Dark Antique Mauve	
3860	Cocoa	
3861	Light Cocoa	

2 skeins each:

315	Medium Dark Antique Mauve
3013	Light Khaki Green
3033	Very Light Mocha Brown

DMC LIGHT EFFECTS METALLIC THREAD

E703	Metallic Light Green Emerald
E898	Metallic Dark Oak
E3685	Metallic Rosewood

DMC PERLÉ COTTON #12

Ecru	Ecru
316	Medium Antique Mauve
524	Very Light Fern Green
642	Dark Beige Grey
644	Medium Beige Grey
778	Very Light Antique Mauve
822	Light Beige Grey
3042	Light Antique Violet

SAJOU FILS DENTELLE AU CHINOIS

6308	Ecru
6844	Dark Olive

DI VAN NIEKERK'S HAND PAINTED SILK RIBBON

2mm:

21	3 m	Antique Brown
32	6 m	Sunny Green
72	3 m	Victorian

4mm:

36	3 m	Avocado
98	3 m	Softest Mink
135	3 m	Tuscany

BEADS

MIYUKI BEADS
Round Rocailles

15° 5F	6g	Matte Silver Lined Dark Topaz
15° 459	6g	Metallic Olive
15° 1631	6g	Semi-Matte Silver Lined Safron
15° 1883	2g	Transparent Wine Gold Luster
11° 577	2g	Butter Cream Gold Lined Alabaster
11° 641	2g	Rose Bronze Silver Lined Alabaster

HEX CUT BEADS

15H459	2g	Metallic Olive

3.4 MM DROP BEADS

DPMix 04	2g	Merlot
DP 454	2g	Metallic Purple Iris

3 MM BUGLE BEADS #1

#1.2442	4g	Crystal Ivory Gold Luster

DELICA BEADS

DB11-24	4g	Metallic Olive Green Iris
DB11-108	4g	Cinnamon Gold Luster
DB11-109	4g	Crystal Ivory Gold Luster
DB11-624	2g	Light Rose Silver Lined Alabaster
DB11-1016	4g	Metallic Rhubarb Luster

PRECIOSA GLASS PEARLS

2 mm	2g	Cream

CZECH BEADS:

20 x 3 mm Fire Polished Smoke Topaz Light AB

SUPERLON BEADING THREAD

C-Lon AA	Ash
C-Lon AA	Burgundy
C-Lon AA	Cream
C-Lon AA	Olive
C-Lon AA	Pink

FOR WALL HANGING

8mm wooden dowel rod (cut to size)

Unless otherwise instructed use:

- Good quality machine sewing threads in beige, dark green and rose pink, a size 70 needle and the standard foot for the crazy patch and for finishing the project. (We don't supply these in our kits.)
- two strands of thread when working with stranded cotton;
- one strand of thread when working with perlé cotton, special dentelles and Diamant thread;
- one strand of stranded cotton, doubled over and threaded onto a bead embroidery needle for the bead embroidery;
- one strand of beading thread for the beadwork.

INSTRUCTIONS

Referring to the instructions for paper-pieced crazy patchwork in the crazy patchwork techniques gallery, you will need 4 photocopies of the crazy patchwork pattern for *Rambling vine* in the back section of this book.

- Using the first photocopy, cut out all of the paper patches;
- Referring to the fabrics listed above, place and pin each paper template onto the relevant fabric;
- Cut out the patches. Make sure that you leave a **seam allowance of at least ¼" (6 mm)** all the way around each template.
- When trimming that patches at the end of each step in the joining process, **do not trim away the seam allowance on any of the patches that are placed on any of the four outer edges of the panel**. You will need them for the assembly of the project.

Referring to the green area in diagram on this page, using the second photocopy as the foundation onto which you will stitch the patches:

- Place and stitch block 1;
- With right sides together, flipping trimming and pressing with an iron after each and ever stage, continue to place blocks in the following order:
- Block 2 to block 1;
- Block 3 on the edge created by blocks 1 and 2;
- Block 4 on the edge created by blocks 3 and 1;
- Block 5 on the edge created by blocks 4 and 1;
- Join blocks 6a and 6b to create a strip. Place and stitch on the edge created by blocks 5, 1 and 2;
- Join blocks 7a and 7b to create a strip. Place and stitch on the edge created by blocks 6a, 2 and 3;
- Join blocks 8a and 8b to create a strip. Place and stitch on the edge created by blocks 7a, 3 and 4;
- Join blocks 9a and 9b to create a strip. Place and stitch on the edge created by blocks 9a, 7a and 7b;
- Join blocks 10a, 10b and 10c to create a strip. Place and stitch on the edge created by blocks 9a, 8a and 8b;
- Join blocks 11a and 11b to create a strip. Place and stitch that strip on the edge created by blocks 9a and 9b;

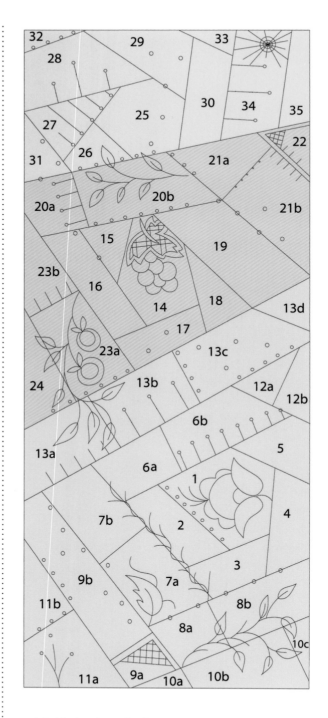

- Join blocks 12a and 12b to create a strip. Place and stitch that strip on the edge created by blocks 6b and 5;
- Join blocks 13a, 13b, 13c and 13d to create a strip. Place and stitch that strip on the edge created by blocks 9b, 7b, 6a, 6b, 12a and 12b;

Referring to the lilac area in the diagram on the previous page, and using the third photocopy which you have cut out, with a generous border, and which you are going to use as the foundation for this section of the panel:

- Place and stitch block 14;
- Place and stitch block 15;
- Place and stitch block 16 on the edge created by blocks 14 and 15;
- Place and stitch block 17 on the edge created by blocks 16 and 14;
- Place and stitch block 18 on the edge created by blocks 17 and 14;
- Place and stitch block 19 on the edge created by blocks 18 and 14;
- Join blocks 20a and 20b to create a strip. Place and stitch on the edge created by blocks 16, 15, 14 and 19;
- Join blocks 21a and 21b to create a strip. Place and stitch that strip on the edge created by blocks 20b and 19;
- Place and stitch block 22 on the edge created by blocks 21a and b;
- Join blocks 23a and 23b to create a strip. Place and stitch that strip on the edge created by blocks 20, 16 and 17;
- Place and stitch block 24 on the edge created by blocks 23a and b;

Remove the foundation paper from the back. With right sides together, place and stitch the edge created by blocks 24, 23a, 17, 18 and 19 to the edge of the original panel created by blocks 13a, b, c and d.

Referring to the grey area in the diagram on the previous page, and using the fourth photocopy which you have cut out, with a generous border, and which you are going to use as the foundation for this section of the panel:

- Place and stitch block 25;
- Place and stitch block 26;
- Place and stitch block 27 on the edge created by blocks 25 and 26;
- Place and stitch block 28 on the edge created by blocks 27 and 25;
- Place and stitch block 29 on the edge created by blocks 28 and 25;

- Place and stitch block 30 on the edge created by blocks 29 and 25;
- Place and stitch block 32 on the edge created by block 28;
- Place and stitch block 33 on the edge created by blocks 29 and 30;
- Place and stitch block 34 on the edge created by blocks 33 and 30;
- Place and stitch block 35 on the edge created by block 34;

Remove the foundation paper from the back. With right sides together, place and stitch the edge created by 31, 26, 25, 30, 34, and 35 to the edge created by blocks 20a and b, 21a and 22.

Remove the foundation paper, press the entire panel with an iron. Keeping it as flat as possible and referring to the directions at the end of the paper piecing section in the crazy patch techniques gallery, attach the panel to the foundation panel taking note of the following:

- Prepare the foundation fabric by first transferring the embroidery design onto the left side, making sure that you mark the lines on the right of the embroidery that marks the placement of the crazy patch panel. You do not need to transfer the lines of each individual crazy patch block to the foundation fabric;
- With right sides together, on the side that starts at the top with patch 32 and ends at the bottom with side 11, pin the crazy patch panel to the line adjacent to the embroidered panel. It is wise to check that placement is correct before you stitch.
- Flip the panel to the right and iron the seam.
- Pin and tack the top, right and bottom edges to the foundation fabric along the lines that indicate the outer edge of the blocks.
- With a zig-zag stitch on a sewing maching, stitch the edge of the seam allowance to the foundation fabric on these three sides. This will prevent fraying while you are hand stitching the embellishement and will ultimately make it easier when assembling the wall hanging. Do not trim away any of the excess foundation fabric.
- Back the entire piece with 1 of the squares of voile. Overlock or zig zag around the four sides.

EMBELLISHMENT INSTRUCTIONS: JACOBEAN EMBROIDERY PANEL

Flower 1

This flower appears on the top, right hand side of the embroidered panel.

1. Referring to pattern 9 (music staves) in the needle weaving gallery, fill the centre of the flower with music staves. Use perlé #12.822 for colour 1 and 1 strand of 3021 for colour 2.
- Using the colour image as your guide, work the music notes using 2 strands of 3371 for the straight lines and beads 15° 5F for the dots.

2. When you have completed the bead embroidery and shading that surround this area, outline the ovate shape by couching a line of 1 strand of E3685 in the ditch.

3. Fill the outer area of the flower with long and short stitch shading, guide lines for which are in the embroidery stitches gallery.
- Working from the inner edge, start with 1 strand of 642, shading through 822 and 778 to 3726 on the edge.

4. Using 1 strand of 902, outline the shading with outline stitch.

5. Referring to the bead embroidery gallery, using bead 15° 1631 and stranded cotton 3013, bead couch a line of beads onto each of the lines.
- Using 2 strands of the same thread, work a bullion knot between each of the bead lines, using the colour image as your guide.

Flower 2

This flower appears below flower 1 on the right hand side of the embroidered panel.

1. Referring to pattern 9 (music staves) in the needle weaving gallery, fill the centre of the flower with music staves. Use perlé #12.822 for colour 1 and 1 strand of 3021 for colour 2.

- Using the colour image as your guide, work the music notes using 2 strands of 3371 for the straight lines and beads 15° 5F for the dots.

2. When you have completed the embroidery that surrounds this area, outline the shape with bead couching using beads 15° 1883 and stranded cotton 902.

3. Fill each of these leaves with checks and stripes 4, found in the needle weaving gallery. Use perlé #12. 822 for colour 1 and perlé #12.642 for colour 2.

4. When you have completed the surrounding embroidery outline each leaf with bead couching using bead 15H459 and stranded cotton 934.

- Thereafter, couch a line of E703 metallic thread immediately adjacent to the inside of the bead couching line.

5. Referring to the embroidery stitches gallery fill each of these petals with woven trellis using 2 strands throughout: 316 for shade 1; 3726 for shade 2; 822 for shade 3, the first round of weaving and 3727 for shade 3, the second round of weaving.

6. When you have completed the embroidery in the next section, outline each petal with backstitch using 315, whipping it with E3685.

- Using stranded cotton 902 and bead 15° 1883, stitch beads along the exposed edges of each petal, spacing them apart and using the colour image as your guide.

7. Pad each of the semi-circles with horizontal satin stitch using 2 strands of 3053.

- Using 1 strand of the same thread, work vertical satin stitch over the padding.
- With 1 strand of 3051, work simple trellis couching over the satin stitch and outline the top edge with outline stitch using the same thread.

8. Using 2 strands of 3052, fill the leaf at the top of the flower with stain stitch. Start at the tip with a straight stitch, which extends to the top of the vein. Thereafter, work pairs of satin stitches which go into the vein, fanning around for the first few pairs, until you reach a diagonal angle, continuing at this angle to the bottom.

- Working with 2 strands of E898, couch down the vein of the leaf, continuing to the bottom for the stem. Work the two side branches and the semi-circle in the same way.

Flower 3

This flower appears on the top, left hand side of the embroidered panel, just below the leaf.

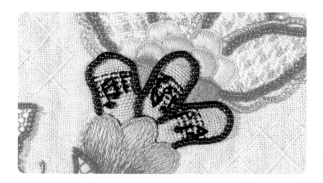

1. Referring to pattern 9 (music staves) in the needle weaving gallery, fill the centre of the flower with music staves. Use perlé #12.822 for colour 1 and 1 strand of 3021 for colour 2.

TOP TIP

Light Effects Metallic thread is inclined to stretch, particularly after washing. Make sure your stitches are tight and, if necessary, tighten it after washing and before quilting your project, by pulling from underneath and securing the threads with a single strand of cotton at the back.

2. Using the colour image as your guide, work the music notes using 2 strands of 3371 for the straight lines and beads 15° 5F for the dots.

3. When you have completed the embroidery that surrounds this area, outline the shapes with bead couching using beads 15° 1883 and stranded cotton 902.

4. Fill each of these leaves with checks and stripes 1, found in the needle weaving gallery. Use perlé #12. 822 for colour 1 and perlé #12.642 for colour 2.

5. Using bead 15° 459 and stranded cotton 934, outline the woven area with bead couching.
- Thereafter, couch a line of E3685 metallic thread immediately adjacent to the outside of the bead couched line.
- Using bead 15° 1631 and stranded cotton 3013, work bead couching on the outer outline of each petal.

6. Each of these shapes is filled with padded buttonhole stitch. The padding is horizontal satin stitch worked with two strands of thread whilst the buttonhole stitch is done with 1 strand and should fan around the shape. Use 3726 for the darkest, 316 for the medium and 3727 for the lightest semi-circles.

7. The three shapes at the top of this section are filled with long and short stitch shading using 1 strand of cotton. Starting at the base use 934, shading through 3051 and 3052 to 3726 at the tip.

- Outline each shape by couching two strands of E703 around the top edges as pictured in the colour image above.

8. Pad the calyx at the bottom with horizontal satin stitch using 2 strands of 3053.

- Using 1 strand of the same thread, work vertical satin stitch over the padding.
- With 1 strand of 3051, work simple trellis couching over the satin stitch.
- Outline the entire calyx with bead couching using 1 strand of 934 and bead 15H459.

Flower 4

This is the large flower at the bottom of the branch.

1. Referring to the needle weaving gallery, fill each of the 3 small leaves with checks and stripes 12. Use Sajou Dentelles 6844 for colour 1 and 6308 for colour 2.

- Outline each of the leaves with bead couching using bead 15° 459 and stranded cotton 934.

2. Fill the scalloped section at the top with lines of bead couching that radiate from the middle section to the outer edge. Using bead 15° 1631 and stranded cotton 3013, and working from the inside outwards, leave a very small space between each line at the beginning and a slightly larger space at the outer edge. Use the colour image as your guide.

- Using strands of the same thread, work a bullion knot between each of the bead lines.

3. With 2 strands each of 822 and 3013 threaded onto the needle at the same time, fill the middle section with 10-wrap French knots – great big knobbly things that create texture, spilling over the edge to cover the start of the bead couched lines and the 3 small leaves.

- Using stranded cotton 3013, stitch single beads 15° 459 and 11° 641 here and there, evenly spread, between the knots.

4. Referring to pattern 9 (music staves) in the needle weaving gallery, fill the centre of the flower with music staves. Use perlé #12.822 for colour 1 and 1 strand of 3021 for colour 2.

- Using the colour image as your guide, work the music notes using 2 strands of 3371 for the straight lines and beads 15° 5F for the dots.
- When you have completed the outer edge, work an outline of bead couching in the ditch using bead 15H459 and 1 strand of 934.

5. Work rows of chain stitch to fill the outer edge of these petals. Starting from the inside, work a complete row with 2 strands of 642. For two rows thereafter, and using the colour image as your guide, work incomplete rows that create the bulges of the outer edge.

- Change to 2 strands of 644, working two rows that follow the shape you have created.
- Change to 2 strands of 822, fill the rest of the outer edge with rows that follow the shape, adding extra short rows here and there if you need to adjust the shape along the way.
- Outline the outer edge with outline stitch using 1 strand of 3371. With the same thread stitch a single bead 15° 5F at intervals outside and adjacent to the outline stitch. Use the colour image as your guide.

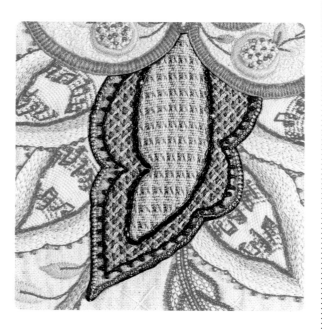

6. Working from the inside of this section and referring to the needle weaving gallery, fill each of these leaves with checks and stripes 4. Use perlé #12. 822 for colour 1 and perlé #12.642 for colour 2.

7. Moving outwards and referring to the embroidery stitches gallery fill this section with woven trellis using 2 strands throughout: 316 for shade 1; 3726 for shade 2; 822 for shade 3, the first round of weaving and 3727 for shade 3, the second round of weaving.

- Outline the outer edge with backstitch using 315, whipping it with E3685. Stitch a single bead 15° 1883 at evenly spaced intervals adjacent to and on the outside of the outline using a single strand of 315.
- Bead couch a line of beads 15H459 in the ditch between the weaving and the woven trellis. Use a single strand of 934.
- Thereafter, couch a line of E703 metallic thread immediately adjacent to the inside of the bead couching line.

8. Using bead 15° 1631 and stranded cotton 3013, work bead couching on the outer outline of this section. Couch a single strand of E3685 immediately adjacent to and on the outside of the bead couching.

- Fill the outer "skin" of each of the berries within this section with padded buttonhole stitch using 2 strands of cotton for the stem stitch padding and 1 strand for the buttonhole stitch, fanning it as you go around the circle. Use 3726 for the darker and 316 for the lighter berries on each side.
- Fill the insides of the berries with two layers of 2-wrap French knots using 1 strand each of 822 and 642 in the needle. With a single strand of 3371, intersperse the knots with evenly spaced single beads 15° 5F.

9. Each of the small leaves is worked with raised herringbone stitch using 2 strands of 3051 for those that attach to the stem, 3052 for the darker leaves that come out of the top of the berry, and 3053 for the lighter leaves.

- The veins and stems are couching worked with E898.

10. Fill the background with seeding done with 2 strands of 644.

11. Finally, work the border of the petals. Using 2 strands of 3726, work buttonhole stitch all the way around the border, leaving a gap between each stitch. Fill this gap with straight stitches using E3685. Start at the base, burying the end of the stitch under the ridge of the buttonhole.

- Using 1 strand of 3726, work outline stitch on the lower edge and adjacent to the buttonhole and straight stitch, to neaten up the bottom edge
- Using 1 strand of 902, work outline stitch all the way around the outer edge, adjacent to the ridge of the buttonhole stitch. Stitch a single bead 15° 1883 at intervals on the outside of the border that is exposed. Use the colour image as your guide.

Large leaves no. 1

There are two of these leaves:
- The first comes out of the branch at the top left of the design;
- The second comes out of the large flower at the bottom of the design.

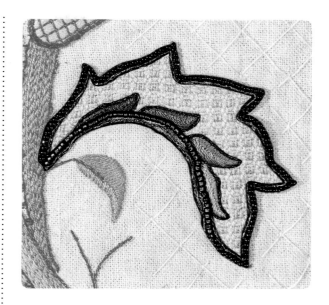

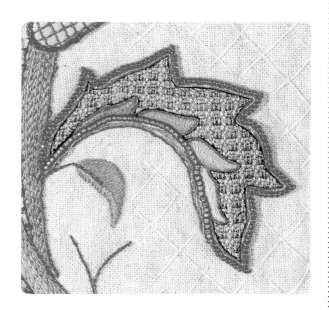

1. Referring to the gallery of needle weaving techniques, fill the main body of the leaf with checks and stripes 15. Use perlé #12.642 for colour 1 and perlé #12.524 for colour 2.

2. Fill each of the pink petals with raised herringbone stitch using 2 strands of thread. Starting at the tip, use 3727, moving through 316 and 3726 to 315 at the base. Couch an outline around each petal with E3685.

3. Starting at the base of the leaf, where it comes out of the stem, bead couch beads 15° 5F up the line that runs under the pink petals using 1 strand of 3371. When you get to the point where this bead line joins the lower outline of the leaf, start picking up beads 15° 459 and continue outlining the outer edge of the leaf until you get back down to where the leaf goes into the stem again.

- Couch a line of E703 along the lower outline and also between the bead line and the weaving, starting from the top of the lightest pink petal, continuing all the way around in the ditch and finishing where the green bead outline goes into the stem.
- Using 1 strand of 3021, work outline stitch below the metallic green along the lower outline and, also, on the inside of the couched metallic green line that is in the ditch between the bead outline and the weaving in the main body of the leaf.

Large leaves no. 2

There are two of these leaves:

- The first curls over the main branch at the top centre of the design;
- The second comes out of the large flower at the bottom right of the design.

1. Referring to the needle weaving gallery, fill each section of the leaf separately with checks and stripes 12. Use Sajou Dentelles 6844 for colour 1 and 6308 for colour 2.

1. Outline each section of the leaf with bead couching using bead 15° 459 and stranded cotton 934.

2. Outline each side of the vein with bead couching using 15° 5F and stranded cotton 3371.

- Couch a line of E703 metallic thread between the two lines of beads that form the vein. When doing the leaf at the top of the design, continue this line of couching along the branch that holds the leaf, until it joins the branch that it comes out of.

Tatted flowers

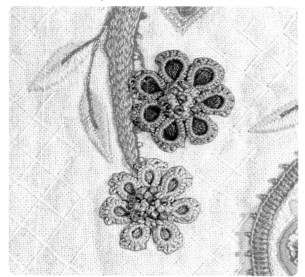

1. Referring to Rambling Vine Tatted Flowers in the tatting techniques gallery:

- The single tatted flower, which is at the top of the branch, is worked using variation 1 and perlé #12.778.
- The larger flower on the branch of two at centre left of the design is worked using variation 1 and perlé #12.316.
- The smaller flower on the branch of two at centre left of the design is worked using variation 2 and perlé #12.778.

2. Fill the centre of each flower with two layers of 2-wrap French knots using 2 strands of 3013 and 1 strand of 822 threaded on the needle on the same time.

- Stitch 7 beads 11° 641 here and there between the knots, spreading them evenly over the centre of each flower using 1 strand of 3013.

Branches, stems and leaves

1. The main branches are filled with two shades of chain stitch using 2 strand of cotton.

- Thread up two separate needles, the first with 3860 and the second with 3861. Work each segment of the main branch separately.
- Referring to the colour images and taking note of which side is which, come up on the edge of the darker side with the darker thread and work a line of chain stitch up that side.
- Work a line of chain stitch on the other side with the lighter thread.
- Keep working rows of dark and light chain stitch, alternately, until the rows meet up in the middle.
- Outline the outer edge of the lighter thread with outline stitch using 1 strand of 3371.

Once you have stitched any leaf stems that need to go into the main branch, place 15° 5F beads at intervals adjacent to the outline stitch.

- Couch an outline of E898 metallic thread up the darker side of each segment of the main branch.

2. The small ovate leaves, which appear throughout the design, are worked with raised herringbone stitch. Referring to the colour images as your guide, working with 2 strands of cotton, use 3051 for the dark leaves, 3052 for the medium and 3053 for the lighter leaves

- The stems and veins of all of the sets of leaves are couched with E898. Start within the leaves working the vein and continuing down into the stems without a break.
- Work tendrils that come out of the stems in the same way, always making sure that where any of the stems or branches join a branch or a stem, it is buried under what it joins.

The trellis couching background will be covered under Finishing at the end of these instructions.

THE INTERSECTION OF THE EMBROIDERY AND THE CRAZY PATCH PANELS

It is important to work and attach the tatted daisy intersection before moving onto the embellishment of the crazy patch panel, as the edge of the tatting will, in places, determine the placement of the stitching.

1. Referring to the instructions for the tatted daisy chain in the tatting gallery, work a chain of approximately 21 daisies using perlé #12.644.

- Placing it so that the centre line of the daisy chain corresponds to the join of the embroidery and crazy patch panels, pin it into place.
- Working with a single strand of stranded cotton 644 and starting at the bottom, stitch the daisy chain to the fabric base. Place a couching stitch over the base of all four petals, through the loop of each picot and over both sides of the picot that lies between each of the daisies.
- With a doubled over strand of the same thread on a beading needle, stitch a bead #1.2442 inside each petal and a single bead DPMix04 in the centre of each daisy.
- With 2 strands of stranded cotton 3727, work a lazy daisy stitch around each bugle bead.

2. Referring to the leaf of the spiral tatted flower in the tatting techniques gallery and using the 11 ds, p, 11 ds variation, work approximately 20 single leaves using perlé #12.524.

- Using the colour image as you guide, place and stitch each leaf between the daisies of the chain about ¼" (10 mm) from the join of the two panels. Catch the base of each leaf and stitch through the loop of the picot to secure it to the fabric. Also catch the sides of the leaves with a small couching stitch that goes between the double stitches about halfway up on each side.
- With stranded cotton 644, secure a bugle bead #1.2442 in the middle of each leaf.
- With 2 strands of stranded cotton 3053, work a lazy daisy stitch around each bugle bead.

EMBELLISHMENT INSTRUCTIONS: CRAZY PATCH PANEL

Every block has been described in detail. The order in which the blocks are described is not necessarily numerical. Many have been grouped out of sequence so that the embellishment is described in a logical way. Because of the nature of crazy patch, embellishment that may encroach on a block but starts inside another will be described in the block where it started.

Block 1

1. Fill the centre of the Jacobean flower with padded long and short stitch shading.

- Pad with lines of stem stitch using 2 strands of 3727.
- Work long and short stitch shading over the padding starting at the base with 1 strand of 644, working through 822 to 3861 at the top.
- Using 1 strand of 779, work trellis couching over the shading.

2. Pad the small wedge shape below the shaded area with horizontal satin stitch using 2 strands of 779. With a single strand of the same thread, work vertical satin stitch over the padding.

- When you have woven and outlined the calyx leaves, bead couch a line of bead 15° 5F in the ditch above the satin stitch, using a single strand of 3371.

3. With 2 strands of 640, pad the scallops above the shaded area. With a single strand of the same thread, work vertical, slightly fanned satin stitch over the padding. You should try to achieve an even outer edge at the top of the satin stitch. If this hasn't happened, outline the top edge of each scallop with outline stitch using the same thread.

- Using a single strand of 3371, work outline stitch in the ditch below the scallops. Stitch a single bead, at intervals, over the outline stitch, using the same thread.

4. Referring to the needle weaving gallery, fill each calyx leaf with checks and stripes 12. Use Sajou Dentelles 6844 for colour 1 and 6308 for colour 2.

- Bead couch an outline around each leaf using beads 15H459 and a single strand of 934.

TOP TIP

Padding is usually done with the same colour thread as the stitch that will go over it. When working shading, however, it is best to pad with a thread that is the same colour as the fabric base, to avoid confusion during the stitching of the shading.

5. To create the stem at the base of the flower bead couch a line of bead 15° 5F, using a single strand of 3371.

6. Using the colour image as your guide, work the three stamens at the top with fly stitch, which transitions into backstitch, using 1 strand of 3371, and stitching a single bead 15° 5F at the tip of each stamen using the same thread.

Blocks 2 and 6a

1. Referring to the combination embroidery and silk ribbon embroidery stitches gallery, work combination 09 along the border between block 1 and 2. Use 2 strands of 822 for the lazy daisy stitch, a single strand of E703 for the straight stitches and bead 11° 641. The lower straight stitch encroaches on block 1.

2. Referring to the needle lace techniques' gallery, work edging no. 7 using perlé #12. Ecru and 2 mm ribbon 21.

Start in the top left hand corner of block 7a and finish in the top right hand corner of 6a.

3. Starting in the bottom left corner of block 6a and using the colour image as your guide, work combination 02 along the bottom edge, turning the corner on the right, continuing up the right hand side until you reach the edge of the needle lace and finishing on the side of the needle lace, encroaching on block 6b.

- Working with 2 strands of cotton throughout, use 3053 for the lighter green chevron stitch, 3015 for the darker green chevron stitch, 452 for the lighter lazy daisy trefoils and 451 for the darker trefoils.
- Place bead 15° 459 at the base of the darker and 15° 1631 at the base of the lighter chevron stitches.

Blocks 6b, 5 and 4

1. Referring to the combination embroidery and silk ribbon embroidery stitches gallery, work combination 19 along the lower edge of block 6b. The first flower on the left will end just under the chevron stitch combination, which encroaches from block 6a into 6b.

2. Use ribbon 4mm 135 for the pink flowers and 2 mm 32 for the leaves.

3. Use 2 strands of 3051 to work the straight stitches that form the veins of the leaves and the stems of the flowers.

4. Referring to the needle lace techniques' gallery, work needle lace edging 8 on the border of block 4 that runs along the sides of blocks 1 and 3. Use perlé #12.Ecru.

- With the same thread, whip the top row of backstitch that is the anchor for the needle lace.
- Using a single strand of 822, attach the picot at the bottom of the edging to the fabric block. Stretch the lace downwards as you do this and then stitch a bead 11° 577 over the tip of the picot.
- If the needle lace edging has not stretched evenly, work a few invisible couching stitches over some of the rows of needle lace, using 1 strand of 822 and keeping going until you are happy that it is lying flat and even.
- Referring to the colour image to guide you, attach a pair of beads 11° 577, one at a time, above each area made up of single detached buttonhole stitches in the needle lace edge. Use 822 and come up above the whipped backstitch, returning into the fabric below the whipped back stitch.

TOP TIP

The single strand trellis couching that forms the background in blocks 1, 7b, 11b, 12b, 24, 20b, 21a, 25 is worked in the finishing process and instructions are found in that section.

5. Moving to block 5, work stitch combination 01 on the border that joins the sides of blocks 1 and 4, making provision for the lace edge in block 4 by missing parts of the stitch combination as you work along to the end.

- Use 2 strands of 822 for the lighter chevron stitch, S469 for the darker, placing an 822 lazy daisy stitch above and below the green stitches and a bead 11° 641 above and below the light chevron stitch.
- In the space available on the border that joins block 6b, work stitch combination 13. Use S3685 for the up and down buttonhole stitch, E703 for the lazy daisy stitches and stranded cotton 3727 for the extended French knots.

Blocks 3, 7a and 7b

1. Referring to the combination stitches in the techniques' galleries, work stitch combination 07 along the edge that is common with blocks 1 and 2. Use 3726 with beads 15° 1883 for the herringbone stitch, 3860 and 3861 for the double lazy daisy stitch and beads 15H459 for the additional line of vertical beads.

2. Referring to the needle weaving gallery, fill the main section of the leaf in block 7a with checks and stripes 12. Use Sajou Dentelles 6844 for colour 1 and 6308 for colour 2.

- Bead couch the vein and stem of the leaf using beads 15° 5F and a single strand of 3371.
- Bead couch an outline around the leaf using beads 15° 459 and a single strand of 934.
- Bead couch the tendrils on the right of the leaf using beads 15° 1631 and a single strand of 3013.

3. Using 2 mm ribbon 21 work the main branch of the rose creeper that goes up the borders on the right of 7 a and 7b with whipped backstitch.

- Using the colour image as your guide, each leaf is a silk ribbon stitch done with 4 mm ribbon 36. The veins and leaf stems are straight stitches done with 2 strands of 934.
- The rose buds are done with silk ribbon stitch using 4 mm ribbon 98. Working with 2 strands of 934, do a fly stitch around each pink ribbon stitch, combined with a straight stitch down the middle of the pink ribbon to make the calyx of each bud. The leg of the fly stitch should be long enough to become a stem that joins the bud to other stems.

4. Work stitch combination 4 along the border between blocks 7a and b, tailing off when you reach the rose branch. Use 3052 for the short Cretan stitch, 822 for the long Cretan stitch, 3051 for the backstitches on the intersections of the Cretan stitches, bead 11° 577 at the tips of the long stitches and bead 15° 459 at the tips of the short stitches.

5. Referring to the beading gallery, make:

- 5 x 4-bead flowers using bead DB11-1016 and burgundy beading thread;
- 6 x 10-bead leaves using bead 15° 1631 and Ash beading thread.
- Referring to the guidelines in the beading gallery for attaching flowers and leaves to fabric, and using the colour image as your guide, attach the flowers and leaves to the border between blocks 7a, 3, 4 and blocks 8a and b. Add twigs that are made up of 4 to 6 x 15° beads 5F, with a bead 11° 577 at the tip.
- Stitch a bead 11° 577 in the centre of each flower.

Blocks 8a and b; 10a, b, and c

1. The leaves are worked with raised herringbone stitch. Referring to the colour images as your guide, working with 2 strands of cotton, use 3051 for the dark leaves, 3052 for the medium and 3053 for the lighter leaves.

TOP TIP

It is best to attach 3-dimensional components, like tatted or beaded flowers and leaves, after all other embroidery is complete. If they are stitched in place before that, you will catch your threads while stitching.

- The stems and veins are couched with E898. Start within the leaves working the vein and continuing down into the stems without a break.
- Work the tendrils that come out of the stems in the same way, making sure that where they go into the stem, the join is buried under the stem.

2. Using two strands of S3685, work up and down buttonhole stitch on the border between blocks 8a and b, going under the stem of the leaves making the gap as invisible as you can.

3. Starting in the far left corner of block 10a, work stitch combination 12 on that edge, continuing along the top edges of 10 b and c. Use 1 strand of S469 for the whipped stems and leaves and 2 strands of 452 for the trefoil flowers. Leave gaps where you encounter the stems and leaves, making those gaps as invisible as you can.

4. Work the same stitch combination between blocks 10b and c, using the same green thread for the stems and leaves. Use 2 strands of 316 for the trefoil flowers.

5. Using 2 strands of 3053, work a short line of feather stitch between blocks 10 a and b. Stitch single beads 15° 459 at the tip of each feather stitch.

Blocks 9a and b; 11a and b

1. Referring to the gallery of needle lace techniques and to the colour image, work edging 7 facing into block 11a, using perlé #12.Ecru and 2 mm ribbon 32.

2. Working combination stitch 16, using purple silk ribbon 2 mm 72 for the flower stitch and green silk ribbon 2 mm 32 for the leaf stitches, place seedlings facing into 9a and b along the top of the needle lace edge. Use a single strand of 934 to work the fly stitch calyxes, the stems and the veins of the leaf. With the same thread work outline stitch along the tip of the needle lace edge.

3. With 2 strands of 934, work the trellis couching in block 9a. With 2 strands of 640, and using the colour image as your guide, work Sorbello stitch between the trellis couching and the two edges.

4. Work stitch combination 11 on the border between 11b and 9b, continuing down the border between 11b and 11 a – but eliminating one pink lazy daisy stitch – see colour image. Use 2 strands of 3726, 1 strand of E703 and bead 11° 577.

5. The stem of the spray of flowers in block 11a is whipped backstitch worked with 2 mm silk ribbon 32.

- At the tip of the right hand stem is a 6-bead flower made with beads DB11-624 and pink beading thread. Using the same beads and thread, work a 4-bead flower for the tip of the left stem.
- The centre stem needs a 4-bead flower worked with DB11-109 and cream thread. Place a bead 11° 641 in the centre of each of the flowers.
- Work 3 x 8-bead leaves with 15H459 beads and olive thread, placing them on the stems, using the colour image as your guide.

6. Referring to the spiral tatted flower and leaf in the tatting gallery, work the following:
- Variation 1 (7ds) perlé #12.3042
- Variation 1 (7ds) perlé #12.778
- Variation 1 (9ds) perlé #12.316
- Variation 1 (11ds) perlé #12.778
- Variation 1 (11ds) perlé #12.Ecru
- Variation 2 perlé #12.Ecru
- Variation 2 perlé #12.316
- Variation 2 perlé #12.3042
- In addition to the above, work about two dozen leaves of varying sizes using perlé #12.524.
- Using the colour image as your guide, attach the flowers and leaves along the edge of 9b on the side that intersects with 7a and b. Place a drop bead DP 454 in the centre of each flower.

Blocks 12a and b

1. Starting on the left top of block 6b adjacent to the top of the chevron stitch combination, work stitch combination 20 to the right. When you get to the corner, carry on down the side of block 6b where it intersects with blocks 12a and b, until you are adjacent to the tip of one of the pink ribbon flowers. Use 2 strands of 822 for the feather stitch, 3053 for the lazy daisy stitches with beads 15° 5F and 15° 1631.

2. Work part of stitch combination 7 along the borders of 12 a and b using 3726 and bead 15° 1883 for the herringbone stitch. Use 3051 and 3053 for the double lazy daisy stitch. Do not add the additional line of vertical beads.

Blocks 23a, b and 24

1. Encroaching onto blocks 20a, 16 and 17, work stitch combination 05 along the border of blocks 23a and b. Use 3861 for the short Cretan stitch, 822 for the long Cretan stitch and 3860 for the vertical backstitches on the intersections of the Cretan stitches. Add an additional straight stitch in the diamond shapes created in the pattern using E703. Stitch single bead 11° 641 at the tips of the long stitches and bead 15° 1631 at the tips of the short stitches.

2. Referring to points (9) and (10) of flower 4 in the embroidery panel, work the leaf and berry stem that roams over blocks 23a, 24, 13a and 13b in the same way, using the same threads and beads.

3. Work stitch combination 17 on the bottom border of block 23b using 2 mm ribbons 72 and 32 for the ribbon stitches and 1 strand of 934 for the thread embroidery stitches.

4. Making provision for the stem that runs through it, work stitch combination 10 on the border between blocks 24/23a and blocks 13a/b. Use 2 strands of 3726 for the horizontal lazy daisy stitches, E703 for the bottom lazy daisy and top diagonal straight stitches. With the same thread, work a straight stitch on the line of the border between each group. Use E3685 for the top vertical and bottom diagonal straight stitches. The bead is 11° 577.

Blocks 13a, b, c and d

1. Using 2 strands of 316, work a line of knotted cable chain stitch adjacent to the needle lace that is at the top of blocks 7b and 6a. Place a single 2 mm pearl inside the loop of each chain stitch.

2. Using the colour image as your guide and referring to stitch combination 12, work vertical individual lazy daisy and whipped backstitch stems starting adjacent to the knotted cable chain stitch. Use S469 for the stems and leaves. The trefoil flowers are, alternately, light and dark. Use 452 for the light and 451 for the dark trefoils.

3. Using 2 strands of 640, work a line of whipped backstitch up each of the stems depicted in block 13b.

• Turning to the tatting techniques' gallery and referring to the trefoil flower, work 3 x variation 1 flowers using perlé #12.822. Lining up the centre of each flower with the circle at the top of each stem, attach the flowers as instructed, placing a drop bead DPMix04 in each centre.

- Referring to the tatted leaves, the instructions for which are to be found under spiral tatted flowers and leaves, work 6 x 5ds leaves using perlé #12.524. Attach them individually about halfway up on each side of the stems.

4. Moving to block 13c, work stitch combination 10 on the border between blocks 13b/c and 13c/12a. Use 2 strands of 3726 for the horizontal lazy daisy stitches, E703 for the top diagonal straight stitches and E3685 for the top vertical and bottom diagonal straight stitches. The bead is 11° 577.

5. Referring to the beading techniques' gallery, work the following bead flowers and leaves:

- 1 x 10-bead flower using bead DB11-109 and cream beading thread;
- 2 x 6-bead flowers using bead DB11-109 and cream beading thread;
- 1 x 6-bead flower using bead DB11-108 and burgundy beading thread;
- 1 x 8-bead flower using bead DB11-108 and burgundy beading thread;
- 1 x 8-bead flower using bead DB11-624 and pink beading thread;
- 5 x 10-bead leaves using DB11-24 (15° 459 – see Tips) and olive beading thread.
- 3 x 12-bead leaves using DB11-24 (15° 459 – see Tips) and olive beading thread.
- 2 x 14-bead leaves using DB11-24 (15° 459 – see Tips) and olive beading thread.
- 5 x 10-bead leaves using 15° 1631 and ash beading thread.
- 2 x 12-bead leaves using 15° 1631 and ash beading thread.
- 1 x 14-bead leaves using 15° 1631 and ash beading thread.
- You will only want to attach the flowers and leaves when you have finished all the embroidery. Using the colour image as your guide, place and stitch them, spreading over blocks 13c and 17.
- The centre of each flower is 1 to 5 stamens consisting of 3 to 5 beads 15° 5F with a 2 mm glass pearl at the tip.
- With the thread tails – using more thread if necessary – work twigs radiating from the components. These consist of beads 15° 5F for the stalks, with a bead 11° 641 at the tip. Vary the number of beads in the stalk to fit in with what you need to have for the placement of the twig.

6. Using 2 strands of 934, work a line of knotted cable chain stitch on the border between blocks 13 c and d. Place a single 2 mm pearl inside the loop of each chain stitch.

7. Using the colour image as your guide, work stitch combination 16 on either side of the knotted cable chain stitch. Use 2 mm 72 and 32 for the silk ribbon stitches and 1 strand of 934 for the thread work.

Block 14

1. Pad each of the grapes with horizontal satin stitch using 2 strands of cotton. Thereafter, work single strand vertical satin stitch over the padding. Use 779 for the single dark grape and 452 for the 3 x light grapes. The very top grape is worked with 451. The one that is directly below that one is worked with 3860, followed by 451 again for the grape directly below. The grape at the bottom is worked with 3861.

2. Using the colour image as your guide, fill the woven blocks within the leaf with needle weaving checks and stripes 12. Use Sajou Dentelles 6844 for colour 1 and 6308 for colour 2.

TOP TIP

Delica beads are quite bulky if used at the tip of a Delica-bead leaf. When picking up the first row of beads, instead of a Delica, pick up a size 15° bead of the same colour at the end of that row, then carry on as normal.

- Work the lines that outline the woven blocks and continue through the inner leaf with whipped backstitch using the dark green Sajou thread.
- With 1 strand of 934, work two large diagonal straight stitches (or part thereof) with a small couching stitch over the intersection in the wider vacant blocks.
- Using the same thread, stitch a single bead 15° 459 in the remaining, square vacant blocks.
- Starting from the inner edge, work a row of chain stitch in the border around the leaf using 2 strands of 3052, followed by the outside row worked with 2 strands of 3052. Outline both edges of the chain stitch with outline stitch using 1 strand of 934.
- Fill the branch of the leaf with rows of chain stitch using 2 strands of 3051.

Blocks 17 and 18

1. Work combination stitch 21 on the border between block 17 and 16/14. Use 4 mm 135 and 36 for the silk ribbon stitches, 2 strands of 934 for the feather, fly and straight stitches and 2 strands of 822 for the French knots.

2. Starting in the corner that forms the intersections of blocks 17, 18 and 13c, work needle lace edging 3 along blocks 18, 19 and 21b, facing into those blocks and bordering on 13 c and d. Use perlé #12.Ecru and 2 mm ribbon 32.

- Using 2 strands of 779, work a line of feather stitch along the top edge of the needle lace, encroach on the lace and also, on blocks 13 c/d. Stitch a single bead 15° 1631 at the tip of each stitch using 1 strand of 3013.

3. Work stitch combination 12 on the border between blocks 18 and 14 using S469 for the stems and leaves along with 2 strands of 316 for the trefoil flowers.

Blocks 15 and 16

1. Referring to the Blocks 6b, 5 and 4 instruction (2), and using the same thread and beads, work needle lace edging 8 along the short border between 15 and 16.

- Using 2 strands of 779, work a line of feather stitch along the border between 15 and 14. Don't encroach on the leaf in block 14, leaving a gap or stitching 'half-stitches' where possible. Stitch a single bead 15° 1631 at the tip of each stitch using 1 strand of 3013.

2. From the point at which block 15 intersects with blocks 14 and 16, work stitch combination 13 on the border between 14 and 16. Use S3685 for the up and down buttonhole stitch, E703 for the lazy daisy stitches and stranded cotton 3727 for the extended French knots.

3. Referring to the beading gallery, make:

- 2 x 6-bead flowers using bead DB11-1016 and burgundy beading thread;
- 6 x 10-bead leaves using bead 15° 1631 and Ash beading thread.
- Referring back to the instructions for the flowers along the top edge of blocks 8a and b, when you have finished the rest of the embellishment of the crazy patch panel, attach them in the same way, with the same twigs and centres. Use the colour image above for placement guidance.

Blocks 20a and b

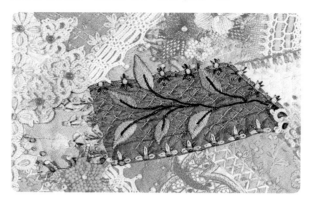

1. Referring to the combination embroidery and silk ribbon embroidery stitches gallery, work combination 19 along the border between block 20a and b. Use ribbon 4mm 135 for the pink flowers and 2 mm 32 for the leaves. Use 2 strands of 3051 to work the straight stitches that form the veins of the leaves and the stems of the flowers.

2. Referring to points (9) and (10) of flower 4 in the embroidery panel, work the leaf stem that roams over block 20b and encroaches on blocks 25 and 26, in the same way, using the same threads and beads.

- Work stitch combination 09 along the bottom border of block 20b, using the same threads and beads that you used for the same combination stitch on the border between blocks 1 and 2.
- Making provision for the stem that runs through it, work stitch combination 10 on the border between block 20b and blocks 25/26, continuing down the side of block 21a. Use 2 strands of 3726 for the horizontal lazy daisy stitches, S469 for the bottom lazy daisy and the top diagonal straight stitches. With the same thread, work a straight stitch on the line of the border between each group. Use E3685 for the top vertical and bottom diagonal straight stitches. The bead is 11° 577

Blocks 19, 21a and b, 22

1. Work stitch combination 13 on the border between 21a and 30/34. Use S3685 for the up and down buttonhole stitch, E703 for the lazy daisy stitches and stranded cotton 3727 for the extended French knots.

2. Work stitch combination 07 on the opposite border between blocks 21a and b. Use 3726 with beads 15° 1883 for the herringbone stitch, 451 and 452 for the double lazy daisy stitch and beads 15H459 for the additional line of vertical beads.

3. Work block 22 as you did block 9a. Using the colour image as your guide, work stitch combination 16 on either side of the Sorbello stitch. Use 2 mm 72 and 32 for the silk ribbon stitches and 1 strand of 934 for the thread work.

4. Referring to the spiral tatted flower and leaf in the tatting gallery, work the following:

- Variation 1 (9ds) perlé #12.316 x 2
- Variation 1 (9ds) perlé #12. Ecru x 1
- Variation 1 (11ds) perlé #12.778 x 1
- Variation 2 perlé #12.778 x 1
- In addition to the above, work about 22 leaves of varying sizes using perlé #12.524.

- Using the colour image as your guide, attach the flowers and leaves along the edge between blocks 19 and 21b. Place a drop bead DP 454 in the centre of each flower.

5. Once you have placed the tatted flowers, work about 5 lazy daisy trefoil flowers in the available space on the border between 21a and b. Use 822 and place E 3685 straight stitches between the lazy daisy petals.

6. Work stitch combination 01 on the border opposite the tatting flowers using 3052 and then 822 for the chevron stitches, E703 for the lazy daisy and straight stitches and bead 11° 641.

Blocks 25, 26, 27 and 31

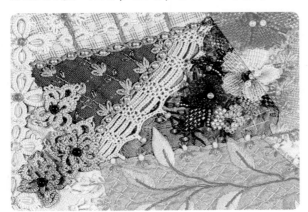

1. With 2 strands of 934, work feather stitch on the border between 25 and 26. Place a bead 11° 641 on the tip of each stitch.

2. Referring to the Blocks 6b, 5 and 4 (2), and using the same thread and beads, work needle lace edging 8 along the short border between blocks 25/26 and 27.

3. Work stitch combination 12 on the vertical lines in this block. Use S469 and 2 strands of 452.

4. Using 2 strands of 3861, work knotted cable chain along the top border of block 27, continuing to the end of the block 25/26 lace edge. Work a second line along the top of the lace edge. Stitch single 2 mm glass pearls into the loop of each chain.

5. The two sides of block 31 require tatted spiral flowers and leaves as under, attached as you have previous arrangements:

- Variation 1 (7ds) perlé #12.778 x 1
- Variation 1 (9ds) perlé #12.316 x 1
- Variation 2 perlé #12.3042 x 1
- About 9 leaves in a variety of sizes using perlé #12.524.

6. Following the guidelines set down for block 13c (5), blocks 25 and 29 accommodate a similar spray of flowers, which will be attached at the end. You will need the following flowers and leaves:

- 1 x 10-bead flower using bead DB11-108 and burgundy beading thread;
- 1 x 8-bead flower using bead DB11-109 and cream beading thread;
- 1 x 8-bead flower using bead DB11-624 and pink beading thread;
- 1 x 6-bead flower using bead DB11-108 and burgundy beading thread;
- 1 x 4-bead flower using bead DB11-109 and cream beading thread;
- 1 x 4-bead flower using bead DB11-624 and pink beading thread;
- 6 x 10-bead leaves using DB11-24 (15° 459 – see Tips) and olive beading thread.
- 5 x 12-bead leaves using 15° 1631 and ash beading thread.
- Flower centres and stamens are the same as block 13c.

Blocks 28, 29 and 32

1. Referring to the instructions for block 13b (3), work the same arrangement using 3021 for the whipped backstitch stems, perlé #12.778 for the tatted trefoil flowers perlé #12.524 for 6 x 7ds leaves and 2 x 5 ds leaves.

2. Work stitch combination 09 along the bottom edge of block 32 using 3860 for the lazy daisy petals, E703 for the straight stitches and bead 11° 641.

3. Work stitch combination 04 on the border of 28 and 29 using 315 for the first line of cretan stitch and 3053 for the second. Use E703 for the straight stitches finally adding beads 15° 1883 and 1631.

Blocks 30 and 33

1. Work needle lace edging 7 along the border between blocks 30 and 34 using perlé #12.Ecru and 2 mm ribbon 21.
2. Work featherstitch on the bottom border of 33 encroaching on 29 and 30, including over the side of the lace edging. Use 3860 and stitch a single bead 15° 1631 at the tip of each stitch.
3. Work stitch combination 12 up the border between block 30 and 25/29. Use S469 for the stems and leaves and 2 strands of 451 for the trefoil flowers.

Blocks 34 and 35

1. Using 2 strands of 934, work a line of knotted cable chain stitch on the border between blocks 34 and 30/33. Place a single 2 mm pearl inside the loop of each chain stitch.
2. Referring to the instructions for block 13b (3), work the same arrangement using 3021 for the whipped backstitch stems, perlé #12.822 for the tatted trefoil flowers perlé #12.524 for 4 x 7ds leaves and 2 x 9 ds leaves (centre stem) which are placed diagonally at the bottom of each stem.
3. Work the spider's web with 1 strand of 822 and 1 strand of 3000 Glamour #12 threaded on the needle at the same time. The spokes are long couched stitches. When these are in place, using the colour image as your guide and starting from the centre, whip over each spoke in a circle. Work a second circle further out. The spider is a 5-wrap French knot and a 2-wrap Frend knot worked with 2 strands of 3371.
4. Work a vertical line of stitch combination 18 up the border between blocks 34 and 35. Use 4 mm ribbons 135 and 36, along with 1 strand of 934 for the leaf veins and 1 strand of S469 for the stems.

FINISHING OFF

Referring to the finishing techniques gallery, you now need to stabilize your crazy patchwork.

1. Cut a piece of cotton voile that is at least 8″ (200 mm) larger than the outer measurements of your project. This will allow a border of 3″ (75 mm) all the way around with extra space to re-stretch the project in the frame.

2. Cut a piece of batting that is the same size as the cotton voile.

3. On a large, flat surface place the voile, followed by the batting and then the crazy patchwork/ embroidery project.

4. Place a few pins, here and there, all over the project, pinning the three layers together. Replace the pins with large tacking stitches, as the sandwiched layers will need to stretch when you place them in an embroidery frame.

5. Pin and tack all the way around the outer four edges.

6. Add the border:

- Cut four 22″ x 2½″ (560 x 65 mm) strips using fabric 14.
- Referring to the butt joint instructions in the finishing gallery, attach these strips to each side of your project, machine stitching through the sandwiched layers.
- Stitch the outside edges of the border down with zig-zag stitch, to keep it stable when you put it back into the embroidery frame.

7. Stretch the sandwiched project in the embroidery frame.

- Secure the beads and work the block intersections as instructed in the finishing techniques gallery.
- Referring to the colour images and to the guidelines for trellis couching in the finishing instructions work the following backgrounds, with a single straight stitch over each intersection:
  · Embroidery panel: 2 strands 3033;
  · Blocks 7b & 20b: 1 strand 451;
  · Blocks 1, 11b, 12b and 25: 1 strand 3727;
  · Blocks 8a, 12a, 21a & 24: 1 strand 3033
- Working with 1 strand of 315, work a straight running stitch on the border, all the way around and about ³/₆₄″ (1 mm) from the inside edge.
- Using the same thread, work meandered running stitch over the entire border, using the colour images as your guide.

8. Making sure that its width is the same on all four sides, trim the sandwiched layers back to the edge of the border.

9. Following the instructions for the continuous binding in the finishing techniques gallery, add a binding with a casing added for the hanging rod, using fabric 15.

Savannah winter

The original of this design measures 9⅔ x 7⅞"
(245 x 200 mm) and has been used as the lid
of a covered storage basket, the top of which
measures 9½ x 7½" (240 x 190 mm). Instructions
on how to make a basket cover are at the end of
the embellishment instructions.

Materials

FOUNDATION FABRIC AND BATTING

15¾ x 15¾" (400 x 400 mm) stable linen or cotton foundation fabric;

20" (½ m) cotton voile;

20" (½ m) lightweight polyester batting.

100% COTTON QUILTING FABRICS

Fabric 1
6 in² (250 mm²)
- Block 1
- Block 10
- Block 16c
- Block 18b

Fabric 2
6 in² (250 mm²)
- Block 11

Fabric 3
6 in² (250 mm²)
- Block 3

Fabric 4
6 in² (250 mm²)
- Block 4
- Block 13

Fabric 5
6 in² (250 mm²)
- Block 2
- Block 5
- Block 13

Fabric 6
6 in² (250 mm²)
- Block 6
- Block 9
- Block 18a

Fabric 7
6 in² (250 mm²)
- Block 7a
- Block 12
- Block 15c

Fabric 8
6 in² (250 mm²)
- Block 7b
- Block 16a

Fabric 9
½ yd (½ m)
- Block 16b
- Block 17
- Basket Cover Base

Fabric 10
6 in² (250 mm²)
- Block 15b

Fabric 11
6 in² (250 mm²)
- Block 8
- Block 15a

Fabric 12
6 in² (250 mm²)
- Block 14

Fabric 13
- A Fat Quarter
- Continuous Binding
- Basket Lid Lining

The 14" hoop of a Morgan Lap Stand was used to stretch the crazy stitch panel during the embellishment process of this project.

Unless otherwise instructed use:
- A standard good quality machine sewing thread in a golden colour, a size 70 needle and the standard foot for the crazy patch. (We don't supply these in our kits.)
- two strands of thread when working with stranded cotton;
- one strand of thread when working with perlé cotton, special dentelles and Diamant thread;
- one strand of stranded cotton, doubled over and threaded onto a bead embroidery needle for the bead embroidery;
- one strand of beading thread for the beadwork.

The design is divided into sections. Each section has been described in detail.

HAND STITCHING NEEDLES

Size 7	Embroidery Needle
Size 10	Embroidery Needle
Size 10	Bead Embroidery Needle
Size 12	Bead Embroidery Needle
Size 22	Chenille Needle
Size 26	Tapestry Needle

THREADS AND RIBBONS

DMC STRANDED COTTON
1 skein each:

422	Light Hazelnut Brown
433	Medium Brown
434	Light Brown
436	Tan
437	Light Tan
926	Medium Grey Blue
928	Very Light Grey Blue
3011	Dark Khaki Green
3012	Medium Khaki Green
3013	Light Khaki Green
3041	Medium Antique Violet
3042	Light Antique Violet
3354	Light Dusty Rose
3731	Very Dark Dusty Rose
3733	Dusty Rose
3740	Dark Antique Violet
3866	Ultra Very Light Mocha Brown

DMC PERLÉ COTTON #12

437	Light Tan
927	Light Grey Blue

DI VAN NIEKERK'S HAND PAINTED SILK RIBBON
2mm:

32	Sunny Green

LIZBETH TATTING COTTON #40

603	Ecru

LIZBETH TATTING COTTON #80

626	Light Shell Pink
627	Medium Shell Pink
639	Light Antique Violet
640	Medium Antique Violet

BEADS

SWAROVSKI 34SS 2028 FLATBACK RHINESTONES

246	7 beads	Light Colorado Topaz

MIYUKI BEADS
Round Rocailles

15° 26F	2g	Matte Silver Lined Olive
15° 457L	2g	Metallic Bronze Light
15° 556	2g	Rose Silver Lined Alabaster
15° 1627	2g	Semi-Matte SL Light Cranberry
15° 1631	2g	Semi-Matte Silver Lined Saffron
15° 1650	2g	Semi-Matte Silver Lined Lavender
15° 1655	2g	Semi-Matte Silver Lined Mulberry
15° 2422F	2g	Matte Silver Lined Topaz
15° 2442	6g	Crystal Ivory Gold Luster
8° 2035	2g	Matte Metallic Khaki Iris

3 mm Cube Beads

SB3.2035	2g	Matte Metallic Khaki Iris

3.4 mm Drop Beads

DP251	2g	Light Gold Crystal AB

3 mm Bugle Beads #1

#1.26	2g	Silver Lined Olive

ADDITIONAL FOR BASKET COVER

8mm Wooden Dowel Rod (cut to size)
2 x 20" (½ m) 25 mm satin ribbon
1¼ yd (1 m) ¼" (6 mm) wide elastic

CRAZY PATCHWORK INSTRUCTIONS

Referring to the instructions for paper-pieced crazy patch-work in the crazy patchwork techniques gallery, you will need 4 photocopies of the crazy patchwork pattern for Savannah winter in the back section of this book.

- Using the first photocopy, cut out all of the paper patches;
- Referring to the fabrics listed above, place and pin each paper template onto the relevant fabric;
- Cut out the patches. Make sure that you leave a **seam allowance of at least ¼" (6 mm)** all the way around each template.
- When trimming that patches at the end of each step in the joining process, **do not trim away the seam allowance on any of the patches that are placed on any of the four outer edges of the panel.** You will need them for the assembly of the project.

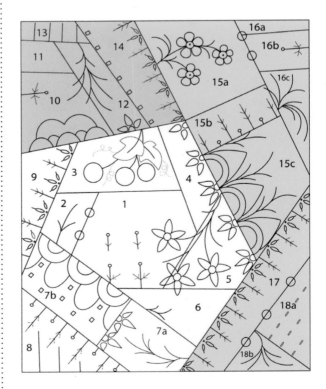

Referring to the white area in diagram above, using the second photocopy as the foundation onto which you will stitch the patches:

- Place and stitch block 1;
- With right sides together place and stitch block 2. Flip, trim and press with an iron;
- With right sides together, place and stitch block 3 on the edge created by blocks 2 and 3. Flip, trim and press with an iron;
- With right sides together, place and stitch block 4 on the edge created by blocks 3 and 1. Flip, trim and press with an iron;
- With right sides together, place and stitch block 5 on the edge created by blocks 4 and 1. Flip, trim and press with an iron;
- With right sides together, place and stitch block 6 on the edge created by blocks 5 and 1. Flip, trim and press with an iron;
- With right sides together, join blocks 7a and 7b to create a strip. With right sides together, place and stitch blocks 7a and 7b on the edge created by blocks 6, 1 and 2. Flip, trim and press with an iron;
- With right sides together, place and stitch block 8 on the edge created by blocks 7a and 7b. Flip, trim and press with an iron;With right sides together, place and stitch block 9 on the edge created by blocks 7b, 2 and 3. Flip, trim and press with an iron.

Referring to the lilac area in diagram above, and using the third photocopy which you have cut out, with a generous border, and which you are going to use as the foundation for this section of the panel:

- Place and stitch block 10;
- With right sides together, place and stitch block 11. Flip, trim and press with an iron;
- With right sides together, place and stitch block 12 on the edge created by blocks 10 and 11. Flip, trim and press with an iron;
- With right sides together, place and stitch block 13 on the edge created by blocks 11 and 12. Flip, trim and press with an iron;
- With right sides together, place and stitch block 14 on the edge created by blocks 13 and 12. Flip and press with an iron.

Remove the foundation paper from the back. With right sides together, place and stitch the edge created by blocks 10, 12 and 14 to the edge of the original panel created by blocks 9, 3 and 4. Flip, trim and press with an iron.

Referring to the grey area in diagram above and using the fourth photocopy which you have cut out, with a generous border, and which you are going to use as the foundation for this section of the panel:

- With right sides together, join blocks 15a, 15b and 15c to create a strip;
- Place and stitch them to the paper;
- With right sides together, join blocks 16a, 16b and 16c to create a strip;
- With right sides together, place and stitch the strip the edge created by blocks 15a, 15b and 15c. Flip, trim and press with an iron.

Remove the foundation paper from the back. With right sides together, place and stitch the edge created by blocks 15a, 15b and 15c to the edge of the existing panel created by blocks 14, 4 and 5. Flip and press with an iron.

Referring to the green area in diagram above and working on the original foundation paper:

- With right sides together, place and stitch block 17 on the edge created by blocks 15c, 5, 6 and 7a. Flip and press with an iron;
- With right sides together, join blocks 18a and 18b to create a strip;
- With right sides together, join this strip to the edge created by block 17.

Remove the foundation paper, press the entire panel with an iron. Keeping it as flat as possible and following the directions at the end of the paper piecing section in the crazy patch techniques gallery, attach the panel to the foundation panel taking note of the following:

- Calculate the parameters of the embellishment according to the size of the basket that you wish to cover. Buy one from one of your local suppliers (because you can't order one from us. Some countries have strict quarantine laws and they don't like grass or wooden products from Africa, because of nasty bugs that we have, that burrow into and eat things). Try to find one with outside measurements as close as possible to those we have use and adjust where necessary, working your tacking lines according to your own basket, not mine.

- Make sure that the foundation fabric fits into the hoop you are going to use for stretching the panel during the embellishment process. If you use the recommended size of hoop, you should be able to expose the entire panel, not having to move it and damage beads and stitching in doing so.

EMBELLISHMENT INSTRUCTIONS

Every block has been described in detail. Because of the nature of crazy patch, embellishment that may encroach on a block but starts inside another will be described in the block where it started. Likewise, stitching on the edges of the blocks will be described in the instructions for one of those blocks.

Block 1

1. Referring to the trefoil flower in the tatting techniques gallery make the following:
- 2 x trefoil flowers variation 1 using Lizbeth #80 626;
- 2 x trefoil flowers variation 2 using Lizbeth #80 627.
- Stitch the flowers into place using the small circles at the top of the four stems as the guide for placement. Stitch a bead 8° 2035 in the centre.

- Following the instructions for twisted couching in the embroidery techniques gallery, work twisted couching over the upright stems using stranded cotton 434.
- The leaves coming out of the stems are silk ribbon stitches done with 2mm.32. The veins and short leaf stems are straight stitches done with a single strand of 434.

2. The lace edging on the side that abuts block 3 is needle lace edging 6, instructions for which are in the edgings section of the needle lace techniques gallery. Use Lizbeth #40.603 and thread silk ribbon 2mm.32 into the insertion area.

Block 2

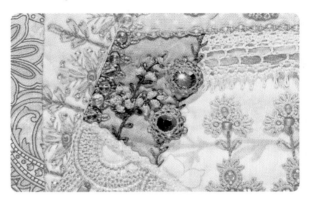

1. Using stranded cotton 434 work the stems of the branch in whipped back stitch. Place 5 drizzle stitches towards the tip of each stem using 3866. Work a small lazy daisy stitch under and around the drizzle stitch bud using 3013. Intersperse the drizzle stitches with 3 beads 15° 1631 using stranded cotton 3013. Using the colour image as your guide, work lazy daisy leaves that come out of the stems using 3011.

2. Using the guidelines for the caged flat back crystal in the bead embroidery techniques gallery, attach a flat back crystal on each of the circles that appear on the border between blocks 1 and 2. Use perlé #12.437. Using stranded cotton 926, work feather stitch along the remaining spaces.

Block 3

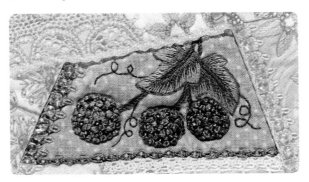

1. Fill each of the berries with a layer of French knots. Place a second layer over the first on the inner two thirds and another layer over inner one third. Use 1 strand each of 3041, 3042, 3733 and 3740 threaded onto a single needle. With the darkest purple thread, stitch 15° 1655 beads at evenly spaced intervals between the knots.

- Pad the leaves with stem stitch using stranded cotton 437. Fill the leaves with long and short stitch shading. Use 3011 shading out to 437 for the leaf on the left and 3011 shading out to 436 for the other. Using the image as your guide, work intermittent outlines around these leaves in outline stitch using 1 strand of 434.
- Work the veins of the leaves and the stems with twisted couching using 433. Using 1 strand of the same thread, work the tendrils with small backstitch.

2. Following the guidelines for variation 1 of the shell border in the tatting techniques, work 13 shells with perlé #12.437. Attach this border up the left side of block 2, continuing up the side of block 3. Place a drop bead 251 in the centre of each shell.

3. Work a line of knotted cable chain stitch on the border between blocks 1 and 3 using perlé#12.927. Place a 15° 2442 bead in the centre of each chain stitch using stranded cotton 3866.

Block 4

1. Each of the three petal flowers on the right side of this block, continuing into block 5, is done in the same way.

- Using stranded cotton 3866, pad the semi-circle at the base with horizontal satin stitch. With 1 strand of the same thread, work vertical satin stitch over the padding.
- Fill the petals and leaves with satin stitch that starts at the tips with a vertical stitch into the middle vein, followed by pairs of diagonal satin stitch which start on the edge and meet in the middle, to create the look of a vein. Work the pink petal with stranded cotton 3733 and the two green leaves with stranded cotton 3012.
- Bead couch a semi-circle of beads 15° 2422F in the ditch between the petals and the flower centre. Use stranded cotton 434.

2. Following (2) in the instructions for block 2, create an identical shell border. You will need approximately 16 shells.

Block 5

1. This spray of flowers starts at the base of block 5 and encroaches into blocks 1 and 6.

- Referring to needle weaving in the techniques gallery, fill each of the petals with single weaving. Use Lizbeth #80.640 for the warp stitches and 639 for the weft stitches; Outline each petal with whipped back stitch using 1 strand of 3740; In the centre attach bead 8° 2035 with bead 15° 1631; Work an 11-bead circle of beads 15° 1631 around the centre large bead.
- Work the branches and the stems with twisted couching using 433.
- Stitch a triangle of 3 single beads 15° 1631 around the tip of each branch that does not end with a flower. Using the colour image as your guide, stitch similar triangles of the same beads adjacent to the branches.

Block 6

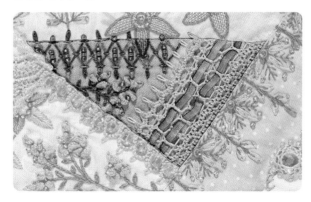

1. Following the guidelines for the branch in block 2 (1), work an identical branch on the lines provided.
2. Following the guidelines for the needle lace edge in block 1 (2), work an identical lace edging on the side that borders block 17.
3. Moving to the edging on the side that borders block 1 and 2 and using stitch combination 3 in the gallery of combination embroidery and silk ribbon embroidery stitches, work a chevron, lazy daisy, bead and straight stitch combination from the left to the right. Work around the petal that encroaches in the block and stop working the edge when it meets the needle lace edge. Use 3011 and 3013 for the two stages of chevron stitch, 3011 for the lazy daisy stitches and 3733 for the straight stitches. Using the same pink thread, stitch single bead 15° 556 on the outer edge between the

outward facing lazy daisy stitches on each side. The 3 beads in the middle are 1 x 15° 1637, 1 x 15° 556 and 1 x 15° 1637, using the same pink thread.

Block 7a

1. Each of the three petal flowers is identical to those in block 4 (1).
2. The branch of buds is done in the same way as that in block 2 (1). Use 422 for the drizzle stitch buds and 3042 for the lazy daisy stitch that goes under and around the bud. The branch remains 434 and leaves are 3011.
3. Moving to the edging on the side that borders block 6 and following (2) in the instructions for block 2, create an identical shell border. You will need approximately 10 shells.

Block 7b

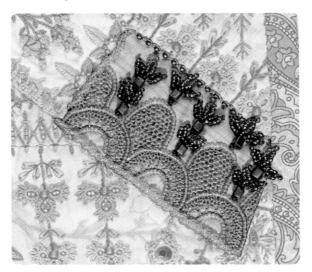

1. Starting at the base of the block, as it appears in the colour image above, pad the semi-circles with stem stitch using 928. Work vertical satin stitch, fanning around the shape, over the padding using 1 strand of the same thread.

- Referring to extras no. 4 at the end of the needle lace section of the techniques gallery, work a 4-row arch over the padded satin stitch in each of the semi circles. Use perlé#12.927;
- Fill the half-oval shapes above the arches with needle lace numbered stitch no. 2.
- Outline each of the lace components with bead couching using 15° 2442 beads and stranded cotton 3866.
- Referring to the bead embroidery section in the techniques gallery, work a line of bead stem stitch along the lower edge of the lace, on the border of this block and blocks 2, 1 and a small section of 6. Use beads 15° 2442 and stranded cotton 3866.

2. Using stranded cotton 434, bead couch 1 x 15° 457L, 1 x SB3.2035 cube bead and 1 x 15° 457L onto the small squares depicted, making sure that the cube bead sits on those squares.

- Following the instructions for simple bead flowers and leaves in the bead embroidery section of the techniques gallery, come up through the fabric above the small brown bead, using stranded cotton 3041. Pick up bead 15° 26F and 5 x 15° 1650 beads. Return down the second last

bead, pick up a further 3 purple beads, go through the green bead and back into the fabric.

- Make two identical side petals using beads 15° 26F and 15° 1655 beads.
- To make sure that the petals of the flowers lie the way you want them to, place a small couching stitch over the thread just above the green bead at the base of each petal.

3. Work a line of knotted cable chain stitch on the border between blocks 7a, 7b and 8 using perlé#12.437. Place a 15° 2422F bead in the centre of each chain stitch using stranded cotton 437.

Block 8

1. Referring to the trefoil flower in the tatting techniques gallery make the following:

- 5 x trefoil flowers variation 1 using Lizbeth #80.626;
- Stitch the flowers into place using the small circles at the top of the four stems as the guide for placement. Stitch a bead 8° 2035 in the centre.
- Following the instructions for twisted couching in the embroidery techniques gallery, work twisted couching over the stems leading to the tatted flowers and the upright leaf stems in between using stranded cotton 434.
- The leaves coming out of the stems are silk ribbon stitches done with 2mm.32. The veins are straight stitches done with a single strand of 434.

2. The three branches that face downwards from the edge of block 8 are done with a fly stitch variation.

- Using 3011 work a straight stitch. Then work two fly stitches with a gap of about ⁵/₆₄" (2 mm) between each. Continue by working two to three back stitches, continuing with two to three fly stitches, starting narrow and going wider as you move down. Depending on the length of the branch, continue in this way until you reach the edge of the block.
- Using the same thread, whip back to the top, taking in each of the backstitches and also the legs of each fly stitch.
- Using stranded cotton 3866 work a straight stitch in the upper half of the gap between each fly stitch.
- Using stranded cotton 437 work a straight stitch in the remaining half of the gap between each fly stitch.

Block 9

1. Referring to stitch combination 6 in the gallery of combination embroidery and silk ribbon embroidery stitches, work the semi-circles in this block using 3731 for the inner and 3733 for the outer lazy daisy stitches. Use a single strand of 3041 for the fly stitches. The large bead is 8° 2035 and the small bead is 15° 1631.

2. Following the instructions for twisted couching in the embroidery techniques gallery, work twisted couching over the upright leaf stems in between the semi-circles using stranded cotton 434.

- The leaves coming out of the stems are silk ribbon stitches done with 2mm.32. The veins are straight stitches done with a single strand of 434.

Block 10

1. Working from the base of the wide lace edge, do needle lace numbered stitch no. 2 in each of the semi-circles. Use perlé #12.927.

- Moving to the two small wedge-shapes between the semi-circles, pad each one with horizontal satin stitch using 2 strands of 928. Cover the padding with vertical satin stitch using 1 strand of the same thread.
- The top section is filled with needle lace number stitch no. 1 using perlé #12.927.
- Referring to extras no. 2 in the needle lace techniques gallery, work 3-stitch picot bars around the entire upper edge of the lace.
- Outline each section of the lace edge with bead couching using 15° 2442 beads and stranded cotton 3866. Secure each picot of the picot bar by stitching it down with the same bead, pulling it up and out at the same time.
- With the same bead and thread, work a line of bead stem stitch along the bottom edge of block, continuing until you meet up with the intersection where block 3 meets block 4.

2. Referring to the Trefoil Flower in the Tatting Techniques gallery make 1 x trefoil flowers variation 2 using Lizbeth #80.627.

- Stitch the flower into place using the small circle at the top of the stem as the guide for placement. Stitch a bead 8° 2035 in the centre.
- Following the instructions for twisted couching in the embroidery techniques gallery, work twisted couching over the upright stem using stranded cotton 434.
- The leaves coming out of the stem are silk ribbon stitches done with 2mm.32. The veins and short leaf stems are straight stitches done with a single strand of 434.

Block 11

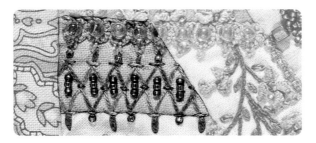

1. Using stitch combination 3 in the gallery of combination embroidery and silk ribbon embroidery stitches, work a chevron, lazy daisy, bead and straight stitch combination from the left to the right along the bottom half of the block, encroaching slightly into block 10.

- Use 3011 and 3013 for the two stages of chevron stitch, 3011 for the lazy daisy stitches and 3041 for the straight stitches.
- Using the same lavender thread, stitch single bead 15° 1650 on the outer edge between the outward facing lazy daisy stitches on each side.
- The 3 beads in the middle are 1 x 15° 1655, 1 x 15° 1650 and 1 x 15° 1655, using the same lavender thread.

2. Moving to the top edging on the side that borders block 13 continuing over the short top side of block 12, and following (2) in the instructions for block 2, create an identical shell border. You will need approximately 9 shells.

Block 12

1. The branch of buds is done in the same way as that in block 2 (1). Use 422 for the drizzle stitch buds and 3354 for the lazy daisy stitch that goes under and around the bud. The branch is done with 433, the leaves are 3011 and the bead is 15° 1631.

2. Following instructions (1) in block 4, work the 3-petal flower in the same way using the same threads and bead.

3. Work a line of knotted cable chain stitch on the border between blocks 12 and 14 using perlé#12.927. Place a 15° 2442 bead in the centre of each chain stitch using stranded cotton 3866.

Block 13

1. The four branches that fill this block are done with a fly stitch variation.

- Using 3011 work a straight stitch. Then work two fly stitches with a gap of about 5/64" (2 mm) between each starting narrow and going wider as you move down. Continue by working back stitches until you reach the edge of the block.
- Using the same thread, whip back to the top, taking in each of the backstitches and also the legs of each fly stitch.
- Using stranded cotton 3866 work a straight stitch in the upper half of the gap between each fly stitch.
- Using stranded cotton 437 work a straight stitch in the remaining half of the gap between each fly stitch.
- Using 3866, work 3 x drizzle stitches at the base of each stem.
- Using 3013 work a small lazy daisy stitch under and around the drizzle stitch bud using 3013. Intersperse the drizzle stitches with 2 or 3 beads 15° 1631 using stranded cotton 3013.

Block 14

1. Following instruction (1) in block 9, work the semi-circular shapes in the top half of this block in the same way. All the threads and beads used are the same but for the fly stitch. Work this with 1 strand of 3041.

2. Following instruction (2) in block 7b, work the simple bead flowers in the bottom half of this block in the same way using identical beads and threads.

Block 15a

1. Following instruction (1) in block 5, work the spray of flowers in the same way using identical threads and beads.

2. Following instruction (2) in block 1, work an identical lace border along the edge that abuts block 15b.

3. Work a line of knotted cable chain adjacent to the top edge of the lace border using perlé#12.437. Place a 15° 2422F bead in the centre of each chain stitch using stranded cotton 437.

Block 15b

Referring to the trefoil flower in the tatting techniques gallery make the following:

- 3 x trefoil flowers variation 1 using Lizbeth #80.626;
- Stitch the flowers into place using the small circles at the top of the three short stems as the guide for placement. Stitch a bead 8° 2035 in the centre.
- Following the instructions for twisted couching in the embroidery techniques gallery, work twisted couching over the long upright stems using stranded cotton 434.
- The leaves coming out of the stems are silk ribbon stitches done with 2mm.32. The veins are straight stitches done with a single strand of 434.

Block 15c

1. Working from the base of the wide lace edge, do needle lace numbered stitch no. 2 in each of the semi-circles. Use perlé #12.927.

- Moving to the arch above each semi-circle follow the instructions for extras no. 3, the 3-row arch in the needle lace techniques gallery using the same thread.
- The top section is filled with needle lace number stitch no. 1 using perlé #12.927.
- Outline each section of the lace edge with bead couching using 15° 2442 beads and stranded cotton 3866.
- With the same bead and thread, work a line of bead stem stitch along the bottom edge of block, continuing up the left side of block 15b.

2. The branches of buds that come out of the dips in the needle lace are done in the same way as those in block 2 (1). Use 422 for the drizzle stitch buds and 3354 for the lazy daisy stitch that goes under and around the bud. The branch is done with 434, the leaves are 3011 and the bead is 15° 1631.

3. Follow instruction (1) in block 11 to work the top edge of the block where it abuts block 16c. Use identical threads and beads.

Blocks 16 a and b

1. Following instruction (2) in block 2, place flat back crystals along the left borders of both blocks a and b, using identical threads and beads.

2. Following the instructions for stitch no. 8 in the combination stitches gallery, work the edge between blocks 16 a and b. Use perlé #12.927 for the knotted cable chain stitch, stranded cotton 3013 for the lazy daisy stitch and bead 15° 2442.

3. Referring to the trefoil flower in the tatting techniques gallery make 1 x trefoil flowers variation 2 using Lizbeth #80.627.

- Stitch the flower into place on block 16b using the small circle at the top of the stem as the guide for placement. Stitch a bead 8° 2035 in the centre.
- Following the instructions for twisted couching in the embroidery techniques gallery, work twisted couching over the upright stem using stranded cotton 434.
- The leaves coming out of the stem are silk ribbon stitches done with 2mm.32. The veins and short leaf stems are straight stitches done with a single strand of 434.

4. Moving to the bottom edging on the side that borders block 16c, and following (2) in the instructions for block 2, create an identical shell border. You will need approximately 6 shells.

Block 16c

All of the branches in this block are done with a fly stitch variation.

- Using 3011 work a straight stitch. Then work fly stitches with a gap of about ⁵/₆₄″ (2 mm) between each some way down the branch, using the colour image as your guide. Continue by working back stitches to the base of each stem.
- Using the same thread, whip back to the top, taking in each of the backstitches and also the legs of each fly stitch.
- Using stranded cotton 3866 work a straight stitch in the upper half of the gap between each fly stitch.
- Using stranded cotton 437 work a straight stitch in the remaining half of the gap between each fly stitch.

Block 17

1. Follow instruction (1) in block 9 to work the semi-circles in this block. Use 3733 for the inner and 3354 for the outer lazy daisy stitch. Use 3041 for the fly stitch. Use beads 8° 2035 and 15° 1631.

2. Following instruction (2) in block 9, complete the leaf branches in the same way using identical threads and ribbons.

Blocks 18 a and b

1. Following instruction (2) in block 2, place flat back crystals along the left borders of both blocks a and b, using identical threads and beads.

2. Starting at the base of each stem depicted in 18 b, bead couch 1 x 15° 26F, 1 x #1.26 short bugle bead and 1 x 15° 26F onto the small rectangles depicted, making sure that the bugle bead sits on those small rectangles.

- Following the instructions for simple bead flowers and leaves in the bead embroidery section of the techniques gallery, come up through the fabric above the small green bead, using stranded cotton 3041. Pick up bead 6 x 15° 1650 beads. Return down the second last bead, pick up a further 4 purple beads, go through the first bead and back into the fabric.
- Make two identical side petals using 5 x beads 15° 1655, returning down the second last bead, picking up a further 2 x 15° 1655 beads and going through the first bead back into the fabric.
- To make sure that the petals of the flowers lie the way you want them to, place a small couching stitch over the thread just above the green bead at the base of each petal.
- Work identical simple flowers about each green bead stem.

3. Following the instructions for block 16 c, work identical fly stitch branches using the same threads.

FINISHING OFF

Referring to the finishing techniques gallery, you now need to stabilize your crazy patchwork.

1. Cut a piece of cotton voile that is large enough to fit into the hoop.
2. Cut a piece of batting that is the same size as the cotton voile.
3. Sandwich the quilt as directed in the finishing techniques gallery.
4. Secure the beads and work barely visible running stitches around the edge of each block, hiding them where possible.

- Leaving a border of ¾" (20 mm) all the way around the edge of the embellishment, rule lines with a washout pen and trim the panel back to those lines.
- Measure the trimmed panel and cut a lining for the back of the panel. Use Fabric 13 listed in the materials section.
- Following the guidelines for the continous binding in the finishing techniques gallery, cut and join strips of fabric 13. These should be 2½" (65 mm) wide. Cut as much as you need to make binding that is the required length.
- Place the sandwiched panel on top of the lining, putting a few pins here and there to stabilize and keep the layers together.
- Pin and stitch the continuous binding to the panel and lining, starting and finishing in the middle of one of the long edges so that the join will be hidden by the ribbon on the basket cover.
- Hand stitch the back of the binding as instructed.

Making the basket cover

THE LID

- From where the binding joins the back, measure the width of the lid of the basket cover. Add 1¼" (30 mm).
- Cut a strip of fabric that measures that length and is 1¼" (30 mm) wide.
- Turn of hem of ⅔" (15 mm) on each end.

- Turning it under on each side, pin and hand stitch it to the horizontal mid-line of the back of the basket cover, to a finished width of ¾" (20 mm).
- Trim the dowel rod so that it will run the length of the casing.
- Using a 3 mm drill bit, drill holes through the dowel rod about ¼ to ½" (5 to 10 mm) from each end. It's a good idea to do this in a vice of some sort, or find a man who knows about these things, because it is easy to make a crooked hole and break the wood.
- Push the drilled dowel rod through the casing and, pushing first one end a little out and then the other, thread a piece of satin ribbon through each of the holes.

THE BASE AND INNER
Measure the inside base of the basket.

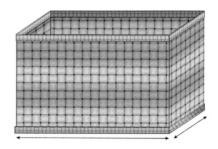

- Cut a piece of fabric 9, a piece of cotton voile and a piece of batting that is 1¼" (30 mm) longer and wider.

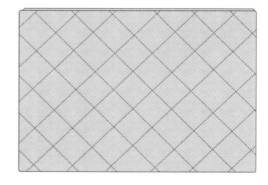

- Using a pencil or a washout pen, rule a trellis of diagonal lines that are 1" (25 mm) apart.
- Sandwich the voile, batting and fabric together, pinning

them firmly. You can tack lines if you wish, but this is a small item and pins will probably do the trick.

- Machine stitch along those lines, starting from the centre and working out on either side and in both directions.
- Place the quilted rectangle inside the basket, pushing it down to the base. Mark it off to the correct size with pins and trim it, leaving a seam allowance on the outside of the pins of ¼" (6 mm).
- Overlock or zig-zag stitch around the trimmed edge to neaten.

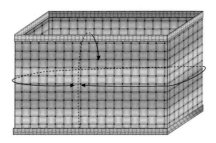

- To calculate the size of the basket inner, measure around the basket and add 4" (100 mm).
- Measure from the inside base of the basket, to the top, over the side and to halfway down the outside. Add 2" (50 mm) to accommodate seam allowances and a casing.
- Cut a strip of fabric to the correct size using the above measurements.
- Fold it in half with right sides together, pin a stitch the raw ends together to make a continuous piece.

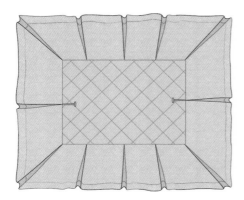

- Still folded, mark the centre point, opposite the join seam with a pin. Also mark the centre of each of the short sides of the quilted base with pins.

- With right sides together, pin the continuous piece to the quilted base creating a pleat on each corner and thereafter as many small pleats – the same distance apart – as you need for it to fit the base.

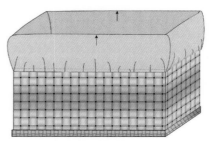

- Fit the inner into the basket, making sure that the base fits snugly into the base of the basket.
- Pull the inner up and over the top of the basket, then pull it down the sides of the basket.
- Decide how far down you would like it to go and place a pin to mark that line.
- Now trim away the excess, making sure that you leave approximately 1½" (40 mm) for the elastic casing.
- Turn over and stitch the casing, thread elastic through it, close the hole of the casing and fit the basket inner into the basket.
- With a ruler or tape measure, determine the middle point of each long side and work a long bullion – about ⅔" (15 mm) bullion – over that centre point.

- Thread one side of the ribbon that goes through the dowel rod on each side of the lid through the ribbon, tie a bow in each case, and you have a covered basket.

PATTERNS

Gussy up
Enlarge to 7½" (190 mm) diameter

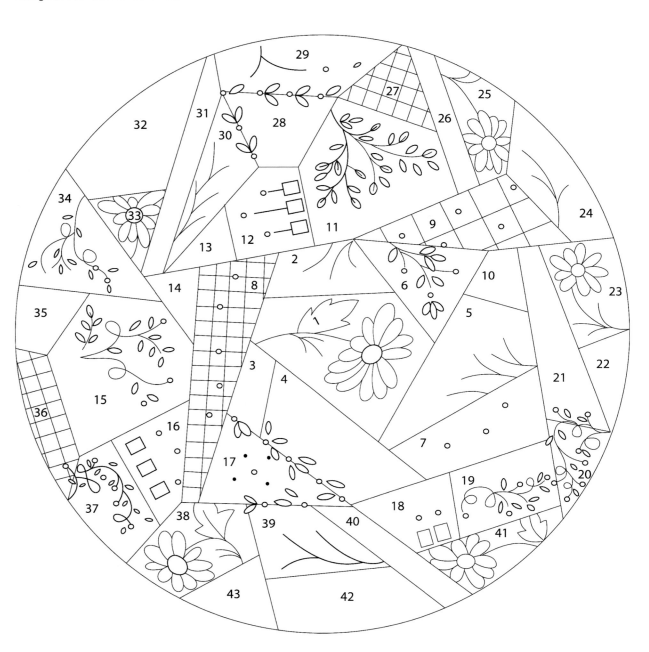

Nightshade
Enlarge to 9⅞ x 7⅞" (250 x 175 mm)

Waiting for santa
Enlarge to 14⅛ x 4⅓" (360 x 110 mm)

STOCKING PATTERN
Enlarge to 11 x 17⅝" (275 x 420 mm)

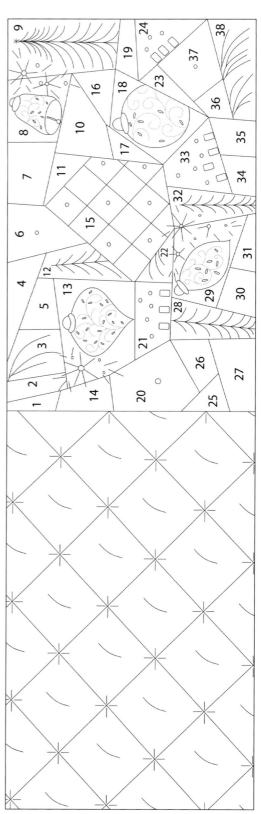

Rambling vine
Enlarge to 15½ x 15¾" (395 x 400 mm)

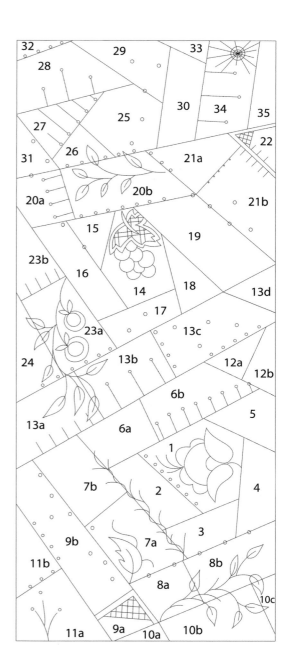

Savannah winter
Enlarge to 9 x 7" (225 x 180 mm)

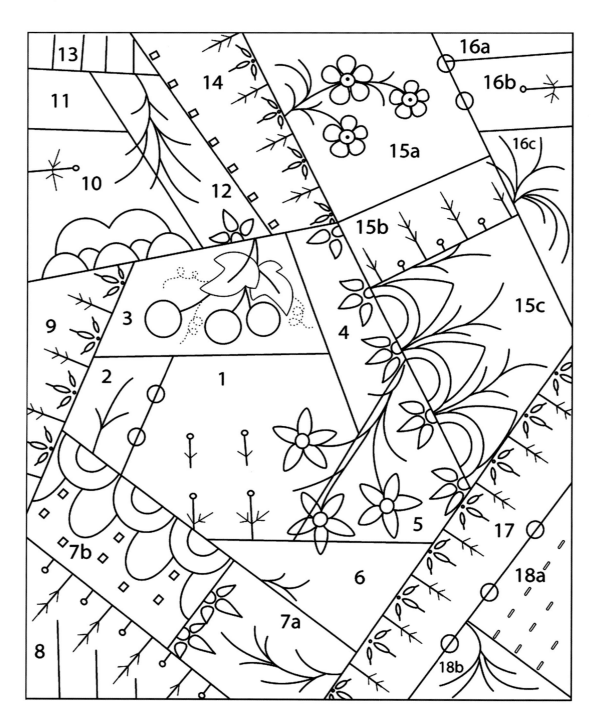